A HUMAN CREATION

Revised and Updated

W. R. Frederick

authorHOUSE®

AuthorHouse™
1663 Liberty Drive
Bloomington, IN 47403
www.authorhouse.com
Phone: 833-262-8899

Published by AuthorHouse 06/24/2022

ISBN: 978-1-6655-6222-5 (sc)
ISBN: 978-1-6655-6221-8 (hc)
ISBN: 978-1-6655-6220-1 (e)

Library of Congress Control Number: 2022911143

CONTENTS

To Mary and John
for their invaluable support
in realizing this work

PREFACE

As the belief in God and the theme of religion reflect very personal and fundamental human emotions, I have decided to express the views in this work in the first person. I have my beliefs; it is up to you, the reader, to judge them according to your views.

A while ago I read a book on atheism that had been highly touted by a respected journal. I came away with the feeling that the book came nowhere near doing justice to the case for atheism. The fault, in my view, was that the author had so heavily emphasized the supposed corporal humanitarian superiority of atheism over theism that the true arguments for atheism were lost. In other words, religion inflicts so much pain on humanity that it must be bad, and God, therefore, does not exist. Clearly, the superiority or inferiority of a religion or belief relative to the happiness or suffering of humankind has nothing to do with the existence or not of God. Pain and suffering do have an effect on belief, but they are not the determinants of the existence or not of God. I researched other works and found that many arguments of the "experts" were so compartmentalized that they exposed their works to weakness on the flanks. Other considerations could undermine their conclusions. I felt encouraged, therefore, to compile the arguments across the spectrum of disciplines that impact the atheist-theist controversy.

I have since read several notable exceptions, in that the authors do truly present a cross-disciplinary mastery of history, philosophy, and science. However, there are not enough of these speakers.

I will not stress the superiority or inferiority of atheism with respect to theism. Whether religion is good or bad is immaterial. And, yes, religion may provide solace and hope, but that does not prove or disprove the existence of God. The fact that atheists have not been the bad guys of history means nothing as well. Atheists never had the numbers and clout to matter at all.

Another factor spurring me to express my thoughts and conclusions is the state of political debate in the United States involving an unprecedented degree of religious fervor. When the president of the United States wears his religion so visibly on his sleeve, and when the political process is being driven often by intense lobbying by religious groups, there arises an urgent need to place these drives in their proper perspective. Hopefully these times will pass. But I doubt it. There are signs that the pressure for theocracy is on the rise. The radical religious right is very alive, and it will not go away.

Who am I to take on this task? I am not a theologian, a medical doctor, a neuropsychologist, an archeologist, a biologist, a psychiatrist, or one in a few more disciplines. I am a generalist with background in engineering, languages, and business. I have lived nearly a third of my life outside of the United States and have traveled through a very large part of the world. New and exciting experiences have been a constant factor in my life. I have had my life and death experiences. I have developed what I think is a very respectful skepticism, and I am a contrarian.

What do I know about religion? I was brought up on Long Island, New York, and it was there that I had the privilege of benefiting from the teachings of a respected biblical scholar. But that is surely not enough to earn any credibility, and a great deal of research has been undertaken to support this book.

Although I will attempt to put a new slant on the arguments, I do not intend to break new ground in the area of research and investigation. The true experts have put time and assets into research that I cannot match. Facts, theories, and conclusions will be cited without footnote generally, while providing attribution as necessary. Again, my goal is to piece together, somewhat in the form of an anthology, a convincing case based on the investigations of several disciplines. In a sense I am reviewing some of the current literature and its arguments.

It is worth noting that the many ideas that have occurred to me as I put together this text have all arisen before, expressed by many others active in the several areas addressed in this book. That should be no surprise. The debate has been going on for millennia, and the more I research, the more

I find that there are few new ideas. The exception is the proliferation of scientific undertakings that provide new underpinnings or contradictions of theories long ago expressed. The deciphering of the human genome is a good example.

In any case, where I state my views, there is no intent to plagiarize, recognizing that someone may have already stated a similar view.

I have been cited by critics for giving short shrift to the arguments of the theists. However, this book reflects my views, and where a theist's ideas make no sense to me, I am not going to waste time in unnecessary debate. I do cite numerous experts who attack those same theist arguments.

I have emphasized sources critical of god belief that support the central theme of this book. As one looks at the sources, one could say I am creating a bible of atheism, citing certain works as gospel. Is this, then, an unbalanced analysis? No, it is not. The religious texts are of a clearly opposing view, and I do cite them. In fact, this book spends considerable time on the theist proponents.

The centuries of studies to back up the various scriptures are readily available. The theists promote them and make them available at every turn. They inevitably strongly engage in defense and explanation of the ancient and original texts central to the religion involved. On the other hand, works critical of God's existence have received far less exposure and great resistance, and I believe a comprehensive presentation of atheist thought provides the balance needed. Yes, a number of great philosophers, writers, and scientists throughout the centuries, as well as several very recent authors, have gained notoriety for their atheist views, but if one examines how society views those voices in religious, educational, and literary institutions, it is clear that they are thought to represent a ho-hum fringe presence and not much more. This needs to change!

Fortunately, or unfortunately (I am not sure), Sam Harris, Richard Dawkins, William Dembski, Michael Behe, Christopher Hitchens, Victor J. Stenger, Stephen Hawking, and several others have come out with books that impact my thesis overwhelmingly. They have a credibility factor that I may never enjoy, and the question arises as to why I would entertain publishing a book that examines their many themes. The answer is in the very authenticity of our messages. They are in most cases the experts. They play by defined rules. I, on the other hand, am a layman. I see things as they may be, but I can describe them with more subjectivity, although, hopefully, responsibly. I will state again that the writings of some of these luminaries that emphasize the terrible human record of religious history do not encompass the theme of this book. The good or bad acts of the religious do not prove God's existence one way or the other.

My thesis does depart from those just mentioned. I am out to show that humans created God. I will show the supporting history, the evolutionary evidence, the biological data, and the cultural/societal influences that prove that God did not create humans but just the opposite. I delve into the cosmological because it is here that the theist has his last argument, and it is my intent to show that no god has ever been involved, that there was never a need for such an involvement, and that there is no evidence of a god involvement.

Let me address Richard Dawkins's *The God Delusion*. Throughout his book I encountered a remarkable parallel with the basic thoughts and arguments that I had proposed to address in my book. A prime example is his discussion on page 154 of the "bandwidth" that God would have to enjoy to be able to do all that he is supposed to do. He says the capability exceeds that of the "largest computer we know." I would say the largest computer imaginable! I thought that I had come up with a unique thought well before I read Dawkins's book. No such luck! (Both of us, however, are off base. If God is what they say he is, numbers are of no account. God is everywhere. God is everything. He knows no limits). And similar parallels with Dawkins come up over and over again. It is worthwhile repeating the arguments.

There are some lessons to be gained in this challenge to my original thinking.

First, as stated above, I have no desire whatsoever to plagiarize and will defer to whomever rightfully claims the point. I do hope I can add some new slants.

Second, it is worth repeating that there are few if any truly new ideas in the debate, although there is a tremendous amount of new scientific data. The crunch comes in how we evaluate the ideas.

Third, it should be noted that the layman can reach the same (hopefully correct) conclusions as the professors and doctors. I described above my background, but here I would like to emphasize that my education, both formal and informal, includes heavy doses of mathematics, archeology, and electronics. I am a layman like millions of others and cannot match the true experts in all ways, but I am no dummy, and I can interpret the facts as well as most.

The fourth observation is maybe the most important. Repetition of the atheist message, the ideas, theories, hypotheses, and conclusions regardless of their origin and who states them is an absolute necessity if the overwhelming quantity of theist expression and literature is to be engaged.

I have presented the argument in five areas of interest.

Chapter 1 on history shows that primordial psychological and societal imperatives have encouraged humans to appeal to the supernatural, and that it is specifically the earliest stages of humankind's development, and not the later polemics, that determine god belief.

The chapter on evolution and the numbers shows that no divine intervention is necessary to arrive at an advanced genome such as that of *Homo sapiens.*

The chapter on the human brain and its manifestations tells us why a belief in God is a direct result of the neurological processes and philosophies that determine our outlook on the world in and around us.

The chapter on society, culture, and politics shows us how the human being is coerced into the worship of a god.

Then we enter a review of the cosmos, the universe, and the universes beyond, all of which show no need for any divine or other intervention.

Lastly, we review the continuity of the conversion of the inanimate to life.

One could slice this cake in many different ways, but I believe these five areas of scrutiny present the burden of proof that God is a creation of humankind and nothing more.

CHAPTER 1

History and God

A Doubtful Record at Best

The Geologic, Archaeological, and Textual Background

What is this first chapter supposed to reveal?

First, it can be shown that the idea of gods and the supernatural has roots in the most ancient biological and cultural background of humankind and is pertinent to this day. In all cultures there has been, at the beginning, a plethora of gods—human creations. In essence, humankind has conveyed its most intimate fears and expectations into belief in the supernatural. The true test of God's existence lies in these early times, not in the immense amount of discourse of the last few millennia that merely work over and refine ancient predispositions.

Second, the historical record itself is extremely suspect and is probably untrue or fabricated. Let us dispense with the just-mentioned discourse over the recent millennia, most of which represents disputes internal to religious organizations over minutiae that have no bearing whatsoever on the existence of God. They deal with how one is to observe an already accepted belief in certain historical assertions. The stories that are the underpinnings of today's religions were dreams, fabrications, and cultural explanations of ancient commonly accepted traditions.

What has history recorded? What, in fact, qualifies as history?

The average person's understanding of history is the text in a book that addresses some slice of events in the recent past. But it is, of course, much more than that. Taken in its broadest sense, history is everything that records geological, archaeological, biological, and societal events encompassing the course over time of things and organisms from their beginnings up to *Homo sapiens* and the world of today. A multiplicity of scientific disciplines shed light on the process. For the purposes of this book, history includes all that has come to light through archaeology, paleontology, geology, written symbols—whether cave drawings or gospels—and a myriad of other disciplines to include the media. Many significant texts of early biological and human history were recorded in stone.

And scientists in numerous disciplines have been interpreting the evidence over many years. The true history of humankind begins, in fact, in the earlier stones that preserve the archaeological evidence of life as far back as 3.8 billion years. I propose to begin, therefore, as far back as the archaeological record can take us, to the very beginning of life on earth. This will show how gods (or a god) were created. Let the stones speak.

Life on earth began over three and a half billion years ago. Life-forms were simple, of course. But from the very beginning, life was driven by two fundamental necessities: the need to survive (i.e., to obtain sustenance and protection from life-threatening dangers) and the need to procreate. Lacking either of these two meant that that form of life was terminated. A microbe two billion years ago needed a source of energy. It would do everything within its power to ensure access to that energy source. The energy source was like a god. Likewise, a reproductive strategy had to take into account the environmental support elements and the dangers for the organism.

At some time several billion years ago, replicators arose, and organisms could pass on to their offspring the essential characteristics that gave the offspring the means to survive. There are differing strategies for survival, but regardless of the strategy selected, it protected the organism from certain hazards and took advantage of certain environmental factors. The hazards and the beneficial factors became the gods to be worshipped if one was to survive.

Where in the world does this bizarre discussion lead us? The answer lies in that, for the basics, little has changed since those microbes swarmed the earth billions of years ago. For today's animals, plants, fungi, archaea, and bacteria, the imperatives have not changed. The life supports and the dangers to survival and reproduction are still here, and they must be revered if life-forms are to persist. This need to pay homage to the necessities of life is in us today. In short, organisms take the necessities of life and turn them into gods. They will sacrifice, change behavior, and defer to genealogical alteration to satisfy the gods of necessity.

But simply paying homage to the necessities of survival and reproduction is one thing. Paying homage takes on a new meaning when animals start to think or cognition becomes apparent.

In line with the general approach to facts and opinion taken in this book, I am not going to quibble about exact figures when it is not necessary. Let's say that several hundred thousand to a million years ago, early hominids were capable of thinking. Perhaps we should be referring to calculating, and if that is the case, we must include many more members of the animal kingdom in our thinking model. Certainly predators of all sorts calculate or think as they hunt. If you have ever watched a hawk, a cat, or a killer whale in action, you have seen true calculation bordering on real thinking.

I cite a March 2008 feature story in the *National Geographic* magazine as some evidence of the complex evolutionary development of intelligence. The message is that many others of the animal kingdom demonstrate at least beginnings of the mental capability heretofore attributed only to *Homo sapiens*. Cognition, episodic memory, and theory of mind have been demonstrated by parrots, crows, jays, elephants, dogs, dolphins, and octopi in scientific experiments, studies, and numerous nonscientific reports. We should not take such a presentation as gospel, but let me remind my readers that the National Geographic Society has a stellar reputation; what it publishes has to be taken seriously.

The lesson inferred by this report is that evolution has pursued several paths toward an intelligent organism or genome and that although *Homo sapiens* seems to be at the top of the heap, it leads the pack only by a step or two. Since 2008 much more has come out concerning the Animal Kingdom's advances in mental capabilities. To my mind, this makes the creationist view of humankind's dominance over the animal kingdom nothing more than an egotistic hypocrisy.

Daniel Dennett, in his book *From Bacteria to Bach and Back*, attributes nonhuman behavior to competence as opposed to comprehension, and he draws a neat line between the two. Human language and consciousness are far removed from the capabilities of the other animals. I believe he overdoes it. The differences in cognitive capability found across the animal kingdom should be viewed as a continuum since each species displays a certain level of competence approaching or bordering on comprehension. Humans have merely come much further.

In fact, it is at the early stages of the hominoid species evolution that we enter an underlying thesis of this work. This was the ability of *Homo sapiens* to go beyond mere calculation and to consciously link its needs and the environment with survival and societal relations and to contemplate the means to influence the future in its favor through appeals to gods and the supposed influence they bring. Humankind thus became inclined to pay reverence to those essential needs and elements of the environment that meant the most to survival, and this led to a related series of gods. *Homo sapiens* was clearly conscious to the degree needed to create gods. Neanderthals probably could conceive of gods—as could the Denisovans and maybe *Homo heidelbergensis*. Just how far back in the line of *Homo erectus* we can go is an open question to me.

Homo sapiens has only existed for a few hundred thousand years, with ancestors going back millions of years—still a blink of an eye in geologic time. The search for humanity's past is still on, so the commonly accepted distance back in time is sure to change. (If the readers are of the view that humankind was placed on this earth by an all-powerful being in a far reduced time frame, then they may as well forget it!) Nevertheless, humankind, along with its predecessors, has existed for a very long time by our contemporary reckoning, through the Pleistocene and the Paleolithic, which amounts to at least four hundred thousand years.

If we accept the fact that *Homo sapiens* and its immediate predecessors have been here for such a long time and that somewhere along the way humans exhibited a degree of consciousness that could balance needs and wants with human action, then we must agree that gods and religions did not simply pop up in the more recent times, which many of us assume. Humankind spent a lot of time creating gods, religions, and religious institutions, and such creation began early on.

How Gods and Religion Began

For a moment, we will assume the mind, body, and environment of a member of the species of *Homo sapiens* many thousands of years ago. This individual can think in the real sense of the word. He or she is mature and has lived long enough to understand a lot about his or her surroundings. There are the various sources of food, and there are the dangers represented by the big cats and other creatures. He or she has noted the rhythms of nature. There is also the presence of a social/familial group, with its sexual imperatives, support, and historical wisdom. We can refer to this as the hunter-gatherer phase of human societal development. Parts of this communal and individual, wisdom are the familiar and unchanging elements of the environment such as weather and the true nature of that orb that appears on one side and travels across the blue to the other side.

If we are to get into the head of this early person, we must put aside much of what we know today. Only then can we see that our subject would puzzle over the reason for the tide to come and go as it does. And what is that warm, radiant orb up there? It was clear that it was sorely needed, but who or what is that thing? Suppose it doesn't come back some day? And then there is the bright thing at night. It looks like an eye. Is it watching me? The nuts that we gather are sometimes very scarce. Who or what changes the crop? Can I influence the change? Since most of these natural phenomena had a strong influence on early humans' very existence, they surely became an object of reverence.

In my view somewhere in the very distant past individuals and communities had to have established a reverential relationship with those elements of nature that clearly meant so much to their existence. The old man of the tribe came out one day and, upon observing the rise of the sun, bowed in an anticipation of its beneficial warmth. The next day the youngsters of the family group bowed the same way in an imitation of the old man. "Ah!" said the old man, and he told his family that we should do this every day. This is a playful little story to illustrate the point, and there must be innumerable just-so stories to illustrate how worship of the elements became a part of the human experience, applied to the sun, the moon, lightning, rain, the prey humans hunted, fecundity of human, animal, and plant, etc., etc.

The authors of *Why God Won't Go Away* visualize a more detailed and complex story involving the stag hunter. This ancient being, suffering physical and mental stress, experiences somewhat sublime visions of himself and the stag before he eventually makes his kill. The authors are primarily interested in the workings of the human brain, and they spell out the story in terms of the brain's processes. The result of these rudimentary experiences leads through the workings of the mind of the hunter to placing of the stag as a god, tribal acceptance of the mystery, and nascent theology involving sacrifice, spells, and rituals. The authors claim that the resulting religious atmosphere gives a survival advantage.

These just-so stories led to ritualistic observances and the establishment of religion. In fact, archeological evidence presents a believable record of burial traditions among Paleolithic communities, cult followings that possibly presumed a belief in an afterlife, and an animistic human relationship with wildlife prey. Artifacts unearthed in the Middle East and elsewhere infer a reverence for the fertile female. Much of what has been uncovered is still in debate as to its exact meaning, but there is no doubt that humans had many thousands of years ago come to pay reverence to the processes that were vital to their survival such as food sources, procreation, and life after death.

As humans identified those elements requiring their reverence, they converted those elements into gods. And how did Man perceive those gods? In *GOD An Anatomy* Francesca Stavrakopoulou describes our early tendency to see the gods in bodies like ours. She addresses the many gods and the many body parts they share with us. Humans could thus better understand how to deal with the gods and commune with them. Although a modern understanding of religion makes God a non-physical entity, the signs of human-like gods are still seen over much of the world.

Stephen Hawking in his most recent work *The Grand Design*, chapter two, mentions the generally supported evidence of early humans' tendency to invent gods to explain their natural surroundings. A physicist and cosmologist? Of course! Why not? In a later chapter he refers to the creation myths of African peoples, the Mayans, and other Central American cultures. I refer to Hawking because this human tendency to explain the unexplainable in terms of gods comes up in the debate about the beginning of the universe and related cosmological interpretations, which we address later in this book.

Here is another unlikely insert taken from Augustine. It makes the point that nature's reality can lead to fantasy. Augustine cites Cicero in chapter 30 of Booklet IV, *City of God*. Cicero's Lucilius Balbus says, "Do you not therefore see that from true and useful physical discoveries the reason may be drawn away to fabulous and imaginary gods?" The generalization is, I believe, true. Augustine would not apply this to the "one God," of course. Not he!

Nicholas Wade came out with his *The Faith Instinct* in 2009. In it he lends considerable support for the beginnings of god belief and religion in the early hunter-gatherer human groupings fifty thousand or more years ago. Early on he makes a pertinent observation that "religious behavior can be studied for its own sake, regardless of whether or not a deity exists." And then,

> An instinct for religious behavior is indeed an evolved part of human nature. Because of the decided survival advantage conferred on people who practiced a religion, the behavior had become written into our neural circuitry by at least 50,000 years ago, and probably much earlier.

He bases much of what he espouses on research conducted with some of today's aboriginal societies and cultures, which should reflect on the historical hunter-gatherer societies of yore. Although god belief is assumed, Wade lays emphasis on religion as a binding communal force that bestows benefits on the group in terms of the hunt, the gathering, and warfare among other human desires. He considers moral standards as a mainstay of religion, and appears to consider them as part and parcel of early religion. I can only observe that morals—that is, the code of conduct of societies and cultures—came first. Primates exhibit moral conduct in their groups, but there is no evidence that they have a god belief. God belief or religion co-opted moral codes to its own benefit much later in our evolution.

Wade makes numerous comments to the effect that god belief is in our neural circuitry or is in our genes. However, he not once offers evidence to support that belief. What parts of the brain? Which genes? What research and by whom? I believe there may very well be a genetic inclination toward god belief, and some scholars have, in fact, researched the topic and reached conclusions, but there does not appear to be enough evidence to conclude one way or another. Richard Dawkins makes religious belief more a cultural, societal effect along the lines of memes.

Nicholas Wade places the beginning of religion more or less as we know it at around fifteen thousand years ago when agrarian and urban societies developed but again makes the point that the roots of religion went far back from those times.

I must therefore emphasize here one of the fundamental arguments of this book, and that is the view that what is often called prehistory, as opposed to the written recorded history that we all cite, is the true source of how humans created God. By the time that humans institutionalized religions, created theocratic bureaucracies, and established dogma, gods were long established as focal points of human existence. This means that much of the last four or more thousand years were devoted to solidifying God's status rather than creating him in the first place. This recent period has great importance, nevertheless, because it represents a period during which belief in God was encouraged and most times forcibly required.

In this book I am concerned with where and when the belief in gods began and why, as well as why beliefs persist. I address the later historical record mainly in the sense that humankind reinforces and enforces beliefs established long, long ago and thereby extends the so-called truths and myths of earlier times into today. Theological experts and historians are all too often locked into a severely constrained world view. They postulate their dogmas based on already solidified dogma. It's too late! God was created many thousands of years ago for very basic primeval reasons, and all efforts to extend or expand god belief are mere reflections of societal and institutional pressures.

Humans Begin to Record Their Religious Beliefs

Move onward to the time when humanity began to record its history, and by record, I mean not only written accounts, but human history passed on by word of mouth through recital of legend and tale. We are probably talking about twenty to forty thousand years ago. By all accounts humankind had by this time deified numerous elements of their natural surroundings and had generated beliefs such as the afterlife. Cave drawings, carved figures, statues, and other forms of expression show humans' veneration for some identity of great importance to humans. The cave paintings found in several locales in Europe certainly show the human tendency to pay reverence to, if not deify, elements of the environment. Unearthed figurines in archeological sites all over the world attest to a godlike reverence for the female. There are other objects of obvious reverence, such as wildlife prey, that digs around the world have produced This unwritten early history is pertinent to what we call recorded history today.

As writing appeared and was able to elaborate peoples' thinking for generations to follow, it became clear that societies had long been paying homage to numerous gods. They were what one would suspect: a sun god, the fertile female, the god of abundance (crops), the god of the hunt, the thunder/storm god, and many more. The animist paid homage to the bison and other animals. Many peoples worshipped their ancestors. Built up around these beliefs emerged societal structures to support and enforce the beliefs. Humans had created God and the religions to institutionalize their worship.

In the early 1960s I came into possession of Time Life's publication, *The World's Great Religions*. Time Life over many years published a long series of photo-enhanced documentaries and reviews of any number of topics, and generally provided very professional treatment of the subjects addressed. I, for instance, have a collection of Time Life cookbooks, which I treasure, covering the cuisine of the entire world, but they are the bane of my fellow cooking enthusiasts because they are in German.

In the case of the *The World's Great Religions*, we have a reasonable summation of the essentials of the dominant half dozen or so religions that exert the most influence on the peoples of the world. The text can be outdated, but the introduction by Paul Hutchinson, a well-recognized Methodist minister, impressed me and seems very cogent decades later. His introduction is a short treatise on comparative religion, and despite being a Christian, he provides a well-balanced appraisal of the other religions. I believe it is worth quoting two of the passages in his introduction that have a bearing on the theme of this book, one of them at the very beginning and one at the end of his contribution.

In order:

> Endless are the forms man's religion has taken. The names of his gods and goddesses will never be completely catalogued. The rituals through which he has sought protection or blessing run the gamut from the horrible to the sublime. The explanations of his rites may fill ten thousand volumes, and many of them disagree violently. Such young and fascinating sciences as anthropology, archaeology and paleontology are constantly uncovering new evidence concerning the life of our Paleolithic ancestors. The evidence brings to light infinite variations, but on one thing it agrees. Man is a religious being.
>
> However, and wherever he developed, from the time he became man, man has worshiped, and has shown a belief that he possesses an immortal soul. His irresistible urge to worship has been explained by a leading American anthropologist, William Howells, who says that man, unlike other animals, is "the creature who comprehends things he cannot see and believes in things he cannot comprehend.

And toward the end:

> In their religious aspirations men do not differ much from one another, no matter where they live, or when. They seek assurance of the favor of their gods, protection against the dangers of life, community with their fellows, courage in the hour of conflict, comfort in the hour of grief, guidance in their daily concerns, release from the pangs of conscience and, for most but not all of them, hope for some sort of immortality. The ways by which followers of the different faiths pursue these common ends vary beyond all telling, though within all the great faiths

there have been mystics who have risen above the level on which most of us live to a sense of the Divine which has made them much akin.

Before commenting on the above quotes, let me cite a small something that appeared in a piece by Sam Howe Verhovek in the *Los Angeles Times* on April 1, 2007. In that piece he cites an American Indian's reference to a wise man's saying that "there are as many ways to pray as there are blades of grass."

To me the above statements, with which I can agree, simply define humans' tendency, or better said, need, to appeal to a god. Some that I have quoted might say that God exists, and that humanity is naturally inclined to acknowledge him and to seek his support. I turn the argument around and contend that humans need a god and therefore create him to provide the solace for which they yearn.

The Religious Institutions

The earliest of the identified great religions is Hinduism, although the early Chinese folk religions or practices taken as a body may compete for this honor. There are Hindu rituals and practices going back as far as six thousand years that provide the basis for its practice, and I would note that this religion relies greatly on the Indo-European Aryan incursions and the very ancient beliefs that they brought. Written records came very late. Hinduism involves the worship of a pantheon of gods but does recognize a central, unifying entity. A derivative of Hinduism (my words) is the following of Gautama, the Buddha. His activities have been described as a revolt against the predominant Hinduism of his time much like a Martin Luther or Muhammad. Although the emphasis by Buddha was essentially on the conduct of humans in their society, he incorporated much of the religion of the time, and the gods were ever present. I intend to address the Eastern religions later, because the debate regarding the existence of God appears to be most intense in the context of the three Middle Eastern great religions of the book, and I would prefer to start there.

I am not going to get into the many other religions of history such as those of the Mayan, Aztec, Andean, Polynesian, or Nordic cultures other than to say that, despite very different circumstances, they all display the same human tendency to create gods.

The Middle Eastern Religions

The Middle East gave birth to three of the great religions recognized today: Judaism, Christianity, and Islam. In each of these religions there is a wealth of writings to describe the origins, the precepts, expected behaviors, awards and punishments, the future, and much more, all in exquisite detail. Each of them is monotheistic, the many gods of earlier history having been vanquished, albeit after long and bitter battles. The written history of the three is embodied in the Torah, the Bible (Old and New Testaments), and the Koran. There are many other sources, but these are the central ones. These works are often taken as being absolute statements of fact and of truth such that there can be no challenge to the texts as written. They can be the words of God! Barring that extreme, most believers accept the texts as a broad statement of generally acceptable facts and truths. Genesis of the Jewish and Christian Old Testament is an example of the authors' attempts to put God's seal on the world as humans see it. The sun, light, night, land, and sea are those things that impinge mightily on human existence. If they had to have a beginning, and not knowing what that might have been, humans defaulted to deity. Clear as night and day but nothing to do with the truth.

The Middle Eastern religions are referred to as "religions of the book," since they rely so much on ancient and then later texts for their central themes, their rituals, their rules of conduct, rewards, and punishments. But how factual can the written word be, and how can it account for the beginnings of god belief? For any student of literature and history, it is obvious that the written word must be taken with a great deal of skepticism. If the writings are two or more thousand years old, there is all the more need to be skeptical.

The question applies not only to the religions of Middle East origin but to any holy texts.

The ancient texts are usually an attempt to record verbally transmitted experiences of individuals and, more often, third-party descriptions of events. This often happened many decades after the events described. The records appeared in an ancient language. They had to be translated, which any decent linguist will contend is a sure way to introduce significant error. Then we see centuries of commentary, new translations, cultural and political pressures, loss of texts, and efforts of the powerful to adjust the texts to their likes, all of which contort both text and meaning of what was originally recorded.

We must understand that the texts, as accurate as they may be in recording what witnesses reported, could not be assumed to portray what, in fact, occurred. Those who originated the description of events may have been and probably were biased. Even if they were not, witnesses are famous for coming up with very different views of the same events. The potential for inaccurate reporting is assured. Once the description of an event was promulgated, history tells us that the bards and sages did a very efficient job of passing on accurate versions of a story. But that by no means assumes the original story to be true to the facts. As an example of these hazards, consider the "Codex Sinaiticus," the world's oldest Bible. Compiled in the mid-fourth century, it has been scattered in pieces throughout Europe. It shows clear signs of significant editing and rewriting. Once collected, one has to wonder what value the codex truly has.

The writings of Hinduism, Buddhism, Judaism, and Islam cannot be any less suspect.

There has been a centuries-old battle over the authenticity or accuracy of specific religious texts. Dan Brown in his *The Da Vinci Code* jumped into the fray with a vengeance. He seized on a clearly established historical theme, whether true or not, and embellished it with a modern suspenseful context. He has been answered by several biblical scholars with an equal vengeance. Timothy Keller, an acclaimed religious advocate, has aimed an interesting amount of criticism at Dan Brown. His and other responses appear to be typical of the response of the church throughout history. For example, Darrell L. Bock, in his *Breaking the Da Vinci Code*, challenges the ideas raised by Dan Brown by reference to biblical studies conducted over the centuries. In other words, he attacks texts and their interpretations with even more texts, those officially supported by the church. They may, in fact, be more recognized, but that does not infer truth. There will always be contradictory descriptions of events that upset the "accepted" views. Two-thousand-year-old documents exposed to two thousand years of translation, interpretation, and manipulation are not reliable depictions of occurrences then, much less thousands of years even earlier, as, for example, the Old Testament and the early Hindu scripts.

When reviewing the Hebrew, Christian, and Muslim historical texts in the context of archeological discoveries in recent decades, it is clear that those religions borrowed tremendously from earlier religions. Here we have evidence of manipulation at the very beginnings. The cultures and the gods, who were passed on in some form or other, of early Sumer, Egypt, and Persia provide examples. The Hindu background to Buddhism is also pertinent. In order to suit the masses, the religious hierarchy had to take in various gods and practices from the religions with which the masses were comfortable. The end effect was a complex historical intermixing of myth, practice, loyalties, custom, and, sometimes, truth. The texts central to the great religions must be seen in this context. To take them literally as they exist today is preposterous.

I advise a bit of caution at this point. The discussion here and in much of what follows revolves around written scripture, and in most recent religious debates the written word seems to be the central point. We must, however, not forget that humanity has since ancient times searched for and evolved ways to explain and cope with its environment. Hopes and fears led early humans to establish elaborate oral representations, rituals, sacrifices, and practices to placate the forces and gods that represented the unexplainable world around them and life in the hereafter. Does the scripture surviving today adequately represent that history?

In her recent book, *The Lost Art of Scripture*, Karen Armstrong contends that it does not. Her work presents an impressive amount of information clearly based on her years of research and more than a dozen acclaimed books on religious themes. Here the author explores the history of the religions of China, the Indian subcontinent, and the Middle East (Judaism, Christianity, Islam) in great detail. She argues that religious scripture is essentially the oral, ritual, emotional, and physical expression of Humanity's search for success, well-being, relief from pain, fear, and defeat, and, above all, meaning in a cosmic context. She narrates an ever changing environmental, psychological, cultural, social, political, religious kaleidoscope. Religious thought changes over time. It is subject to human intervention. It is not necessarily what is in the written scripture.

I find Karen Armstrong's arguments regarding Mankind's religious self to be more than reasonable and very much in tune with the basic themes in my book. Humanity develops and evolves a religious environment to its liking.

I am supportive of Karen Armstrong's themes. Why, for instance, do I argue the weakness of the written texts when my view is that god belief was a fact of life long before the scriptures were first inscribed. I do because the written histories, stories, and myths do have an impact on today's debate. They substantiate and codify humanity's beliefs, and if they are suspect, the beliefs become suspect as well.

Early Less Recognized Religions/Cultures

What I have just stated needs some substantiation. The effects of earlier civilizations on religious beliefs of today cannot be overemphasized. The religions of the book are copies of religions and cultures far their seniors. The civilizations of Sumer and Akkad bequeathed much of their practice to the later Judaic/Christian/Muslim philosophies and practices. Myths such as the flood and Noah probably originated from factually attested overflowing of the Tigris and Euphrates Rivers (Sir Leonard Woolley). The law code of Hammurabi has its clear reflections in the law and religious codes of later cultures. Before him, the culture of Mari probably had an influence on the religious thinking of those of the Fertile Crescent regarding the commercial precedents for inheritance and the place of judges in society. The Mari are a Finno-Ugric peoples found traditionally and today in the Volga River region.

From there to the Fertile Crescent seems far, but peoples then did, in fact, travel far. Invasions and cultural influence from region to region were common in the early history of the Middle East. The discoveries of the ancient settlements of the Hurrians in today's northern Iraq (the Nuzi tablets) led to further evidence of the origins of the basis of Genesis. The evidence predicts early Hebrew practices involving familial relations (wife, consort, slave, adoptions, inheritance, and the so-called sistership relationship).

As a prime example of the influence of ancient and old cultures and religions, consider Zoroastrianism. This religion no longer figures in the modern hierarchy of religions, but it must be appreciated for the significant influence that it had on the religions that did survive.

The ancient Persians (thousands of years BC) at first revered a series of gods, and their beliefs appear to have fundamentally influenced the Vedic traditions of India. Then came the prophet Zoroaster, about 600 BC, who preached the one god or Ahura Mazda. He opposed some of the revolting religious practices of the time such as human sacrifice and offered a more enlightened approach for believers. (Interesting that Siddhartha Gautama at that very time was upsetting the existing religious structure in India.) In effect, Zoroastrianism and its endorsement of Ahura Mazda laid down the foundations for the one God, the concepts of heaven, hell, and the last judgment, all of which are reflected in the Judeo-Christian tradition and in Islam.

What about the Egyptians? Egypt was a major player in the Middle East for millennia. How have the Egyptians contributed to humanity's tradition of god belief? The answers can be derived from a rich archeological record, and Egyptian religion can be traced back to the fourth millennium BC. I am sure that the true beginnings came much further back in time. Religion in the region of the Nile began with animism and then gods representing natural elements such as the sun.

Specific god beliefs and power structures changed, rose, and fell over thousands of years, illustrating very well the fact that the gods ascended or descended in influence depending on the power attained by their human creators. Egyptian religion reflected humans' fear of death and maintained belief in life after death. (Even the gods were expected to die yet retain influence.) And, as was common with early religions, the pharaoh assumed the role of a god or at least an intermediary between humans and a god. Although there were numerous gods, one pharaoh, Amenhotep IV, did flirt with a form of monotheism. That did not last long.

The Egyptians passed on a limited amount of their religion to the rest of the world, and then the religion disappeared. The Greeks and Romans picked up some aspects of the worship of Isis and Osiris. Probably the most significant inheritance was the story of the Exodus. There is evidence that the Jews prospered in Egypt, fell from grace, and were expelled. But just how much of the Exodus itself is fact rather than myth is controversial, and the related interface with the Jewish god are doubtful at best.

We must never forget that today's religions are derived from the most ancient and traditional sources, and that they are conceivably more mythical than real. We could relate any number of records and precedents for the religious philosophies proposed. The main point is that god creation started very early and long before records began.

Judaism

Judaism today is rooted in the beliefs of ancient tribal chiefs, prophets, and poets, dating back roughly six thousand years. Who can really date Abraham? And does Genesis truly provide a viable time frame? The first book of the Old Testament claims a creation around six thousand years ago. It goes on to relate story after story of the older days. There follows a series of books with a vast amount of Hebrew literature devoted to recording the trials, tribulations, and triumphs of the Jews.

There is also a vast amount of commentary analyzing and explaining the resultant religion. We have, therefore, a religion based on beliefs, poems, myths, histories, and gods, all thousands of years old. If one understands what society was five or more thousand years ago, one must also understand that people back then imagined anything and everything to explain their existence and the world around them. There was no archaeology, no anthropology, no microbiology, no science at all in the sense that we know it today. Those early peoples had to create an explanation of what they were and how they related to the forces of nature and to one-another. They created gods, and, as time progressed and thinking matured, they arrived at the one God of Judaism today.

If we look at the book of Genesis, we can see a good example of how and why Judaism and so many of the religions of today came to their core beliefs. Genesis describes how the world and humankind came to be. And how would any thinking person of that time see it otherwise? They had no scientific background, no DNA understanding, no fossil record, and on and on. I am not sure how far back we must go to find the beginnings of the creation story, but it is probably long before the earliest Hebrews. Cultural groupings felt obliged to state how it all came to be, and a clear solution was to spin a tale that the populace would not only believe but enjoy and embrace as a positive for their future. Genesis is not all that positive; it carries some lessons. But it clearly fits the pattern of myth creation. The American Indian, the Aztecs, the Egyptians, and almost all other cultures have employed similar solutions to explaining why and where they are.

It is surprising to me that so many intelligent and well-educated modern people fail to appreciate the cultural and scientific situation thousands of years ago, insisting on taking the myths as reality.

I would like to refer to a book that I read nearly half a century ago and recently reread. It is *The Ten Commandments*, by A. Powell Davies, its latest publication being 1956. I know full well that an immense amount of research related to the Old Testament has been undertaken in the meantime and that conclusions have been revised or abandoned because of archeological and textual examinations. But I believe there is a fundamental validity in Davies's exposition. I take the case of the Ten Commandments as an example of the broader historical weakness of the religious record.

Davies traces the biblical account and the archeological evidence that describe the evolution of the Ten Commandments, and I doubt that any more recent discoveries would cause the conclusions one could derive from his work to be altered significantly. Davies starts with the background of the biblical record, which shows a multiplicity of distortions, concoctions, and contradictions that call into doubt the most basic beliefs of Judeo-Christianity. For example, did Moses really exist? It appears that much of the testimony is merely based on myth. Egyptian records do not even mention the Exodus or events surrounding it, for example.

Christopher Hitchens, in his *God Is Not Great*, discusses the Ten Commandments and says, "It would be harder to find an easier proof that religion is man-made." He goes on to explain that "no society ever discovered has failed to protect itself from self-evident crimes like those supposedly stipulated at Mount Sinai." In other words, we have a policy statement reflecting the views of the powers that be, which in turn reflect the general views of the times. Hitchens, as have others, challenges the entire Old Testament as to its veracity.

It is clear by Davies's account that the Old Testament beliefs and practices were derived from the most basic of humanity's original barbaric striving for survival, fecundity, wealth, and power. We find evidence of ancestor worship in the early Hebrew religion. It appears unlikely that this was imported from the Far East. It may have been indigenous in origin, or it could have been passed on by the Persians or others to the East. The evidence shows that the roots of religion as described in the Old Testament lie with the Babylonians, the Persians, the Assyrians, and the Canaanites, among others, and that the religion espoused in the Old Testament is nothing more than a path described by many other earlier religions. Tellingly, the Hebrew religion described by Davies was not monotheistic! The peoples of Judea fully accepted that there were other gods; they ascribed to one god only for their own region of dominance, and even that was a disputed position. As time passes, beliefs mature, as the record seems to show.

Permit me to quote a lengthy passage from Davies's concluding remarks. It points out the role of humans in the development of moral codes and the role of gods in this process. I will establish the contextual framework by citing Davies's contention that the Ten Commandments represent a great religious symbol "for faith in the God of moral law." He goes on:

> We have studied Israel's religion in its earliest phases: barbaric customs, temple prostitution, degrading forms of worship, infant sacrifice. We learned how massacres were ordered—so the people thought—by Yahweh, Israel's God. We saw that Yahweh was seen as a cruel despot, jealous, capricious, not knowing evil from good.
>
> But this was not peculiar to Israel's religion. In its earliest phases religion has always been like that. All the gods at first were cruel: they were made in the image of their worshippers and could only grow, morally, as their worshippers grew. What the reader must recognize, therefore, is that what he has been following is for the most part a typical religious history. His own ancestors engaged in the same degrading practices as did the Israelites. It is not where Israel started that has ultimate significance— but where she arrived.
>
> Religious progress has come stage by stage. There has been no way of hurrying it. That is how it came in Israel.

The horrors of infant sacrifice gave way to the butchery of animals. The lamb was substituted for the first borne son, as in the story of Abraham and Isaac. Then finally the ritual slaughter ended altogether. In Israel the temple gave way to the synagogue. God was seen in a new light. He was invoked not by splashing blood upon some sacred stone but in the insights of his prophets and the meaning of the law.

That is what, today, the Ten Commandments signify: the turning point in the long struggle to liberate religion from debasing custom and false belief; the difficult ascent from a low moral level toward a high one.

And what can I add to Davies's accounts? Humans create or adopt gods or a god that suits their need for support in life and that depends mightily on their societal and political situation. Myth plays a role. If a god that is revered matches a period of wealth and prosperity, then that god is in ascendancy. If times are bad, a god loses out to another. Blame the god. History shows this. The peoples of the Old Testament followed the gods that gave them the most support and solace. And all of this matures with time.

The point is that humans create the gods that they desire, believing that the created god will improve their life on earth and the life thereafter. An important message that I acknowledge from Davies's exposition is his conclusion that the Ten Commandments as we view them are a result of this process of maturation through the centuries of Hebrew religious ferment. What he is saying is that humankind through the prophets and other modernizing constituencies took the commandments from their barbaric beginnings to their eventual interpretations by means of a long-term humanizing trend. That the end result is a religion of righteousness and law disguises nothing. Humankind derived the code and then modified it to reflect changing times. Humans created gods to provide political/sociological support for ancient and established beliefs of the community such as the requirements of the Ten Commandments.

Beyond the interpretations of the biblical texts there are scientific and archaeological challenges to the Old Testament story. An article in the

December 2010 issue of the *National Geographic* describes the controversy over archaeological discoveries in the "Holyland." To quote the *National Geographic*, "DESPITE DECADES of searching, archeologists had found no solid evidence that David or Solomon ever built anything." Now digs seem to have unearthed some evidence, but the findings are hotly contested. The controversy revolves around findings of supposed structures and mines noted in the Bible and whether they are at all significant.

In this case several experts' egos are involved, but that does not diminish the doubt that we may have for the events depicted in the Bible. The evidence unearthed appears not to be conclusive, and even if it were, the facts can never support the claims for supernatural intervention associated with the biblical texts.

There are, of course, many more investigations into the historical and archaeological background to the Old Testament. Most telling is the conclusion reached by Silberman and Finkelstein of the Institute of Archeology at Tel Aviv University to the effect that there was no flight from Egypt, no wandering in the desert, and no conquest of Canaan. All of this was contrived later.

Judaism is, despite many of its positive sociological elements resulting from the maturation mentioned above, a religion based on mythology rooted in ancient local and foreign beliefs and practices that demanded gods for social, political, and pragmatic economic support. In this sense, it is no different from any of the other known religions.

Christianity

Of all the great religions, only Christianity recognizes the corporal presence of God on earth. Other religions and some pagan sects may place the mantle of God on the shoulders of their worshipped figures, but Christianity proposes that its dominant figure was the son of God in the form of man on earth. I join those who challenge the historical record of the circumstances surrounding the birth, life, death, and resurrection of Jesus of Nazareth as well as the record addressing the earlier biblical prophets.

The challenge is to the gospels and the circumstances that contributed to their development. If one is to disprove a thesis, one must start with the basic assumptions, and the Christian assumptions cannot be sustained. How can Genesis be in any way taken seriously? How can the tales around Abraham and many others be treated other than as popular myths sustaining a cultural identity? How can one reasonably explain a burning bush and a series of engraved stone tablets other than a wonderful way of proclaiming the sanctity of socially desirable rules of conduct through a mass-appealing story? And, of course, we are confronted with the mind-challenging claims of the reality of a virgin birth, healing powers, mystical appearances (fish, wine), and the return from the dead. Given the nature of humans and their cultures of the past millennia, there are many ways and reasons to explain away these contradictions of reality, and it appears to me the only reason they are not generally pursued is the very powerful resistance of organized religion and a thoroughly convinced body of believers who would probably revolt should the fundamentals be denied.

What about the vast libraries of writings accumulated over the many centuries containing so many sacred testimonies to the faith? They are exactly that—testimonies to the faith. Most of what comes after the accounts of the gospels is largely irrelevant to the truth of the events related in the gospels.

Constantine's conversion of the masses was probably a political act. Perhaps the people had already decided for Christianity, and he acted accordingly.

The revered Augustine of Hippo was a forceful advocate whose many writings addressed the means to create a structure to endorse and enforce belief in an already accepted faith. Yes, he agonized in his belief and explored his doubts, but he affirmed his faith even more strongly in the end.

Similarly, Francis of Assisi showed great organizational talents in furtherance of the faith but, as we might expect, little inclination to verify the historical events relative to God's existence or the reality of Jesus's history, a thousand years past.

Though these greats eloquently espoused the good conduct of humans in the imperfect world and the existence of the kingdom of God, they merely built on many centuries of blind acceptance of God's existence and his appearance on earth.

The great American Christian philosophers of the twentieth century, such as Dr. Reinhold Neibuhr, Dr. Georges Florovsky, Dr. Paul J. Tillich,

John Dewey, and others built upon an established faith and interpreted human events in light of an established Christian structure. In my view many of their statements of belief appear nonsensical and very naïve in rationalizing human existence with a relationship based on a two-thousand-year-old myth. Read them and see what you, the reader, conclude.

I would like to continue with two of the supposed heavies of religious philosophy: Augustine and Aquinas. They illustrate the blind adherence to the ancient texts that blocks any intelligent discourse on the existence of God.

Let's briefly examine the works of Augustine. Why not others in the early years of Christianity? The selection is arbitrary but is a reasonable one for our purposes. Here we have a brilliant religious philosopher, clearly a student of history, and a sort of convert, which typically energizes the type. His works display a pattern that underscores the theme of this book.

Roughly a generation ago, more or less fifty years, I read Augustine's *On the Immortality of the Soul*. At that time I wrote a number of caustic comments in the margins of the text. I have recently reread the work. In fact, I have reread parts of the piece several times. My earlier conclusions remain valid, in my view. *On the Immortality of the Soul* is a mess involving false premises, blind assertions, circular reasoning, and one non sequitur after another. It proves nothing, much less the immortality of the soul.

The City of God, by Augustine, though exhibiting some of the literal traits just mentioned, is a work well worth consideration. It is lengthy (six hundred pages plus), and it is tedious, but there are many passages of valuable instruction and religious and historical interpretation. Augustine's familiarity with the Bible is to be expected. His familiarity with the great historians and philosophers of the ages (Horace, Cicero, Plato, Virgil, Seneca, Varro, and others) is impressive. He describes logical, reasonable, and down-to-earth solutions to historical events and narratives. Yet time after time he adds that that is what God ordained/foresaw/proclaimed, etc.

The first ten books of the *City* condemn the peoples and rulers of Rome and the barbarians for their god beliefs, and though undoubtedly justified, he never hesitates to contrast the philosophy and practices of the Christians with those of the heathens. This is probably justified, in that Christianity was an example of maturing religious thought similar to that

that was occurring in Judaism. It had clear attractions for humankind. Score one for the Christians and zero for the Romans.

The remaining twelve books of the *City* are the most instructive for our purposes, and they reflect much of the Christian thinking and philosophy of those early years. Augustine prefers Platonic philosophy because it is nearest to the Christian faith but discusses many of the philosophies and debates of the day. In the *City* Augustine spends far more time on the texts of the Old Testament but then often cites events and statements in light of what is to occur in the New Testament, speaking somewhat as a prophet.

There are some extremely interesting speculations. In book XI, Augustine brings up the question, why was the world created where it is? He addresses infinite space, infinite realms in space, time, innumerable worlds, and hints at the atom (Epicurus), which are amazing predictions of today's twenty-first century scientific debates. In book XIII there are flavors of Buddhism and Hinduism.

However, Augustine's discourses adhere incredibly and slavishly to the texts of the Old and New Testament. In book XVI he defends the scripture regarding the ages of Noah, Terah, and Abram, saying, "because the scripture cannot be contradicted." In book XVIII he addresses Greek and Latin notables, the prophets, translations, the Septuagint, and more in a broad-brush approach to history with added detail. One can see his basic thinking when Augustine says, "We being sustained by divine authority, in the history of our religion, have no doubt that whatever is opposed to it is most false." He accepts the authority of the Septuagint. Note that Augustine writes well after the conclave in Nicea.

In short, Augustine defends the scriptures down to the tiniest detail even when he feels obliged to present somewhat different reasonable explanations of the texts. In light of the serious difficulties in accepting the ancient texts as factual, if not contrived, Augustine can be taken as mainly an intelligent and well-educated religious philosopher whose works are interesting and, at times, informative, but little more. His is all faith. He proves nothing in regard to God's actual being other than one person's dedication to God.

Aquinas is a similar example. He spent his entire life in the service of the church in any number of duties from student to university senior in the church's hierarchy. He had to have had a solid belief in the fundamentals of Christianity to the exclusion of all doubt as to their authenticity. As with Augustine, the only true course of critical debate regarding Aquinas should be the very origins of his belief, not the polemics that follow.

Aquinas's great work is *The Summa Theologica*, in which he lays out and summarizes his version of Christian doctrinal analysis. Of particular interest to us should be the stated "Question II, The Existence of God." One could naively expect a reasonably logical approach to the question of God's existence, but, no, this supposed great philosopher of logic starts the discussion with: "Because the chief aim of sacred doctrine is to teach the knowledge of God." There is no debate. The objective of the discourse is only to "prove" what has already been presumed. *The Summa Theologica* goes on to discuss at length various themes to include angels, for most of which even today's pope would blush.

It may appear that I give Aquinas a cavalier dismissal. Not true! Aquinas is a great religious philosopher and a great contributor to Western thought. Nevertheless, his thought is based on a blind adherence to ancient mores that defy logical thinking. Look at Aquinas's career. He is educated and practices/teaches at theological institutions and surroundings. He suffers an insulated and incestuous religious influence. That has nothing to do or to say about the reality of god belief. The belief is assumed.

It follows that an examination of humans' early history, the historical account, archaeology, evolution, cosmology, and related sciences contain the true answers to the question of God's existence, not the polemics and assertions of faith, however convincing and ingenuous they seem to be.

Why do I even consider Augustine and Aquinas? I do because they illustrate the centuries-old Christian polemics regarding how, what, why, where, and when things Christian are judged. This is an incestuous polemic that achieves nothing! Yes, there are some philosophical jewels that stand out, but nothing more. Why did I not discuss Tertullian? Why not Justin? Why not many more? Because they are more of the same pure faith. They start with the assumption that the Testaments are incontrovertibly true. One could accuse me of the same—that is, that my atheistic view is taken as essentially true—but I contend that I am giving the other side more than due diligence and that the evidence is on my side!

Richard Dawkins in his *The God Delusion* addresses "The Argument from Scripture" and more than adequately undermines the belief in religious texts thousands of years old. Dawkins states early in his book that he would address Christianity primarily as that is his life's experience. He cites the inconsistency of the Gospels relating to the life of Jesus and the events surrounding him as well as the gross historical misstatements they contain. Dawkins cites publications that trace the events of the Jesus legend to earlier religions in the Middle East. The sequence of historical characters is questioned both on historical and biological grounds. He cites the controversy around the "gospels" that were supposed to have been arbitrarily dismissed by the early church hierarchy as potentially embarrassing to the faith. Dawkins places the entire record in the realm of the King Arthur stories. Dawkins sums it up by saying that he "shall not consider the Bible further as evidence for any kind of deity." He cites *The Da Vinci Code* as an equivalent religious fiction.

Karen Armstrong might agree slightly at this point (*The Lost Art of Scripture*). Scriptures serve a purpose beyond things purely logical and factual. They are an art form providing an appealing and meaningful story.

Later in his book, Dawkins addresses "The Good Book and the Changing Moral Zeitgeist." The point here is to show that the ideas, morals, and ethics found in the Old and New Testaments are archaic and not at all with the moral zeitgeist of today. We are confronted with the likes of Rev. Michael Bray, Pat Robertson, and others who take the testaments literally, despite the depraved acts of the biblical characters found in the texts that Dawkins cites. How can anyone condone the felonious acts related in the testaments? Dawkins goes on to recall incident after incident of heinous crimes that show the testaments to be nothing more than sect and clan enforcement of religious dogma.

From my perspective, it is not necessary that anyone elaborate the corruptness in the Bible's stories. It is there to be seen or read. Abraham, Moses, and the other "greats" are anything but saintly! Dawkins accepts that Jesus demonstrates a moral superiority over his predecessors. But the New Testament does display a dark side involving an emphasis on sin, retribution, and clan devotion.

What does all this mean regarding the existence of God or not? Taking the interpretation that Dawkins and others place on the scriptures and the moral lessons of the Old and New Testaments, the entire structure of Christianity comes into question. The written or otherwise recorded history of this religious sect is suspect. I am not examining the goodness or badness of this sect; I believe, as do Dawkins and others, that the contradictory and morally repugnant nature of some of the texts is poor proof that God does or does not exist.

We are discussing Christianity here, but all the religions of today are based on dubious accounts of events long past. Subsequent writings add nothing to the authenticity of the original accounts. Religion and the belief in a god or gods are weakest at their historical beginnings.

I propose to review some of the arguments in *The Human Christ: The Search for the Historical Jesus,* by Charlotte Allen. Choice of this work is somewhat arbitrary. There are many others, but her book tends to underscore the arguments in my thesis. Charlotte Allen's book is a superb piece of extensive research, excellent commentary, and downright interesting and entertaining reading. In her introduction the author states,

> I am not a biblical scholar, and this book is not an attempt to offer a theory of who the historical Jesus was, or whether he actually said or did those things attributed to him in the Gospels. Rather, it examines the way in which the image of Jesus has functioned as a vehicle for some of the best and worst ideas of Western civilization over the past 2,000 years.

Allen does go on later in the introduction to say,

> The quest for the historical Jesus has produced surprisingly little genuine and uncontroverted new knowledge over the past three centuries about the man and his time. We still do not know where the four canonical gospels were written, or when, although it is fairly certain that all of them existed in something like their present form by the end of the first century. We can only make educated guesses as to how they were composed and what source materials their authors used.

The Human Christ provides from cover to cover an immense number of sources, citations, and commentary on the nearly two-thousand-year-old debate about the reality of the figure described in the Gospels. It makes it clear that a broad range of descriptions, many quite radical and doubting, arose in the very early centuries, and that not much original has surfaced in the many centuries up to today. Many new twists have been employed, but the wide range of basic views remains much the same.

It is my observation that the many sources and personages cited in the book tend heavily toward the doubting side. The dogmatic faithful do not appear that often. Allen does show that Catholics were kept out of the debate until only recently when the Second Vatican Council in 1965 allowed Catholics to use all sources in analyzing the Gospels. In a broader sense, it took a lot of courage to enter the debate, and I suspect that many of the faith declined to risk it. Perhaps there was the belief that the arguments were there for all to see in the Testaments and therefore needed no further explanation or defense.

The first conclusion that I would draw from Allen's book is that an accurate description of Jesus is probably impossible and that the facts surrounding his birth, his living years, death, and resurrection are highly suspect. (This is my conclusion and not that of Charlotte Allen.) I am not a biblical scholar. Nor am I a historian. But when I research the works of those who are and the extremely disparate views and conclusions they produce, how can the Gospels and other writings of the period be taken seriously?

Jesus's history is often challenged as to accuracy, and some say may have been coordinated in some way between the Gospels. That source may have been Q. Q is the first letter in the German word for source. In this case it would mean a person or persons who could have written an early unifying text.

It makes ultimate sense to me that the disciples would have shared their views of events and would have had the same motivation in telling the same story. It also makes sense to me that such personages would want to make the most out of their experience and would embellish the facts to their advantage.

As to the resurrection, it was enlightening to me to read that almost all of the technical, liberal explanations of the event were proposed in the early centuries. I cannot add much to the debate. However, I feel obliged to leaf through a few of the explanations that, to be very clear, explain away any return from the dead. First, Jesus did not die and somehow recovered. If so, then there he was! Second, if he did die, the authorities whisked away his body to avoid problems. Or friends did so to make their point. Or this or that! One can imagine any number of reasonable possibilities. Later encounters with Jesus can be explained as delusional or fabrication for some purpose or other. Gnostic teachings took this line.

I cite a passage from *The Human Christ*, again from the introduction.

> Nearly all Jews in Jesus' day believed in the resurrection of the dead, especially in the case of martyrs. It is therefore not surprising that certain of them imagined that Jesus had returned to life in glorious form.

In short, for any student of literature and history, it is obvious that the written word must be taken with a great deal of skepticism.

Let me address the timing of the authorship of the Gospels. Charlotte Allen wrote that the Gospels existed in something like their present form by the end of the first century. Other researchers arrive at a similar time frame. I respect her scholarship and would accept decades of slippage in any direction, so that authorship of the Gospels occurred anywhere from twenty to one hundred years after Jesus's reported death, possibly more. Even in today's era of advanced technology, it is a severe challenge to reconstruct events of only a few years back. Check today's judicial proceedings. A few years after the event, things get very nebulous.

Now, go back two thousand years and try to portray accurately the events that occurred at that time decades in the past. Yes, the bards have had a reputation for passing on verbally events of the past, but we have no evidence of this element of storytelling in the record. Even if we did, the bard only passes on what has been passed on to him, and the truth or not of the story is up to question. To say that the Gospels accurately portrayed anything factual, having been written over the better part of a century and then rewritten, editorialized, and filtered over two millennia, is a real stretch.

Nor am I impressed with the accuracy of description of geography, towns, landmarks, customs, and figures in the early texts such as John's gospel, when it implies a similar accuracy in the definition of specific events. A description of physical things that change little over the years or cultures that also change very slowly is easy. Citing the big wigs or events of regional impact is also not difficult. But a description of purely local events regarding an individual's meetings, discussions, activities, and preaching is something else. The realistic environmental description is by no means a validation of the associated minutia.

Timothy Keller, on the other hand, believes that the description of minor details in the Gospels does, in fact, contribute to their authenticity. Why, he argues, would details appear if not for the accounts of reliable witnesses? C. S. Lewis supports this argument, describing the Gospels as "reportage." I am not convinced!

One of the most instructive aspects of *The Human Christ* is the convergence of the first and last parts of the book in describing the pervasive influence of Hebrew lifestyle and culture on the story of Jesus of Nazareth. The life and actions of Jesus must be evaluated in the context of this Jewish world, a world that survived despite the strong influence of a Greek and Roman overlay. Much has been written about the influence of this Jewish environment not only on Jesus the individual but also on the record of his birth, life, death, and resurrection.

The record, in my view, was bound to incorporate the Jewish symbols and statements that were deemed acceptable to the community. If a certain theme enjoyed acceptance by the people, then it was wise to incorporate it in any new doctrine. The record shows that much of what Jesus preached has a source in Hebrew religious culture and history, which would as well include the Greek and Roman influences.

Charlotte Allen's book reinforces my belief that the incorporation of historic beliefs in the story of Jesus of Nazareth and the two thousand years of alteration of late and questionable texts suffice to deny a story of divinity or of God. That's as simple as I can put it! Charlotte Allen may not agree with the conclusions that I draw from her book, but so be it.

On March 4, 2007, an op-ed contribution by Charlotte Allen appeared in the *Los Angeles Times*. Allen commented on a documentary, *The Lost Tomb of Jesus*, which was to be broadcast that evening on the Discovery Channel. The documentary looks into the 1980 archaeological find in Jerusalem of a number of ossuaries that are purported, by the originators of the documentary, to contain the remains (bones) of Jesus, Judah (son of Jesus), and two Marys (Mary Magdalene and Mary, mother of Jesus). This would, of course lend credence to Gnostic and other interpretations of the life of Jesus and the early years of Christianity, and Allen gives her evaluation of the historical significance of the find and the documentation. Allen refers to the Gospel of Judas, the *Da Vinci Code*, and then:

> A continuing cottage industry of constructing versions of Christianity to the one we already have: the Gospel of Thomas, the Q Gospel, the Gospel of Mary Magdalene (uncovered in Egypt about a century ago) and a host of other Gnostic and related texts and idiosyncratic archeological interpretations that have floated around the Western World since the 18th century.

Allen's point is that despite all these revelations, "Christianity continues to exude power and fascination even among those who seek to debunk its claims." I cannot dispute that point, but I wonder if Allen isn't unwittingly making another point: that Christians are wed to a story that they want to believe, come what may in the historical record, or any challenges that may contest the accepted theses. Any contradiction of their beloved religious history must, of course, be wrong. Don't waste your time challenging what we believe.

I watched the documentary. It was quite interesting, but it did not prove anything, and I would not support the thesis; nor would I reject it. I just do not know, although proof that the thesis is correct would tend to play down the existence of God, and a contrary proof would leave us where we were: believing or doubting as we see the facts. This is one more example of the cloudiness of the historical record and the shaky ground upon which the Jesus story rests. We can extend this controversy to other stories in other religions.

Other Sources

There are several other recent publications that are of interest here. The first, *Misquoting Jesus*, by Bart D. Ehrman, is particularly illuminating. Allen, above, describes the controversies: everything is challenged, and nothing is new. Ehrman describes the inaccuracies: as far as biblical texts are concerned, we have no originals, and what we have is surely quite different from the probable originals.

Ehrman's career has been one devoted to investigating the textual changes in the New Testament. Ehrman rather uniquely bares his soul in his book. In his introduction (picked up later in an annex, *Q & A with Bart Ehrman*) he describes his journey from a born-again Christian experience through fundamentalist and then evangelical commitments to his current agnosticism.

Misquoting Jesus was a *New York Times* bestseller for many weeks and should need no extensive review here for those interested in the book's central theme. In short, Ehrman addresses the New Testament and describes the pervasive textual changes that have been made to the scriptures over time, most of which are minor errors, but some of which are significant. Human error has much to do with the scriptures on which Christianity is based. I quote from Ehrman's summary:

> We do not have the original manuscripts of any of the books of the New Testament, but only copies—over 5000 copies, just in the Greek language in which these books were originally written.
>
> Most of these copies are centuries removed from the originals.
>
> All of these copies contain mistakes both great and small, as scribes either inadvertently or intentionally altered the text.
>
> The vast majority of these changes are insignificant, immaterial, and of no importance for the meaning of the passages in which they are found.
>
> Others, however, are quite significant. Sometimes the meaning of a verse, a passage, or an entire book depends on which textual variants the scholar decides are original.
>
> These decisions are sometimes relatively simple to make; but in other instances they are exceedingly difficult,

even for scholars who have spent years working on the problem.

As a result, there are many passages of the New Testament where scholars continue to debate the original wording. And there are some in which we will probably never know what the authors originally wrote.

Ehrman hints at his doubt of the "originals," the Gospels themselves, and states his belief that the "originals" had to be the result of human attempts to relate events in light of their beliefs, hopes, fears, surroundings, and all that influences a human being. As a responsible historian, he does not make the definitive leap that the gospels were therefore concocted to reflect the all too human tendencies toward beliefs consistent with the cultures of the time.

I am willing to make that leap. It is possible that the story related in the Gospels (with appropriate attention to the Gospels not accepted by the Catholic Church) is that of a charismatic, forceful, and dynamic individual (Jesus) who encouraged an extremely loyal following in the form of the disciples and was somewhat in the league of Moses and Solomon. Islam judges it so to some degree.

It is clear to me that a loyal following would interpret and relate to others a uniformity of story, anecdotes, individuals, and events. There is evidence that, for instance, the Gospel of Mark was the source for much of the material in Mathew and Luke, not to mention the speculative Q. Each of the authors had his own ax to grind, but the stories seem to be coordinated, and that classifies it all as a conspiracy. For what reason? To create a myth in support of personal, social, or political goals or an innocent but naïve attraction to a seductive philosophy or cult? Any combination of these factors would be a likelihood in my view.

It is worth restating that Bart Ehrman found the biblical record to be on such tenuous grounds that it undermined his long-held faith.

Christopher Hitchens, among others, joins Ehrman in doubting the texts and assumptions of the New Testament. He cites Ehrman, in fact, and points out a number of gross contradictions and discrepancies that Ehrman identified in the Gospel texts.

Bart Ehrman has written several books, his latest, *The Triumph of*

Christianity, published in 2017. He has a reputation as a respected historian with a tendency toward levelheaded balanced analysis.

Well worth mentioning is an article in the December 2011 issue of the *National Geographic* that addresses the King James Version of the Bible. The central theme is the influence that the King James Version had on subsequent linguistic and social mores over the last centuries.

However, there is a subtheme. King James intended to come up with a version of the Bible that reflected what his view of what the Bible should represent. To be honest, he may have been trying to be an arbitrator for a version that appealed to all his constituents: he had a vision of what was acceptable. King James assembled a truly diverse set of scholars to produce an accepted version of the Bible. And they did. Nevertheless, there can be no doubt that there were intense pressures to suit current beliefs and institutions. Texts were altered. What more can one say? The *National Geographic* article also displays an impressive chart that shows a full score of biblical versions over the centuries; a challenge to the credibility of what we read today.

Another author, William Lobdell, a former religion reporter for the *Los Angeles Times*, writes about his loss of faith in his book *Losing My Religion*. Lobdell's problems with religion are different from those of Ehrman, being primarily his disillusionment with the performance of the church as well as the nonperformance of God in relationship to humanity's needs. There are, without a doubt, many more of those with intelligence and the scientific spirit of inquiry and critique who have confronted the dogma of the religions and concluded that it has failed.

Nevertheless, there are those who convert the opposite way, and it is only fair to say that there are many of them. The once noted atheist Antony Flew, an academic philosopher, converted and later professed belief in God based on his views on DNA and the statistics that underlie the chance of existence of the species that exist today. Sir Francis Crick, of human genome fame, expresses his belief in God, perhaps for the same or similar reasons.

Now I will address Sam Harris's book *The End of Faith* and its concentration on the evil that faith and religion have visited on humankind. Harris is clearly saying that there is no God. He makes many points to the effect that old traditions and myths are nothing more than exactly that.

However, he places an emphasis on the destructive nature of religion and the evils resulting from faith. Although this is not the proof we seek, it certainly provides a clue. How can a God allow all this evil? What godly logic would allow for the developments of religious history? How can God be the caring, loving God that many presume?

Timothy Keller rationalizes evil as an element of God's way in forming humankind's belief in God. One could say (and many do) that we humans cannot fathom Gods thoughts or logic. It's beyond our comprehension. A reasonable point, but it does not make a good argument that God would allow a situation in which his creations acted in such demonic ways. Or was Satan the creator?!

It makes sense to say that, given the misery that god belief has inflicted on humanity, it is reasonable to assume (but not prove) that God does not exist. Otherwise, he becomes a malicious and spiteful steward of his creations, much as he appeared in Moses's time. Is that what believers want for a god? Harris's alternative is a combination of human qualities and pursuits that can achieve the happiness that humans desire. This is partially a tribute to the philosophy and practice of the Eastern religions. Harris believes that the nature of consciousness and the facts of morality, ethics, honesty, and love obviate the need for God and faith. Humans can do it themselves. At the end, however, Harris's emphasis on evil neither proves nor disproves God's existence.

I cite Christopher Hitchens a few times in this chapter. Hitchens's entire book *god is not Great* levels damning evidence against organized religion. He points out texts, practices, occurrences, and personalities in religious history that clearly show the disaster that religions have and still do impose on humankind. Hitchens is saying that religions, being as terrible as they are, must mean that their gods cannot exist. He cites reasons for God's nonexistence but generally condemns the religious. His approach appears to be to destroy the historical record, the "transparent fables," as well as the rational and philosophical underpinnings upon which all religions rest. I am not sure that this contributes to the debate as to whether God exists, but, again, it could be a clue.

Above all, Harris and Hitchens make the point clearly that religion is based on false premises. God should, therefore, not exist. The evidence for his existence is suspect—more so, it is not there.

There are many publications and studies that generally support the biblical texts and may lend credibility to certain aspects of the texts. However, we must distinguish between fact and fiction and pure faith. The next source does a decent job in this respect.

The National Geographic Society recently published *The Biblical World, an Illustrated Atlas* (which I will refer to as the *Atlas*), which makes a significant contribution to the central thesis of this book. One could ask what the National Geographic could have to say about the religious nature of our study. I would remind the reader that the National Geographic Society has one of the highest standings in the world when it comes to archaeological undertakings across the globe.

The *Atlas* adds to the understanding of the Bible, its context, and subsequent events. It associates numerous passages in the Bible with archaeological discoveries and other research, and it does so in a very balanced and erudite approach. The text is secular and does not proclaim either truth or falseness for the biblical record. It does provide possible explanations for many of the miraculous events depicted in the Bible, based on geographic, geological, archaeological, linguistic, and textual research, but it also states time and again where controversy exists.

Why do I find this publication to be meaningful?

First, the *Atlas* provides further proof that the Bible is a great historical record. Scribes and writers have preserved a very reasonable account of the cultural background, the religious beliefs, the migrations, the conflicts, the wins and losses, and the familial lineage of certain peoples originating somewhere in early Mesopotamia and settling in Palestine, Egypt, and again Palestine. The *Atlas* provides factual underpinning for the texts.

Next, however, there are many "buts."

Let's say the biblical record is historically reasonably accurate as to times and places involving movements and circumstances of peoples of the Middle East. And let's accept the accuracy of the reporting in the *Atlas*. But what about the supposed conversations with God and the angels? The ancient Sumerian culture had its gods. Worship of the gods was a given. When Abraham's father moves the tribe up into Haran, he was surely encouraged to do so because of problems in Ur. The ancient trade routes, being what they were, certainly carried information as well that indicated the existence of a land along the Mediterranean that would offer a better life than that foreseen for southern Mesopotamia. When Abraham assumes the leadership role after his father's death, what makes more sense than an appeal on his part to the gods or, in this case, his select god, to encourage and guide his followers toward Canaan. Any historian would have to accept that this would have been the normal religious and political approach in those days. Any proof of God's existence? None at all.

It is interesting to me that the Bible concentrates so exclusively on Abraham and his descendants. I would attribute this to the view that history is written by the winners. Terah, Abraham's father, could not have been the only patriarch leading his tribes out of Mesopotamia at the time. There had to be many thousands of other migrants. It could be that a report of a clan traveling out of Ur to what is now Turkey and then on to Canaan became one accepted story out of many. Then famous names that matched those in later history could be assigned to the story. There could be numerous twists in arriving at the biblical text.

The reliance on particular linguistic scripts probably helped. By this I mean that the linguistic heritage of the relevant texts proved to be a survivor. Other texts in other languages or dialects did not survive, because their languages or dialects did not survive.

As the story enfolds, we see many subplots, among them Jacob and his trials and Joseph in Egypt and eventually Moses and the Exodus and later historical events. There are constant appeals to the God of the Hebrews, but this can be nothing more than the ancient traditions of god belief. The record has, without a doubt, been adapted to tradition, myth, and political expediency.

Yes, the *Atlas*, which I am highlighting, shows a very close correlation between the texts and the archaeological data as far as location and dates and names in the empires of the time, but that in no manner proves the reality of a god who favors a group of migrant peoples out of the Tigris and Euphrates. Again, it would have been very natural for anyone of that age to claim the support of a god. We must take every reference in the Bible to contact with God in this sense: it was to be expected. This was the mind-set of a person of that time.

The *Atlas* covers the life of Jesus of Nazareth in the same manner as all the Old Testament figures. It covers the environs of Jesus and later those of Paul. Yes, there appear to have been personages of great significance as described in the Bible. There is archaeological evidence to back up the story. Yet, we cannot, and the Atlas cannot, attribute any truth to the tales related in the Bible that deal with miracles or correspondence with God. For that there is no evidence, and as Ehrman has concluded, the biblical stories may very well have been contrived.

To conclude the comments on the *atlas*, I can accept the possibility of the existence of the peoples, places, and major events that the Bible relates and that the *Atlas* corroborates, but I deny the veracity of the communication and the interface with God found in the Testaments. This is also challenged by the *Atlas* in its realistic interpretations of many of the unusual events related in the Bible.

There Must be Evidence

It is difficult, if not impossible, to prove that God does or does not exist. However, Victor Stenger, in his *God, the Failed Hypothesis*, contends that if God exists then there should be scientifically acceptable evidence for his existence. Critical to his argument is the view that evidence of biblical accounts ought to be expected. It is not that there simply is no evidence; evidence should have been there. The obvious lack of evidence where it ought to have appeared thus falsifies the accounts.

Stenger devotes a chapter titled "The Failures of Revelation" to a critique of the historical record. First, he states that there is no evidence whatsoever for the truth of the prophecies stated in the Bible and the religious experiences cited therein. Stenger goes on to examine the biblical texts and other religious beliefs regarding the creation among other phenomena. He concludes that the religious texts cannot be accepted in view of the scientific knowledge that we have accumulated. Stenger then examines the prophecies of the Old and New Testaments and finds them unsupportable in scientific terms. Stenger then goes on to what I believe is the crux of the matter. He starts the section on "Physical Evidence" with:

> Events recorded two thousand years ago and longer
> by superstitious people accustomed more to mythological
> tales than objective observations cannot be taken literally.

Stenger claims that no solid evidence beyond the biblical account can be found that supports the very existence of Abraham, Moses, David, Solomon, and Jesus, or the Exodus or the conquest of Canaan. He concludes:

> The Bible reads as an assembly of myths fashioned by ancient authors who had no concept of historical accuracy. Its description of the world reflects the scientific and historical knowledge of the age in which the manuscripts were composed.

The information and insights contained in scriptures and other revelations look just as they can be expected to look if there is no God who revealed truths to humanity that were recorded in sacred texts.

Stenger's analysis conflicts to a degree with the previously cited National Geographic work. There is a lot of evidence that events described in the Bible are linked to geographic and archaeological discoveries. As I have stated earlier, any storyteller would be a fool and not at all credible if he did not base his story on a recognizable geographic background. However, just because we can trace the journey of a figure called Abraham does not mean we must accept this figure's claim to have communicated with God.

Early Doubters

Two more recent works deserve our attention, those of Elaine Pagels, a recognized scholar in the study of biblical texts. Her book *The Gnostic Gospels* and her book in collaboration with Karen King, *Reading Judas*, are fruitful sources for our study. Of the two books, the first has a more encompassing message, *Reading Judas* being more or less a supporting witness for that which is contested in *The Gnostic Gospels*.

Throughout her first book, Elaine Pagels describes a clear central theme, and that is the intense pursuit by the orthodox early Christian leaders to establish a simple and undisputed religious and institutional structure for what became the universal or catholic church. This was embodied in the trio: doctrine, ritual, and clerical hierarchy, or, in other terms, canon, creed, and bishops/priests. The Gnostic teachings tended to dispute and undermine this religious institution, which was at the time only under development.

As Pagels says in her introduction, "In simplest terms, ideas which bear implications contrary to that development come to be labeled as 'heresy'; ideas which implicitly support it become 'orthodox.'" Conflict then, of course, arose, with debate raging among such greats as Irenaeus, Polycarp, Tertullian, and Ignatius on the orthodox side against Gnostic teachers such as Valentinus, Theodotus, Ptolemy, and Heracleon on the other side. Pagels does not mention anything more than the war of words, but I suspect there was a background of lethal intrigue to accompany the verbal conflict. The orthodox won, and the Gnostic teachings and influence were eradicated. As Pagels restates the standard truism in her conclusion, "It is the winners who write history—their way." That, of course, leaves the question: Is the resulting history truth or fabrication or a bit of both?

In *The Gnostic Gospels*, Pagels uses the chapters to describe the elements of the debate and their impact on the fight to establish the one universal (Catholic) church. I remind the reader that one must appreciate that in the early first and second centuries all of the histories and beliefs were contested and that for Christianity all was chaos. This is exactly where the Gnostic teachings gain their meaning; the currently accepted biblical stories, teachings, and history may not be what they are purported to be.

In Pagels's first chapter, "The Controversy over Christ's Resurrection: Historical Event or Symbol?" the author argues (citing other scholars as well) that belief in the resurrection of Christ—the return from the dead to life of a flesh and blood body—had more than a religious appeal to the emotions of believers and to their deepest fears and desires to overcome death. Pagels states:

> But when we examine its practical effect on the Christian movement, we can see, paradoxically, that the doctrine of bodily resurrection also serves an essential "political" function: it legitimizes the authority of certain men who claim to exercise exclusive leadership over the churches as the successors of the apostle Peter. From the second century, the doctrine has served to validate the

apostolic succession of bishops, the basis of papal authority to this day.

I can see how this might have worked, but it is not very logical to me.

The Gnostics challenged the historical accounts of the resurrection. In the Gospel of Mary, for example, the resurrection appearances are attributed to "visions received in dreams or in ecstatic trance." The Gnostics in general placed belief in the context of the inner spiritual self (there is an interesting relationship inferred with Hinduism and Buddhism). Gnostics, in fact, not only disagreed in the flesh versus spirit debate, but they also disagreed with the canon and the hierarchical demands of the orthodox. The orthodox knew that the Gnostics had to be expunged if the church fathers were to succeed. Pagels concludes that orthodox teaching on the resurrection "legitimized a hierarchy of persons through whose authority all others must approach God." Gnostic teaching "was potentially subversive of this order."

The chapter "One God, One Bishop" follows a similar track. The Gnostics claimed knowledge of the true spiritual god while denouncing the god (demiurge) acclaimed by the church bishops. In certain of their circles there was a devotion to dualism. In any case, they, in effect, challenged the orthodox hierarchy, the bishops and the priests committed to one God. Pagels states: "When the orthodox insisted upon 'one God,' they simultaneously validated the system of governance in which the church is ruled by 'one bishop.' Gnostic modification of monotheism was taken—and perhaps intended—as an attack upon that system. For when Gnostic and orthodox Christians discussed the nature of God, they were at the same time debating the issue of spiritual authority."

The chapter "The Passion of Christ" is telling. Here the orthodox support for the belief in the human Jesus who suffered, died, and arose from the dead underlies the church's faith in the martyrs with the added and welcomed attention to the Christian faith and the sympathy for its adherents. The orthodox (the church fathers) emphasized the elements of the passion to support their temporal political aims. The Gnostics, with their belief in the supremacy of the spiritual over the physical, naturally fought this approach—and lost.

What does Elaine Pagels say in her conclusion? She pays tribute to the strategy, organizational skills, and aggressiveness of the churches' founding fathers who were able to force acceptance of a common canon, ritual, and clerical hierarchy. They won against multiple challenges, and they won, she contends, because the mass appeal of the orthodox was more palatable to the people than the solitary, inner self, and elite secretive aspects of Gnosticism.

Elaine Pagels collaborated with Karen King on a book, *Reading Judas*, that interprets another Gnostic text, *The Gospel of Judas*. Much of what was said about the Gnostic texts in Pagels's book above applies equally to *The Gospel of Judas*. However, there are several additional and supporting points that are worth mentioning.

- Corroborating other investigations, the Gospels were written 40 to 70 years AD, and they were not written by the disciples.
- Mark came first. Mathew and Luke copied Mark.
- The gospel authors changed and added text to match their story with the Hebrew texts and to make the crucifixion plausible and acceptable.
- The Gospels clearly toyed with questions as to historical authenticity. In general, historicity matters less than the moral lessons the gospel writers endorse.
- In the chapter "The Mysteries of the Kingdom," there is shown to have been a great controversy among early Christians concerning the resurrection, one side citing not only Gnostic texts but selected texts in the orthodox gospels, contending that the resurrection was a spiritual event and perhaps a vision. The point is that the facts of the resurrection were not clear at all if all the views of the early Christians are taken into account and not merely the texts adopted by the early church leaders.

What do I draw from Elaine Pagels's and Karen King's works? Ambiguity in the extreme! These accounts are further support for the view that the religious texts that so many Christians rely upon are very, very suspect. The Christian institutions that exist today have from their very beginnings constructed a history amenable to their fundamental beliefs and continued existence as an institution. They have left us with an account that clearly affirms the existence of the Son of God (and hence God himself), while disregarding histories that claim otherwise. They have systematically and aggressively eliminated those who disagreed with their canon, creed, and hierarchy, and they have sought to destroy those texts that they consider heresy. Isn't it a shame that the library of Alexandria was destroyed!

I can accept that the churches' fathers truly believed what they defended as doctrine, but I cannot accept that that doctrine was not contrived, filtered, and doctored to suit the purposes of those in charge and their developing church.

Add to the above state of affairs the error-prone translations and texts described by Bart Ehrman, and I cannot place any degree of faith in the story told by the New Testament, and the Old Testament may be in even more doubt.

Keller's Charms

As a final note on the subject of Christianity, I refer to *The Reason for God*, by Timothy Keller. Keller is the founding pastor of Redeemer Presbyterian Church in New York City and the spark behind as many as a hundred Christian churches in the United States and other countries. I consider this book worth the attention of both the believer and the atheist, and I will now spend a good bit of time addressing it.

The title of Keller's book is a bit of a misnomer. This is an unconstrained advocacy for Christianity, pure and simple. God is an attribute of Jesus Christ. It all revolves around Jesus. His chapter 6 involves the claim that "Science has Disproved Christianity," not disproved God. This book is about support for belief in the Bible. On the other hand, Keller is one of few who have argued against the specific claims of the skeptics and the atheists.

The first five chapters of his book, "There Can't Be Just ONE True Religion, "How Could a Good God Allow Suffering," "Christianity Is a Straitjacket," "The Church Is Responsible for So Much Injustice," and "How Can a Loving God Send People to Hell?", despite their titles, are bound to appeal to the believer. Keller is a master in rationalization. Through anecdotal references, frequent assertions and interpretations, he provides the rationale for belief in the Bible. He is good at it! And in some few instances I can completely agree with him. In most cases, I must disagree.

The Redeemers' basic doctrines---the deity of Christ, the infallibility of the Bible, and the necessity of spiritual rebirth through faith in Christ's atoning death—represent the challenge. These doctrinal points come up over and over again in Keller's arguments, and it is frustrating to read a conclusion to an argument that basically says, if you believe in Christ and the Bible, the contest will be resolved.

In his chapter "Science Has Disproved Christianity," Keller defends miracles. A strong inference is that there is a supernatural dimension that science cannot prove does not exist. Let's refer to this as the religious string theory. He takes a swipe at evolution, claiming "When evolution is turned into an All-encompassing Theory explaining absolutely everything we believe, feel, and do as the product of natural selection, then we are not in the arena of science, but of philosophy. Evolution as an All-encompassing Theory has insurmountable difficulties as a worldview."

He is flat wrong here. Evolution is pure science, and it does present a template for everything we know regarding life, despite the fact that questions need to be answered to fill in the blanks. He goes on to claim that many scientists are believers. This is true. His poll numbers conflict with those of the opposing camp, but that is immaterial. Scientists are humans like the rest of us, and their needs are the same. This neither proves nor disproves God's existence.

Keller defends Genesis. He muddies the water, quite frankly, comparing texts of historical content with those of poetic theological meaning, without providing a reasonable rationale for what Genesis describes. After all this, Keller resorts to what I mentioned above, in effect a cop-out. Believe in Christ and the Bible, and all is resolved. He states what follows.

> What can we conclude? Since Christian believers occupy different positions on both the meaning of Genesis 1 and on the nature of evolution, those who are considering Christianity as a whole should not allow themselves to be distracted by this intramural debate. The skeptical inquirer does not need to accept any one of these positions

in order to embrace the Christian faith. Rather he or she should concentrate on and weigh the central claims of Christianity. Only after drawing conclusions about the person of Christ, the Resurrection, and the central tenets of the Christian message should one think through the various options with regard to creation and evolution.

In other words, keep the faith. Don't let facts get in the way.

Typical of the style in his book, Keller entitles his chapters in the words of Christianity's critics. One chapter is titled "You Can't Take the Bible Literally," and his first three paragraphs summarize the critic's case beautifully. In short, Jesus is a historical figure whose divinity has been challenged and whose life and teachings have equally been disputed and subsequently shaped in the form of approved texts by the church hierarchy. Should this be the case, there then exists a serious challenge to Christianity. Amen! Couldn't agree more! Keller, of course, goes on to discredit the critics. I find him to be less than convincing. He cites one research effort that led the author Anne Rice to reconvert to Christianity because she claimed the liberal scholars' arguments against the Bible's authenticity were so weak. Keller claims that the "skeptical view of the Bible has been crumbling for the last thirty years."

Keller disputes the claim that the gospel accounts were written or assembled far too late to be accurate or true and cannot in most cases be validated. He says the timing was, in fact, right and bases his view on the supposed fact that there were hundreds of witnesses who should have been alive when the Gospels were written and who would have retained their memories of events over the intervening years while orally repeating what they had witnessed. Decent points, but they do not negate the one or two generations delay between Jesus's death and the earliest texts. Were witnesses truly still alive? Memories do fade. Memories are subject to change. And most of all, were witnesses led to believe what they perceived? Were they deceived (maliciously or merely coincidently) into interpreting what they witnessed? Were events misinterpreted? Did witnesses coordinate their views to present a unified front? Were witnesses coerced into the making of supporting statements? Did the writers rely on a central gatherer of the facts? There are many questions, and the passage of time makes them all the more pertinent.

Keller devotes an entire chapter to "The Reality of the Resurrection," in which he makes some well-stated arguments, none of which leads me to abandon the doubts that I have.

Keller proceeds to analyze the gospel texts themselves. They are too counterproductive (against the grain, not politically correct, unexpected) to be put together by the church hierarchy or other authorities. They are just not the style of writing of those times. C. S. Lewis is cited, saying that the Gospels are reportage—that is, written more in the style of modern novels with many details that fill out the narrative. In other words, they are eyewitness reports. This can be convincing argumentation, and I would expect C. S. Lewis to be a key in it, but I do not believe it overcomes the claims for identified errors in reporting, the intentional insertion of anecdotes, conflicts between texts, and the clear influence of the early church in ratifying the Gospels. In fact, I could understand that the church's elders would consciously approve the Gospels' narrative nature in order to support its authenticity, knowing full well the importance of the Gospels for the future of the church.

The chapter "The Clues of God" is, in effect, clueless. In brief and very slanted comments on the universe, Keller, of course, supports the case that some outside source started it all. He neglects to mention that some suggest that there was, in fact, no beginning, not to mention the thought that no outside source was even needed.

Naturally he must endorse the "fine-tuning" argument that postulates that there are so many constants required in the architecture of the universe to arrive at the exact constants critical to the existence of earth's conditions and thus the rise of life as we know it that some hand had to have twiddled the knobs.

Interestingly, Keller displays his lack of knowledge in this field by equating the "fine-tuning argument" to the "anthropic principle." The anthropic principle, in fact, refutes the fine-tuning argument. Keller ignores the fact that things just happened the way they did. No intervention needed.

To illustrate Keller's fixation on unchallenged faith, I cite the following.

Although organic life could have just happened without a Creator, does it make sense to live as if that infinitely remote chance is true?

The answer is, yes, it does!

Keller goes on to make the pointless arguments on the regularity of nature (What would we expect otherwise?), the clue of beauty, and the clue killer, all of which involve a convoluted series of doubtful arguments on the existence of God. I find them far less convincing, much less supported, than they claim, particularly since the chapter ends with the usual "We KNOW that God is there." Blind faith!

Keller has a chapter called "The Knowledge of God." This chapter essentially deals with morals, and it delves into the evolutionary theory of moral obligation, human rights, the violence of nature, and a few other related subjects. The underlying thought is that morals are very debatable based on time, place, and context and that in the end God is a necessary ingredient in their determination. I dispute the last point. Humankind alone has developed codes of moral comportment. Not God! The codes have matured over the many centuries of human existence, and that is not because some something was laying down the laws. The key word is "evolved." Humanity has always known what morals best suited the times, and it has been and always will be a matter of push and shove. To say, therefore, as Keller does, that debates over morality and justice represent "The Endless, Pointless Litigation of Existence" and that therefore we must accept the existence of God as the determiner of acceptable morals, is not credible.

Of particular concern to me are three themes that crop up in Keller's book (and many other theist and philosophical works): the *why* in humans' appraisal of their being, the meaning and reality of a beginning, and the reality of evolution.

First the *why*? It comes up clearly in Keller's book. There must be a reason for our existence and our uniqueness. There is no meaning without God. Our human attributes attest to something beyond the human ken. There is a special something about us. There are many more phrases that point to the special nature of humankind. It is all bull poop, to be politically correct. The real answer is that there is no *why*! We are what we are, pure and simple. We are a product of physical and chemical forces in a universe and an earth that just led to what we are.

But, there must be a reason. No, there isn't, other than what nature can explain! If you wish to view it that way, feel free, but why should there be a meaning? Is this because you think you are something extra special on this tiny fleck of space? You do, of course, which leads you to seek relief in such notions as God, immortality, heaven, and hell. In short, there is no answer to *why*? other than an egotistic emphasis on our selfish nature and refuge in religious beliefs and institutions. Theists and philosophers would prefer to just ignore the fact that there is no plausible answer to *why*?

Second, there is the reality and the meaning of a beginning. Of course, this is fertile ground for the god-believer. If there was a beginning such as the big bang, God did it. But this does not do credit to the many possibilities that might have led to the big bang, some of them purely speculative, but nevertheless as likely as a God-induced beginning.

There are a number of hypotheses that involve no beginning, meaning that natural forces led to a universal continuity that would require no intervention. They would show that there is no indication that a god was involved or needed.

Finally, evolution. Keller makes several comments that challenge evolution. He does acknowledge that even the pope recognizes evolution as a reality, but he clearly states a belief that the so-called philosophical naturalism is off base. The disturbing part of his thinking is the inference that some sort of supernatural influence had to be imposed on the evolutionary process. We can't take his commentary otherwise. Again, however, there is no indication that God was involved or needed. In line with my comment above, people like Keller have a hard time coming to grips with the fact that we are truly the product of a "blind watchmaker."

After reading and rereading Timothy Keller's book, I am more confident than ever in my atheist stance. I find the book to be an affront to the reasoning person. It demands a belief in the infallibility of the Bible and the Resurrection before any argument can be resolved. It is a faith-based text with, I must admit, many forceful arguments that, however, upon scrutiny do not hold up. One of Keller's sources cites the supposed piling of assumption on assumption by the critics of the Jesus story as a reason for her return to belief. I can cite Keller for the same. Alternatively, when Keller says Christianity is "a hospital for sinners," he is stating the very thesis of my book: God is a human creation that meets the needs of a suffering humanity.

Islam

What does history say about Muhammad and Islam? What proof of God's existence can be gleaned from Muhammad's life, the Koran, the Hadith, and other Muslim texts?

We have here a Johnny-come-lately to the Middle Eastern religions. In the late sixth century and early seventh century, Muhammad claims a special relationship with God, and he and his followers proceed to conquer much of the Middle East and more distant cultures by the sword. They thereby inflicted the rule of an Islamic state on the compliant (and historically amenable to whatever the dominant force demands) peoples of the Middle East and the more resistant distant peoples.

Whatever we can conclude about Islam, there is a politically unifying theme to all its teachings, and that is the personal and individual relationship with God. There will be no worship of idols. There will be no caricatures of God and the prophets. Prayer and ritual define an individual's life on earth, subverting oneself to a watchful, demanding, yet merciful God. Yet Muhammad and Islam did not originate God. God was adopted from other cultures.

There is, perhaps, a good reason for this religion's appearance. I am convinced that there was a political-economic motivation behind the founder's strategy, cemented, perhaps, on his honest view of the state of religion in his time. Arabia displayed a mix of god worship practices where fiefdoms were locked in conflict. Muhammad spoke out while Christianity was experiencing troubles, and the political and power relationships in the Middle East were in flux. Byzantium was in trouble. He may have been influenced by these propitious circumstances and they gave him and his followers an advantage. They clearly won. God did not win. God was already in the equation. It was all about how one worshipped God and who made the rules.

We need to trace the historical record as far as it exists to determine what proof, if any, Muhammad and the religion that he established might offer regarding God's existence.

The Koran? I have read the Koran as I have read the Bible. That does not mean I completely understand it. In fact, it is vouchsafed that only the reader of the original Arabic can truly understand the Koran. That's not me! Nevertheless, I can say I have a good feel for what it's all about. The Koran covers a multitude of topics. It is a mixture of history (partly that of the Old Testament), myth, and exhortations to subvert oneself to God and to obey the rituals demanded. It lays out the way in which one conducts one's life and how one worships the one God. It presents lessons learned from the events in the Prophet's life, reflections of a small and insignificant tribal conflict in the desert of Arabia. It says a great deal about God's treatment of the faithful as well as the nonbelievers. It addresses the Jews and the Christians.

In sum, in addition to providing specific guidance to the faithful, Islam as interpreted in the Koran is a repository of ancient beliefs, as are Christianity and Judaism, and the three share a common background. God's existence was imagined long ago. Religious views of gods or God, the rituals to be observed, the awards and punishments, and proper conduct in society had roots thousands of years old. Much of the old traditions are reflected in the Koran. As Christopher Hitchens said, this is a "borrowed belief."

The content of the Koran was purported to have been created over a period of twenty-three years by the Prophet Muhammad ibn 'Abdullah. Supposedly much of the content came from visitations of the angel Gabriel. The Prophet could neither read nor write, but scribes and companions put in writing the pronouncements of the Prophet and the revelations that came to him. All was then collected in what we know as the Koran.

The contents of the Koran as we know it today should be more accurate than most ancient religious texts when it comes to adherence to the originals largely because the Koranic texts were created, collected, and arranged under the direct supervision of the "author" himself. History, however, shows that amateur recorders (they were merely companions and not professional scribes) can and may distort what is related to them and could easily twist what they record to show what they think the speaker (Muhammad) really means or what they want him to mean.

The contents of the Koran might further have been tampered with in the intervening centuries. I am sure that alterations for various motives would have occurred. We have evidence of the history of manipulations of other ancient texts, and the evidence is not good. Some historians do claim a lack of authenticity in the surviving Koranic texts.

My initial take on the origin of the Koran could be called simplistic, but I don't think that's the case. Let's see.

Nicholas Wade discusses the origins of Islam and shows that the traditional account of the beginnings and rise of the religion are subject to serious debate. Islam has apparently not been subject to the scrutiny that has been concentrated on Judaism and Christianity. Traditional inquiry involves the analysis of the Koran itself, the interpretations known as the Tafsir, the Sirah or account of the life of Muhammad and the rise of the Islamic state, the Sunna regarding Islamic law, and the Hadith or sayings attributed to Muhammad. Traditionalists find this trove to be sufficient, with supporting inputs, to justify the basic history of Islam. Muhammad perseveres in a tribal conflict in the Hajiz, the western coast of the Arabian Peninsula on the Red Sea, which subsequently, under his followers, leads to a conquest of the Middle East and much of the Mediterranean region and the establishment of an Islamic religion and empire. Very simple!

Wade, however, brings up a tantalizing and contradicting view of Islam's history. It is not his view but that of the so-called revisionists, and he concedes that their views need to be researched. The revisionists are reported to be a mere small minority among the scholars in this field. Wade cites John Wansbrough, Patricia Crone, Michael Cook, Nevo, Koren, and Karl-Heinz Ohlig, among others.

Essentially, the revisionists claim that Islam originated in the Christian communities in Syria and Palestine where the early leaders were inclined to acknowledge the existence of Jesus as a prophet or messenger, meaning there was only one God and no trinity. Mu'awiyah, the first Arab Umayyad ruler recorded by non-Islamic sources, ruled a largely Christian state. Inscriptions on the Dome of the Rock, the great structure in Jerusalem built by the second Umayyad ruler, Abd al-Malik, infer a Christian place of worship decades after the death of Muhammad. I find it extremely interesting that one inscription among others inscribed there by 'Abd al-Malik, "muhammadun rasul allah," was supposedly meant to say, "The

Messenger of God is to be praised," meaning that a notable person was to be praised and possibly inferring Jesus. However, a central phrase of the Islamic faith makes the inscription read "Muhammad is the messenger of God." Even more interesting is the inferred question as to the very existence of Muhammad.

The revisionists' intent is to show that, when the early supposed Christian-Judeo-Islamic dynasty was overthrown by the Abbasid dynasty, this began a process of establishment of a uniquely Arab religion centered as to origin, not in the north, but in the Hajiz to the south, and championing an Arabian prophet. They had appropriated the early Judeo-Christian history but had made it a singular Arab history.

Suffice it to say that the authenticity of the Islamic texts is no more valid than the very suspect texts of the Jews and the Christians. Although the revisionists are a minority, doubt as to the traditional interpretations must be acknowledged, just as the Coptic texts make us reevaluate the traditional Christian texts. God becomes a big question mark in any case.

At this point I will cite the views of the late Christopher Hitchens, which should amplify the preceding. He is an acclaimed journalist and author of several books, one of which is *god is not Great*. Hitchens claims a familiarity with Muslim religious practices, based on his experiences and acquaintances, saying he has visited 'innumerable" Muslim gatherings and mosques around the world. He appears to have an understanding of the Arabic language. Let's take him seriously. When it comes to the authenticity of the text of the Koran and the facts on the life of Muhammad, he cites in chapter nine of the above-mentioned book several serious difficulties.

Muhammad was illiterate. He had to depend on family, friends, associates, and amateur scribes to record his revelations, orders, thoughts, and actions, a great source of potential error. His life and all that he said and did involve local tribal conflicts. Local scholars of religion may have helped in the reporting.

And then, the first recorded account of Muhammad's life (which basically means the Koran) came long after Muhammad's death. Hitchens cites 120 years. He also declares that there is no account of how the Koran was assembled. (Martin Lings and others, however, do spell out how the Koran was most probably initially put together by close associates of Muhammad at or near the time of his life.) There were attempts to assemble witnesses and writings to establish an authoritative account of the Prophet's life and the Koran, but just as with Christianity, conflicts between prominent individuals, princes, followers, sects, and political and regional entities confused rather than clarified the record. Texts were purged and destroyed in order to maintain the "truth." To add insult to injury, Hitchens cites the many examples appearing in the Hadith (also the Koran itself, I would add) that are simply borrowings from Hebrew, Christian, and other cultural texts. In fact, Hitchens titles his chapter "The Koran is Borrowed."

Hitchens fully supports the view expressed in this book that the texts and practices of religions, to include Islam, go way, way back in origin and lack any claim to authenticity and credibility.

Nevertheless, the real point of contention and the central theme of my book is humanity's tendency to believe in God, while defying any evidence or argument against God's existence. Let's start way back in the earliest times with Abraham and even those generations that came before him. I briefly addressed this period during my look at Judaism and Christianity, but this is a good time to do so again.

One must remove oneself to those ancient times to appreciate what was then imagined and related as history. In those early days there were probably zero individuals who did not believe in the gods. The gods were acknowledged as an integral part of every individual's life. None could even imagine another way. Therefore, stories of intercessions by the gods or visitations by angels or other similar beings were taken seriously and were recited by the sages from generation to generation.

If we look at the probable typical mental state in those days, we will undoubtedly find a tendency to accept any reasonable fantasy that fit the circumstances of the times. Thus, we have great persons such as Abraham corresponding with God. And the people believed that. And it goes on and on. This leads us directly to Muhammad, who was brought up in an intellectual atmosphere reflecting the god beliefs of the previous thousands of years. He would speak in accord with those beliefs.

Muhammad and/or his close associates were clearly familiar with the Old Testament. However, he was presented with an Arabian society that was ruled by idolatry, and he chose to follow the path of the one God in opposition to the accepted mores of the day. Why he did so is not clear to me. It may have been political or tribal conflict or sincere belief or just the lust for power. But he did so within the context of history, while rejecting elements such as the status of Jesus as a son of God. We note a view that takes part of the past for granted while rejecting certain elements of that past, all in the interest of proclaiming his messianic pursuit of a direct and personal relationship with God that is to be a pattern on which his followers are to construct their lives—and deaths.

It seems reasonable that Muhammad was bent on an honest quest: to return the religious to a belief in God, the one God. And then again, he may have been a mere political opportunist. Nevertheless, he was steeped in the practices of the distant past, and he would be expected to invoke the supernatural through revelations whenever possible to achieve his goals. This is not to say that he was being deceptive or false in his preaching; he was doing what came naturally to a person of his time.

Who was this proclaimed prophet? I accept that the individual probably lived and was a significant influence in the places and times cited by the texts, just as Jesus could have lived in the times and places recorded in Christian texts. The revisionists may claim that he was only a mythical figure to fill out the historical story critical to the faith just as some question the reality of a Moses. Nevertheless, Muhammad appears to have been a very intelligent, dominating, and attractive (physically and sexually) individual real or otherwise. He was also aggressive, persistent, and stubborn, yet reported to be socially and humanly responsive. He could also be brutal in his judgments. Above all, he was a leader.

Now we must judge whether or not the background and the dedication can testify to God's existence. I do not believe they do. Given the historical background, how can they?

Much of Muhammad's legacy relies on the revelations that he supposedly receives from God and the angel Gabriel. He relates a number of encounters with the angel. Herein lies the crux of the matter. We have an individual raised in the belief system of antiquity who is bound to maintain at least something of the god belief of his forefathers, even though he may impose a new interpretation of belief. Thus, angels are real. Prophets speak to God. It is interesting that many of the revelations came after an occurrence of some tribal, familial, military, or emotional significance. His state of mind may have convinced him that it was God, but no. There are too many instances of rapture- and stress-induced hallucinatory imaginations of supernatural happenings in history to deny this possibility regarding Muhammad's connection with God and angel. As beneficial as are many of the revelations, and as assertive and brutal as are many others, they are all the product of the mind of Muhammad. And then again, how much of Muhammad's message has been magnified by the scribes and altered through the centuries? Could the miracles he described have been inserted as embellishments to the original texts?

Sam Harris made it one of his basic themes that the Koran and the Hadith (a body of literature providing interpretation of and expansion on the Koran) present a particularly hateful liturgy bent on the destruction of all non-Islamic believers. He cites chapter and verse in his book *The End of Faith*. He describes a very cataclysmic potential world future if Islamic believers are not reined in or reeducated. The fear is grounded in the Muslim word-for-word belief in the Koranic texts. Harris spends pages in quoting the murderous statements found in the Koran and the Hadith.

Christopher Hitchens in *god is not Great* is very critical of Islam and most other religions as well. He is less vociferous. He joins Harris (and others) in condemning Islam as a faith founded on illiteracy, contradictions, and opportunism and displaying arrogance and presumption.

But, of course, this is the way prophets spoke thousands of years ago. Very machismo! One should expect this extreme aggressiveness and look on these texts and practices as reflections of the then warring societies and the god beliefs of the time. Taking them literally is the problem. Harris is dead on when he describes the threat to civilization when billions of humans take the ancient texts literally. This is a very current problem. Harris gives no slack to the Christians either. Their devotion to the scriptures is no less threatening. Does this mean there is no God? No. Nor does this mean there is a God.

In an interesting comment on the reality of conclusions regarding the threat of Muslim assertiveness, I cite a contradictory small article that appeared in the *Los Angeles Times* on April 2, 2008. The authors were John L. Esposito, Islamic studies professor at Georgetown University, and Dalia Mogahed, executive director of the Center for Muslim Studies at Gallup. They write that essentially Muslims worldwide do not fit the role that their critics assert. Gallup was reported to have conducted a six-year poll of a population that would have represented more than 90 percent of the world's 1.3 billion Muslims. They found that a great majority of Muslims supported equal rights for males and females. Only a small minority favored civilian targets in conflicts. There was a general rejection of the 9/11 attacks, and there was little reference to the Koran in support of any violent measures. In essence there was a general rejection of terrorism and the killing of innocents. Meaning? A radical fringe is calling the shots. And this may undermine one of Sam Harris's central themes.

But never fear; there is always the opposing view. *The Economist* in an article in the April 19, 2008, issue makes a point of challenging Gallup's release of the facts that are supposed to support Gallup's polls. And *The Economist* cites another survey that found rising numbers of Muslims with a "very unfavorable" view of America. Relevant? Maybe. Maybe not.

In a recent book, *MUHAMMAD Prophet of Peace Amid the Clash of Empires*, the author, Juan Cole, casts Muhammad as one seeking affiliation with anti-pagan forces and generally in favor of peaceful solutions to conflict. Cole is a Professor of History at the University of Michigan. His analysis has been challenged for selectively choosing supportive parts of the Koran while ignoring opposing citations. Nevertheless, he does make his point that the Koran is not all the fire and brimstone that many have assumed it to be.

Do the peoples of Islam have a place in today's debate about the existence of God? Not really, except to represent a solid front in support of theism. There do not seem to be many, if any, prominent Islamic speakers that question the existence of God. In fact, in recent years declarations of apostasy in Afghanistan and court decisions in Malaysia regarding a woman's desire to change religions show a strong social and broad public resistance to accept other than the Islamic creed. The ferocity of the resistance of the Islamic believers to the Americans and native moderates in Iraq and Afghanistan as well as the offensive of ISIS in Syria and Iraq also show a very strong devotion to Islam. Islam seems exceptionally united in its fervent belief in the one God and the manner in which Man worships him. As far as reinforcing the faith, Islamic entities may be some of the strongest enforcers of god belief that we know.

Yet there are several versions of Islam, as there are many versions of other religions. To say that no Muslims will tolerate other sects and religions is wrong. The Pakistanis appear to be secular to some degree. Tribal areas, however, have seized the initiative, and a minority is forcing the issues in that country. Indonesia, as the most populous Islamic country, has long been known as tolerant and somewhat secular.

And there is another community of belief that merits notice: the practitioners of Sufism. There is reason to believe that this is the practice of most South Asian Muslims. If so, there is a latent tolerance of different beliefs and a clear mixing of Western, Hindu, and Muslim rites and rituals. The Sufists claim unnumbered saints, engage in orgiastic celebrations, and rejoice in a very relaxed version of Islam. They are, naturally, rejected by the Islamist fundamentalists. In these and other cases, however, the communities remain solid god-believers.

How should we summarize our examination of Islam?

First, it, like other religions, is rooted in the distant past. God belief was established long ago, and Islam is just one more effort to institutionalize that belief.

Second, texts upon which the faith is founded are suspect as far as accuracy is concerned and are unable to substantiate the spiritual events they describe, similar to what we have seen with the scriptures of Christianity.

Next, data or proofs that God exists are no more apparent than they are with the other religions of the book. Perhaps the citation of the supposed evils in the Islamist texts could justify questioning how God's existence could be accepted. But again, evil neither proves nor denies a deity.

Finally, there is no reason to question the universal human desire for a god's support in life and death as discussed earlier as well as the societal pressures to adhere to beliefs. The Messenger of God fits the profile.

Religions of the East

Thus far I have concentrated on the religions of the Middle East, Judaism, Christianity, and Islam, the three monotheistic cultures closely linked in their historical backgrounds and exhibiting most of the religious ferment and debate in the Western world over God's existence for the past many centuries. It seems to be in the West that God's existence is most challenged, although the challenge comes from a minority among the vast numbers of Jewish, Christian, and Muslim true believers.

Do we see a similar situation in the other regions of the earth? Probably not, given the unique histories of India, China, and related cultures throughout Asia. For one thing, the three Middle Eastern religions propose a direct relationship with a god—the God of Abraham. Christianity goes as far as to say God appeared on earth in the form of a son.

The East seems to have generally placed its religious emphasis more on the relationship of the individual with his environment, society, and human relations and, most importantly, the sought-after union with the all-encompassing entity rather than upon an individual's or a society's direct relationship with a god or gods. This may partly explain the seemingly intractable differences between the Hindus and the Muslims of the Indian subcontinent: emphasis on a direct correspondence with God versus emphasis on human and societal relationships that lead to union with God. This may be an oversimplification, but I believe it is a valid point.

Nevertheless, no matter how one views the differences between the Near, South, and Far East approaches to religion, there is still the element of the supernatural to be found in every case concerning worship. Whether it be a Hindu seeking nirvana, a Tibetan appealing to the Dalai Lama, a Chinese evocation to Buddha, or a Shinto observer's offering to his ancestors, there exists an assumption of a god or gods, some ethereal existence beyond the real world. If we accept that some religions have matured into forms of monism, then we are dealing with beliefs that entertain some union with a great spiritual all-embracing entity. This assumes belief in the supernatural, a form of god belief, and reflects humanity's need for deference to and help from the gods.

The Eastern religions no longer revolve solely around gods and goddesses and animism, although they began that way. They revolve around a way of life, and this way of life is supported by the supernatural. If we are to accept that God takes many forms over the broad spectrum of human imagination, then the Far Eastern religions certainly qualify as god belief systems. The gods, the institutions, the rituals, and the creeds merely take different forms.

If I now devote far less space to the history of the Eastern religions, it is not because they are less important to our thesis. It is because most of the arguments in the preceding pages apply to all god belief systems. I do not want to repeat them unless there is a need to do so.

God in the Indian Subcontinent

Hinduism

The two major religions for which we can cite the Indian subcontinent as source are Hinduism and Buddhism. There are certainly several more religions or practices or offshoots of these two such as the Carvaka system, Jainism, the Vedanta, Yoga, Nyaya, and others, but these two remain the principal ones. We will look first at Hinduism.

The Indian subcontinent has been home to humans for at least forty thousand years. For tens of thousands of years humans and their cultures spread across a varied geographical and climatic environment. As in the religions farther to the West, anything to do with god worship has to take into account the earliest history of the region and the humans who lived there.

Archaeological finds have shown very early indications of worship of the female as a symbol or embodiment of fecundity. The bull and the cow turn up as well, the implication being rather clear. Just how much the evidence proves god belief forty thousand years ago is not clear to me, but the elements for such belief are there. Does this mean that God was there and caused these early peoples to believe in him? Hard to accept! These early cultures were responding to what we have mentioned before—the need to explain the world around them and to appeal to the forces that meant so much to their individual and communal survival and prosperity. They did so in very elemental terms. They, therefore, display the underlying tendency for god belief that gives a later, more sophisticated theology, a basis for development.

The Indus Valley, Way Station to the East

Indigenous cultures in the Indus River region in the 3000–1200 BC time frame (timing varies by source) give us a clue to the furtherance of god belief. The well-known Harappa culture in the southern Indus valley provides some clues into human god beliefs that are based on antecedent and assuredly ancient anxieties and expectations. The Kulli culture, another perhaps related culture found generally to the west in what today is southern Baluchistan, provides differing but corroborative evidence. There are archaeological finds of Bronze Age deities, figurines of women, some with bangles and bracelets, and perhaps portrayed as mother-goddesses or guardians of the dead. There are indications of household shrines. Some evidence for votive pots, food offerings, protective wrapping, and offering stands points to possible belief in the supernatural and the afterlife. There is also some evidence in the Harappa culture of priesthood, male-god prototypes of Shiva, phallic worship, sacred animals, and mother-goddesses similar to Hindu goddesses of today in the Indian countryside. Stuart Piggott refers to this phenomenon as "gods before the gods."

Nevertheless, subsequent discoveries and analyses challenge support for a Harappa religious culture. There is not enough evidence. We just do not know if religion played a significant role there.

Influence of these Bronze Age cultures on the eventual Indian Hindu religion are conjectural, but let me quote Piggott in reference to the Indus River cultures and their possible influence on the broader Indian religious traditions:

> The religion [Harappa] as implied from the archeological remains is significantly distinct from any others known in Western Asia and is essentially Indian from the start.

He goes on to say:

> [That there are] many features that cannot be derived from the Aryan traditions brought into India after, or concurrently with, the fall of the Harappa civilization.

Vedic and Epic sources certainly show that the arriving Aryan peoples did adopt and adapt local beliefs while bringing in their own. In fact, we are not sure how much direct contact the Aryan had with the Harappa.

With remnants of the civilization, perhaps, but there was probably a gap of as much as a few centuries between the Harappa collapse and the arrival of the Aryan.

There is an interesting sidelight worth mentioning. Research performed by a team at the Woods Hole Oceanographic Institution suggests that the demise of the Harappa civilization was largely the result of the eastward migration of the monsoonal systems, which replaced Indus Valley rains and floods with dry or drought conditions. The Aryan invasions possibly merely took advantage of an already fatally wounded economy and culture.

God belief has thus been around for a long time. In the case of Hinduism, it amounts to thousands of years before recorded history, and it is, at least in part, local in origin. The early civilizations of the Indus Valley and to the east influenced the religious beliefs of the subcontinent in the following millennia. There are interesting signs that gods of the cultures to the west, including pre-Aryan, had crept into the beliefs of the Indus Valley cultures through channels such as trade. But prehistoric god beliefs were maybe there already. We have addressed the Harappa civilization, but it should be taken as only one example, since there were other local cultures in the subcontinent that would have left an imprint of their ancient beliefs on a developing Hinduism.

Then came the so-called Aryan invasions. But we must understand that "invasions" are not all or even most of what occurred there. Better to say migrations or incursions or colonization, although there were probably some battles and wars. Even before the arrival of the Aryan there were earlier arrivals of peoples from the west, and the Aryan may have been a mix of various ethnic and cultural groups more or less attuned to a central culture. In any case, evidence shows that they brought their gods with them.

Since we are discussing Hinduism, I am going to refer to the effects of the Aryan arrivals strictly in terms of those effects on the Indian subcontinent and the peoples and cultures there, knowing full well that the Aryan spread out in all directions from the steppes of Asia like the waves from a stone thrown in a lake. These movements of peoples are clearly established from the evidence for the spread of the Indo-European languages. Recent study of ancient DNA provides some interesting variations on the movements of peoples throughout the region. Analysis of this ancient DNA confirms the general west to east movements, but the specific migrations or invasions were more complex than had been previously thought.

The entry of the Aryan peoples into the Indian subcontinent provides meaningful insights into humanity's very early god beliefs. It is, of course, of note that the subcontinent fell to the sword of the Muslims centuries later; that culture's monotheism derived from the very same Indo-European antecedents.

Gods and Philosophy

This chapter is all about history. If we are looking at the history of god belief related to Hinduism, what then is the record to which we can refer? There is no easy answer. Although writing came into use in varied forms as much as 2 to 4 millennia BC in several cultures of the ancient Middle East, there is scant written evidence of god belief in the Indian subcontinent. Texts were produced only as recently as hundreds of years after the birth of Christ. Why? As Stuart Piggott and others have pointed out, the climate of India does not allow the preservation of documentation on biodegradable surfaces. Instead, the culture favored a tradition of oral presentation of the sacred texts, which showed an incredible demand for the most minute adherence not only to text but to innuendo on recitation. Despite the difficulties, we do now have texts that are, in fact, very voluminous.

Is there such a thing as a Bible in the Hindu tradition? Scholars would probably say no. Instead, in an extremely voluminous oral and written presentation, we are served an elaborate tablet of gods and the mythological, often animistic, stories of their powers and accomplishments along with an elaborate philosophical structure. I possess a large spreadsheet which shows the principal gods and goddesses of the pantheon, and I count seventy. Some sources say there are many more.

The Vedic traditional pronouncements are central to Hinduism's history. The RigVeda is a starting point. It is most probably an Aryan description of the invasion of Western India, and it carries with it the warrior gods of the invading Aryans. From philosophical and religious viewpoints, we see the origins of what is now the dominant religion of the subcontinent, having undergone a subtle progression from polytheism through monotheism to monism. The RigVeda, in whatever Aryan form it may have taken, was mainly inspired by earlier Indo-European cultures and the god beliefs of those primitive peoples. The hymns to the many gods are clearly a reflection of a long-standing religious tradition. These early peoples created their gods and passed on the accepted pantheon and religious doctrines to later generations of the conquerors and the conquered.

There is some additional evidence of what went into the religious philosophy of the Indian subcontinent as the incursions came from the west and moved to the east. There is an inference from preserved clay tablets that the Mittannian rulers in the ancient region of Syria invoked the witness of gods who should "be the gods Mitra, Varuna, and Indra of the ancient Indian pantheon as recorded in the earliest religious texts." This is from Piggott. John Keay cites evidence the Aryan gods such as Indra, Agni, and Varuna predate their arrival in India and can be related with counterparts in Persian, Greek and Latin mythology.

When we address the Hindu religion, we find ourselves immersed in a complex religious and philosophical world. Gods abound. Animism survives. Mythology is in abundance. The rules for the good and proper conduct of one's personal life are lengthy and detailed. One's performance before the judgment of an obscure tribunal sends one on a beneficial trajectory to a later greater life or perhaps on a less fortunate course to a lesser life. Taking into account all that is involved, some say it is better to address the Hindu religion more as a philosophy than a religion. This thought might equally apply to the examination of the Hebrew, Christian, and Islamic traditions, as well as most of the Eastern religions of China and Japan, but it is not substantiated. How does one explain away the clearly supernatural aspects of Hinduism?

As philosophical as Hinduism may be, the supernatural is ever present. Hindu beliefs and philosophy are grounded on or augmented by the mythology of the Hindu pantheon or based on the power of a unifying unembodied entity; gods or an all-encompassing entity are there. It all began millennia before today, and the reverence and philosophy clearly reflect humanity's creation of the godlike in order to benefit their lives on earth. It is worth noting again that belief systems, Hinduism included, tend to codify the conduct of humans in their society and then to ascribe the origin of said conduct to the almighty. This is either a genuine human attempt to justify the rules of human society or a conscious effort by those in power to regulate the activities of their followers. In either case, a god is called in to enforce a certain deportment.

There is, of course, a great distinction between the Hindu tradition and that of Christianity when it comes to the existence of God. Whereas Christians swear by the appearance of God on earth, a Hindu may accept the Christian view as one of many ways to worship the Almighty, but he or she will still insist on the overarching oneness of the spirit, which binds all that exists. Nevertheless, there is a godlike something.

It is also pertinent to look at Hinduism in light of the progression of several of the world's religions from animism, idolatry, polytheism to monotheism, and then in the case of Hinduism, to monism. This reflects a maturation of the religion, as has occurred with Judaism, which reflects a more acceptable social order and standard of human conduct. But we cannot forget that, despite the maturing of philosophy and credo, Hinduism is still rooted in prehistoric and ancient god beliefs, signs of which remain.

Supposedly the Western mind should have a difficult time in understanding these complexities, and there is some truth in this view. However, we must never forget that Buddhism and Hinduism both have their roots in the same Indo-European peoples, cultures, languages, and religions of the peoples of Mid-Eurasia with which we in the West are supposedly familiar. Far-flung as the subcontinent may be, much of the same Mid-Eurasian "stuff" appears in the beliefs that surface there, and, despite sometimes extreme variations of belief, there should be common threads that the Westerner will understand. As we noted with Hinduism, gods and practices did, in fact, derive from inputs from peoples to the west. I suspect that much of the mystery regarding the Eastern religions is simply a matter of translation between the many ancient and modern languages and an understanding of the history. What really happened and what was really said?

Buddhism

Some critics question whether Buddhism can be considered a religion. The very philosophical nature of Buddhism and the fact that certain offshoots from the center tend to be essentially atheist lead some to consider Buddhism simply a philosophy. We discussed this in the section on Hinduism, and the argument applies here as well. The Buddha himself and most of his following depend to a great degree on the Hindu background, which has a god belief history. Gautama was born a Hindu. Buddhist texts have been crafted to mimic the oral presentations of the Vedas (Lopez).

The doctrine of Karma is common to both religions, Hinduism and Buddhism, as is the view of the world and the need to tame the appetites of the flesh to attain Nirvana, a supernatural state. Buddhist tradition describes realms located in this and other worlds including the high realm of the gods. We are told of a heaven of the thirty-three that is populated by the gods of ancient India, ruled by Indra. There are the four cosmological systems involving a predicted time frame for the existence of all beings. But most importantly, the fact that Buddhists believe in rebirth based on one's performance in one's latest life and then the concept of nirvana, which would end the cycle of rebirth, must assume a supernatural element.

I have visited Buddhist temples in China, Cambodia, Vietnam, Thailand, Myanmar, and Japan, and there is everywhere a clear sense of the supernatural. Godlike guardians. Incense clouded stupas. People engaged in prayer. Offerings. Obvious Buddha worship. This for me helps define Buddhism as a religion. Whether or not a practice is considered a religion is dependent on one's definition, and the all too obvious supernatural element is the key, in my view.

I recently (November 2011) concluded a visit to Thailand, Cambodia, and Vietnam, during which I visited numerous temples, among them Angkor Wat. I returned to Cambodia and Myanmar in 2013. I spoke with quite a number of locals and discussed their religious views rather openly. They were not shy.

It is clear to me that Buddhism as practiced by the peoples of the region is based on gods and the supernatural. There was the influence initially of Indian beliefs as they modified earlier animistic beliefs and ancestor worship. The temples of Angkor (eighth to eleventh centuries), influenced heavily by Indian culture, clearly show the god belief of the time, which placed the rulers in the realm of the gods.

That early influence exists today in the form of Theravada Buddhism practiced generally in Thailand and Cambodia. I was impressed by a college graduate's clear statement that most of the ancient animism and ancestor worship are still very strong in the region. Vietnam mirrors some of this, but there is a stronger geographic and cultural influence there from China to the north. That does not mean less belief. One Vietnamese correspondent spoke in detail of how he and his family relied on the support of their deceased parents for decisions in their lives.

Gautama the Buddha spoke out against the practice of Hinduism in his time and encouraged a return to its earlier and basic values. Thus, the Buddha had to have retained much of the god belief of Hinduism. The thesis of this book revolves around the ways and means by which humanity creates gods, and gods can mean more than the identifiable God of the "religions of the book." They encompass the amorphous supernatural cycle of life, death, and rebirth, the human creations pertinent to the subcontinent's religions. We again have an example of the tendency to convert moral and social mores into the realm of god-enforced rules of conduct.

This chapter deals with history, and the historians of Buddhism present at best a doubtful set of evidence for God's existence. There is nothing here that is very different from the histories of the other great religions. Accounts of the Buddha's life and teachings did not appear before four hundred to six hundred years after his supposed nirvana, and he is supposed to have lived (and died) somewhere around 600 to 500 years BC. These numbers should and do present a big question mark. I do not question that a great personality with, perhaps, the name Siddhartha Gautama was born around 500 to 600 years BC, or that this person preached over forty-five years a certain philosophy and then died. Very believable! But we are asked to accept that this person's life events and teachings were accurately related through the oral traditions over four or more centuries. Some experts claim reliance on accounts reportedly much closer to the time of the Buddha's life.

Despite the reputation of the bards for accurately passing on stories and verses without alteration over long periods of time, I strongly suspect that error or deliberate change entered into the account of the Buddha's life and teachings. In fact, the oral presenter, as accurate in transmission as he may be, will only repeat what he has been told, and this may be far from the truth. By the time that Buddhist history and dogma began to be recorded in material form, they could have been doctored to the beliefs and preferences of an innumerable number of interested individuals and communities. The process is a perfect one for the creation of myths. The Buddha, his life, teachings, and deeds therefore probably incorporate a series of myths that represent desired human sociological standards relevant to eventual achievement in the supernatural.

It is not the purpose of this book to debate the myriad interpretations of any of the religions, but it is within the purview of my investigation to highlight the god-reinforcing tendencies that result from the struggle by religious factions to interpret the faith and to enforce its worship. Buddha and his philosophical/religious views of life and death, according to the experts, were a challenge to the Hindu state of affairs of his time. He, like Jesus, Muhammad, and Martin Luther many years later, proposed a repudiation of the practices and beliefs of the then-dominating religion and a return to values that had been lost over the passage of generations, while adding new concepts as well.

Recognizing this movement, there came about a critical self-analysis in the subcontinent by the orthodox systems involving a new emphasis on criticism and analysis as opposed to poetry and religion (Radhakrishnan and Moore). Gautama also set in motion a movement in support of a code of conduct with its ritual and dogma (Dharma) that literally exploded across Asia. The number of texts and sects derived from his teachings and acts has reached an astronomical level. Here is a quote from Lopez's *The Story of Buddhism*.

> This overwhelming ocean of texts, many long unread
> in languages long forgotten, inevitably changed through
> time and translation, presenting doctrines and practices at
> wild variance with one another, all claiming to originate
> from a man whose words can never be recovered.

We have heard this before. The original being and events are debated and altered to such an extent that speculation, myth, and religion become the virtual focus of the movement. The Buddhist religion has its basis in the ancient god beliefs of humans, and while the original Buddhist middle way may be taken more as philosophy than religion, societal activity over the millennia has reinforced the religious aspects and preserved or reintroduced the god or supernatural. Though Buddha himself denied that he was a god, he has since been elevated to that status.

The Asians have come up with their own version of heaven and everlasting life. Whereas the religions of Abraham portray a supernatural heavenly place where humans of good behavior reside forever in wonderful and beneficial conditions, the Asians have been more down-to-earth. If one does good acts, then one enters not a heavenly abode but a new life on earth. If one does not exercise good and selfless behavior, then one assumes a lower form of life. Thus, we have two examples of differing religious cultures that describe humanity's search for eternity. The result in either case is the same; humanity's earthly behavior leads eventually to bliss or pain, and that for eternity.

We must accept that much of what Siddhartha Gautama preached made absolute sense. There was a pragmatic down-to-earth element to his preaching. He asked his adherents to live a good life and to deny corrupting thoughts and actions. This resembled the preaching of Jesus of Nazareth in certain ways. How do humans overcome the burdens of life and at the same time contribute to the lives of their neighbors while understanding that there is an all-encompassing realm of existence that one must seek? I have a hard time faulting his pragmatic approach to life. I do have a problem with the supernatural element based on his background in Hindu god belief. He is cited with frequent references to the gods.

I also have a problem with the Buddha's emphasis on the first noble truth from which all follows: suffering, pain, life dislocation, sickness, and selfishness. In other words, life is brutal. The Buddha prescribes a metaphysical approach that allows one to ignore and overcome these maladies inherent in the life of a human being and thus reach a state of relief from it all. But what the first noble truth describes is the evolutionary, traditional, and normal stresses on human beings over millennia if not a million years.

I fully agree that one should adopt a philosophy and pragmatic approach to one's life that seeks to avoid or overcome the negatives around us. But humans have historically been capable of overcoming all this bad stuff. We cope with it. We have survived. Buddhism, however, seems to take the approach of denial and escape from reality. In effect, Buddhism dodges the challenge. It is defeatist. It represents an escape from reality. How perverse can it be that the monk enters into a denial of reality while depending on the gifts of those who must daily confront the reality of life!

Yet, despite my criticism, I find the Buddha's fundamental teachings to be as acceptable as those of other great religions. Proof that there is a god? Not really.

How can we summarize Buddhism and its lesson regarding god belief? A human being born roughly 600 BC into the aristocracy of the Hindu subcontinent abandons his life of luxury, sees the burden of poverty, disease, and death, experiences the ascetic life of physical misery, rejects asceticism, and eventually develops a pragmatic philosophy of life that overwhelms the thinking of peoples across continents.

He becomes godlike in the minds of his followers. The human propensity to create gods is well in force. As stated earlier, Gautama is reported to have insisted that he was not a god. However, the following centuries, in fact, elevated him to that status. Any reference to Buddhism will contain hints to his godliness. This factor along with the historical religious background, questionable god-supporting texts, and the appearance of myth and fantasy, all that we discussed above show Man's tendency to invent the gods.

Jainism

Jainism is one of the sects that appeared to challenge the trends of the day and sought to return to the ancient traditions. I find little in the thinking of Jainism to directly support god belief, except that the founders of the belief based their movement on the Vedas, while resisting the authority of the Vedas. The Vedas had a solid background in god belief. Jainism is a philosophical religion that emphasizes its grounding in logic and experience. Nevertheless, there is in its teachings a subtle inference of a soul and a being beyond the corporal, all in concert with its origin in the Vedas.

Carvaka

The Carvaka system reflects what seems to appear in all religions, an extremist branch, in this case an essentially atheist offshoot. No god. No soul. No heaven. No final liberation. No afterlife. Only that which is perceived exists. It is hard to believe that the Carvaka system derives from Buddhism, but that apparently is its history. I bring it up to illustrate that at least some Buddhists reacted to the inherent supernatural nature of the religion and elected to establish a counter system. I can only speculate as to whether they went through the same thought process that led me to write this book. They might even be supporters.

On a different theme, I must mention here one of the most curious elements encountered in Indian religious literature, dogma, and practice. So much seems to revolve around six of this and seven of that. Three principles here. Eight there. Despite the centuries of deep thought about the human condition, and the intellectual treasures derived therefrom, the alignment of so much thought with a bunch of numbers is odd. The Chinese obsession with the right numbers is also of note.

Religion, Philosophy of China, Japan, and Korea

China

It would be a great support for my atheist standpoint if one were to take into account the essence of spiritual innovation in China twenty-five hundred years ago without question. There is much to say about the traditional emphasis on harmony with the natural world and the social, familial underpinnings of so much of Chinese philosophy, which came out in that period, and which would appear to dismiss the role of gods and the supernatural. But this so-called harmony of "man and nature" is a snapshot taken at a certain limited period of the millennia of Chinese religious development, corresponding to the era of the great philosophers and teachers—Lao-Tzu and Kung Fu-tzu (Confucius). God belief was there before and in later generations, and, most probably, during the periods of the philosophical greats as well.

Taoism

This religion has as its source or founder the philosopher Lao-Tzu. Extremely little is known of his person, and some would say he is more myth than real. Nevertheless, he is supposed to have written a small book entitled *Tao Te Ching*. It is from this book, antidotes and teachings from his life (real or imagined), and interpreters of the book and his teachings that Taoism emerges.

Essentially, Tao means "the way." That can be the greatest way of ultimate reality, the way of the universe or nature's agent, and the way of human life. This is a simplification, and I am going to leave it at that. Taoism also breaks down into three versions, which do interest us. There is the philosophical way, which espouses the preservation of Tao and its powers. There is the vitalizing or energizing way, which attempts to increase the power flow of Tao through Yoga, meditation, and exercise such as Tai Chi. And there is the religious way with its churches and institutionalized practices involving folk religion, rituals, magical effects, and higher powers.

We can see these three versions of Taoism today, so they do not necessarily reflect what Lao-Tzu would endorse. Taoism, the religion based on his teachings, fell into a state of moral decline as it developed into a mystic, god-populated regime of superstition, alchemy, and idolatry. God belief took over.

Confucianism

Kung Fu-tzu, or Confucius, was born around 551 BC. He lived a professionally unsatisfying life but traveled considerably, teaching his rules of behavior. His philosophy was conservative and one of deliberate tradition, recognizing traditional family and ancestor relationships while emphasizing social life and personal relationships. He thus made a shift from emphasis on the heavens to earthly needs and requirements. He, like Lao-Tzu, believed in Tao. He taught a constant striving to become a more perfect person. One must behave humanly toward others, observe moral rules, be mature, do what's right, and practice the arts. Confucius is reported to have specifically recommended that beliefs in the supernatural be avoided. But, in the words of Huston Smith, Confucius taught a "restrained and somewhat attenuated theism."

During his life and the period of his teaching, Confucius found support at times for his philosophy, but it was only after his death that it truly became accepted, so much so that Confucianism became the law of the land and spread eventually across borders to Japan and Korea. The teachings of Kung Fu-Tzu even today underlie much of the thinking of the Chinese. Although the sage reportedly said, "I know nothing of the gods," Confucianism has, since his time, become hierarchical with religious traits. Humans have again exercised their desire for the supernatural.

In the grand scheme of things, Chinese religious practices take an interesting early, midpoint, and later progression over time. I began with the mention of Lao-Tzu and Kung Fu-Tzu. They represent a middle point. Humankind before then had a different view of the world, and humankind after then fashioned an even more unique and different view of the world. Rice cultivation on the Yangtze is supposed to have had its beginnings as far back as ten thousand years ago. This is contemporary with grain domestication in the Middle East. Humans in China were embarking on the agrarian revolution that was to alter their history all over the world. It was seven thousand years later that the great philosophers appeared! What can we imagine was the spiritual/philosophical/religious template for those times before then?

The template is not at all different from that of other sources of human expression. I must state again a central thrust of this book—that the early and primitive cultures and beliefs determine all that follows in the realm of religious thought. The earliest Chinese, like their contemporaries in Egypt and Sumer, did eventually decipher the movements of the celestial bodies, and they succeeded in a number of scientific endeavors. Yet, the ancient folklore of the Chinese, which involved beliefs in the supernatural, became a fundamental element of later and even modern religious thinking in China. Research points to societies that in the earliest days revered their ancestors as virtual members of the living family. There were animistic practices, and there seemed to be a vision of heaven and gods of the elements and the beyond to whom one must show obedience. There were the usual supernatural representations of the natural elements that so powerfully influenced human existence. There was god belief, just as there was in all ancient societies, and for the same reasons: ignorance of (and, therefore, worship of) the natural elements, favor sought in catastrophe and war, fear of death, and the other vital interests of humankind trying to survive.

The early god beliefs of the Chinese were to some extent honored by the great Lao-Tzu and Confucius, but as stated above, they tended to proclaim an approach more oriented to the proper conduct of humankind in society and in harmony with nature. What became of their efforts? The answer is the near end of the progression. Taoism was partly theistic to begin with. It merged with ideas of deities in the folk religions and stressed magic elements. Confucianism, despite its original earthly and social pragmatism, evolved into a religious cult in which Confucius became a deity. In both cases we see a very human tendency to convert the earthly into godly realms, realms that exist only in the minds of humans.

Japan and Korea

Much of the religious experience in these two nations derives from beyond their borders. Both Japan and Korea have exhibited religious activity in the form of the great religions of India and China, and their observances will resemble those of the originating countries. This is not to say that local folklore in Japan and Korea had no influence on the practice of religion; it certainly did, as the folklore in China influenced Confucianism, Buddhism, Taoism, and other sects there. In Japan, Shinto arose to be the eventual state religion, venerating the ruling elite as gods or at least direct representatives of God. The emperor enjoyed "the mandate of heaven." Was this a perversion of the Confucian dedication to family and ancestor and its emphasis on societal order? Some may say so. Shinto has little respectability today. The god of today's Japanese, though flavored with reverence for family past and present, may very well be the god of abundance.

Of more significance, however, is the cult of Zen Buddhism. It long ago made its mark as a central aspect of religion in Japan, although its ancestry is clearly Chinese. Zen Buddhism is a Mahayana sect, but it is a very distinct version thereof. It takes as its central theme the breaking of the language or the word barrier. It is "not founded on written words, and

[is] outside the established teachings" (Smith-Novak). Masters were known to punish students who relied on established word definitions of the most sacred entities then known such as nirvana. The resultant practice of the religion becomes demanding as the students must approach seemingly absurd conundrums to gain merit, the so-called koan. The intent is to force the mind to indulge in extraordinary thinking. Zen tries to upset the ordinary and to excite the mind to free itself from the confines of accepted definitions.

Zen Buddhism is a mystical religion that relies on a nonconventional challenge to the conventional and textual concepts of Buddhism and at the same time relishes the goodness of life, accepting the adversities of life and death. Zen appears to take a pragmatic approach to its religious fundamentals, much as the original Buddha might have endorsed. Does Zen tell us anything about god belief? Its origins are clearly god-based. Its philosophy envisages an eternal being and a supernatural existence. Yes, Zen Buddhism is another human construction in support of a god, gods, and/or the supernatural in whatever form, all anchored in the past.

And in Korea? The waves of religious thought washed over Korea from the far reaches of India, China, and Japan, and are clearly reflected in Korea's society. However, there has occurred, for me, an unexplainable conversion of many Koreans to Christianity. This needs some further research. Why has this religion of the Mideast and the West become such a fascination for the Koreans? I have yet to encounter a reasonable explanation. It certainly deserves an analysis.

More Thoughts on the Religious Histories

This chapter has dealt with only a limited number of major religions. Throughout history there have been thousands of religions, and there are probably that many still identifiable today. I refer to the beliefs of the American Indians or the Aztecs or the Egyptians or the Greeks or the Nordics and their pantheon of gods. All would illustrate the same tendency of humans to create gods for the same reasons I have explored. For the purposes of this book, I believe that an examination of the majors, as we have done, provides sufficiently the evidence required to support our thesis that God is a human creation.

In the case of every one of the religions examined, it is clear that the foundations of the religion were laid many thousands of years ago. All examples reflect ancient god beliefs involving animism, gods representing the elements, gods of fertility, gods of war, gods of the harvest, and, of course, the fear of death and the desire to continue to exist in an afterlife. Yes, the great religions have "matured" such that they reflect advancing modernity of philosophical, scientific, and political thinking. However, we are to this day still thinking in terms of early Chinese folklore, of pre-Aryan and then Aryan myths in India, of Aztec mythology, of Yahweh in the wilderness, of angels and curses, of floods and pestilence, of God on earth, and so on. God belief remains.

It is interesting to see how powerfully the ancient ways of thinking attract belief even today. It seems that the great teachers, prophets, and God-related are credited with similar execution of miracles such as conversations with angels, multiplying items of food for the benefit of their followers, the entertaining of visions and communications with the supernatural, and a relationship with the dead. These tendencies as seen from religion to religion suggest an ancient expectation of such events and capabilities. Their statement in the texts is probably what one would expect of societies steeped in the ancient traditions. That does not mean we should believe them today. But we do!

A very interesting analysis pertinent to what has preceded in this chapter has been developed by Christopher Booker in his book *The Seven Basic Plots: Why We Tell Stories*. He summarized his thesis in a contribution to the *Los Angeles Times*, and I cite his words. The seven basic plots are: overcoming the monster, rags to riches, the quest, voyage and return, comedy based on confusion, tragedy, and rebirth. These plots, according to Booker, are central to and are repeated in human stories throughout history. Should a story involve most or all of the plots it supposedly becomes most appealing. The stories of Jesus of Nazareth, Confucius, Muhammad, Gautama the Buddha, and others of the religious pantheon evoke these plots somewhat, and if the analysis is at all pertinent, one must ask how much the stories were embellished to appeal to the listener's preferences from the beginning.

Everlasting Life

Never forget the one aspect of religious belief that has been here from the beginning and is with us today: the fear of death and belief in an afterlife.

Let's look at the concept of everlasting life. It seems to be an element in all religions, large and small. In the Christian and Islamic context, one can carry on in a supernatural state, say in heaven. But, if we listen to the Christian biblical texts, perhaps Jesus was only citing the customs of the times. A male was then assumed to have a wife and to have children. What better way to ensure everlasting life than through one's progeny? That is not the accepted Christian view, but it is the best I can advance as plausible for everlasting life. I cannot see a parallel in the Hindu and Buddhist beliefs, but the emphasis on one's worldly achievements as a means to achieve a higher status in a later life certainly comes close.

The good and success that one accomplishes would surely be a key to one's advantages in a later world, and would, of course, benefit the family and friends of the beneficent, whether or not that is the accepted solution for the religious autocracy. Asian ancestral worship looks back, but the idea was always that one's ancestors were in some form or other present. That is, they lived on. Egyptian, African, North American, and Central and South American cultures all display similar or parallel beliefs. No matter how one constructs the model, most religions place an emphasis on an everlasting life.

I must insert here a very personal view of everlasting life. Why would one want to live forever? Can you imagine what that means? In what state would one live? In what surroundings would one live? Would nothing ever change? What would one do? Would one merely float through all time in some sort of a dreamy existence? These questions infer that everlasting life is not all that it is supposed to be. There are classic Greek and more recent tales illustrating that everlasting life may be more hell than heaven!

Evil

At this point I must bring up a topic that one reviewer of this book emphasized: evil. Why have I not delved into this aspect of nature and, of course, so much of humanity's less than honorable history? I have shied away from a discussion of evil because it, in my view, has little if anything to do with God's existence. Evil exists, not as a substantive thing, but as an aspect of reality. It's just here. And evil is in the eyes of the beholder. Is the tsunami that killed two hundred thousand in Indonesia evil? Is the lion feasting on the still living zebra evil? Are incidents of infanticide for the purposes of population control evil? There are innumerable examples of what many would call evil.

But evil, whatever the description, has been with us from the beginning. It is part of nature and part of humanity's history. Now, what does that mean about God? I submit that it means nothing. Timothy Keller tries to show that the existence of evil is part of God's plan to strengthen humankind's faith in God. This is a real stretch. On the other hand, the fact that humanity has displayed so much cruelty in its history is no means to deny God's existence, although it may provide a clue for his nonexistence. In fact, evil is demonstrated far and wide but has no meaning as to the existence of God. It just happens to be the downside of nature, and that's it!

Yet, there is a point to be made. God supposedly created the world and placed his much-favored humans there in the beginning. But humanity's history has been one of constant conflict from the earliest clans to the empires of today. It is a history of killing, torture, wars, atrocities, and incredible suffering. Man has also meticulously gone about the destruction of his environment.

Is this what God is all about?

Is this what union with the All is all about?

It leads to doubt. Doesn't it?

We Conclude

A historical pattern is discernible. The first gods were those that represented natural forces. They provided for good crops, abundant fish, rain, sunlight, etc. As time went on, they protected against predators, invaders, drought, and pestilence. Gods advanced to the status of tribal and cultural protectors, as with the gods of the Rig-Veda or Yahweh of the Hebrews. Such gods remained viable as long as the tribes and cultures won; they declined in adverse times.

The hunter-gatherer was soon gone as a model for humankind. Agriculture had arrived. Great demographic movements were occurring. Wars were waged at ever greater intensity. Urban living arrived. Humankind could take time to think. Humans appear to have then reached a philosophically evolutionary point at which an appreciation of their mysterious surroundings and many of life's unknowns resulted in "modernized" philosophical and religious explanations for these phenomena. Human cultures had matured to the point at which humanity's relationship with the natural and the supernatural must be explained rather than simply endured.

It was always clear to humankind that they depended on gods (gods were always assumed to exist) for their well-being. Then societies and cultures evolved and matured. Persons of great repute melded the ancient beliefs in the gods with the rules and regulations of society. The resultant mix of ancient gods with a matured understanding of society and the rules that must govern it led to innumerable myths and stories that supported the emerging religions. This was purely a case of new concepts or religions absorbing and co-opting existing earlier gods and practices to support the advancement of the newer trends. Gods or God were assumed to provide a legitimate underpinning of newly established social rules. In effect, gods or God were used to authenticate and authorize societal (and thus political) aims. The gods that humans created had always been there.

In the period between roughly four thousand years to one and a half thousand before present, a series of very memorable personages and related or subsequent movements appeared on the scene, and the resulting influence through teachings, evolving doctrine, practice, and institutional structure have led to the major religions of today. The gods of today's modern religions have matured to "feel-good" gods. Do right! The Golden Rule. Human rights.

We have reviewed the record accumulated over these last several thousand years regarding the establishment and maturing of the religions. As stated earlier, the record is a shambles. There were no texts, for instance, in early China or the Indian subcontinent other than the archaeological and oral accounts. The "religions of the book" were written so late and have been so subject to translation, rewrite, theological "correction," political influence, loss, and simple copying error that they are hardly worth accepting as verifiable or reliable as to fact.

So many of our experts quote Socrates, Maimonides, Hume, Spinoza, Paine, Descartes, Nietsche, Aquinas, Augustine, Epecuros, Galileo, Kant, C. S. Lewis, the popes, and on and on. I have been through many of these. They have been part of the great debate. Some are on one side; some are on the other. And the result? Often a lot of hot air. Sometimes brilliant discourse. The theists repeat ad nauseum the same old faith in the history and faith they constructed. The revolutionaries offer a freedom of thought and a challenge to the theists, albeit oft merely polemical. I believe the doubters have the best arguments.

In the end, I see no proof or acceptable reason for God's existence in the study of history. There are, instead, many clues that God does not exist or is, at best, a virtual creation. Everything that we have reviewed in this chapter points at humankind as the source of the gods, with all the goods and bads that that implies. Gods are a human creation.

CHAPTER 2

Evolution and the Numbers

The Evidence Supports
Evolution and Not God

How can something as complex as the human genome develop in the time of the earth's existence without intervention by a supreme being? It did, and it had nearly four billion years to become a fact. This is an exceptionally long period of time, and the effect of time in the process has not been properly appreciated by the critics of evolution. Nor have other factors that made evolution literally inevitable received the credit they deserve.

One factor in the journey from then to now is the implied assumption that the human genome is a unique and isolated case. The human genome is perhaps the most complex of all those known; however, the human genome shares an incredibly large part of its DNA (deoxyribonucleic acid) with many other species. Why do we base so much of our medical research on experiments with primates and mice? Because their genomes are very close to ours; rodents have 88 percent of the human DNA, and orangutans have a 99 percent correlation. In other words, despite the fact that the human genome is more "advanced" than all other known species, it is only one on a list of genomes with related DNA.

For the theist, this can mean that humankind was not the sole beneficiary of sublime intervention. But he was the favored one to benefit from the Almighty's efforts and is a very special case. Of course, this leads us to the question as to why humans are so special and why humans should so reflect the deity or be so favored by a deity. For the person who supports evolution, the broad sharing of DNA among the species becomes one of the keystones in the argument. The true Darwinian contends that the fact that DNA is shared by so many species is one of the reasons why evolution needed no outside help. This fact and evolution's conservative retention of past developments allowed innumerable successes and failures to lead to innumerable outcomes and a diversity of species, some more complex than others.

Numbers have a meaning, but numbers can be made to say whatever the analyst or interpreter desires if basic assumptions are manipulated, assumptions are made, and results of calculations are interpreted. Thus, one can easily construct an algorithm that essentially straight lines an incremental evolutionary path starting four billion years ago and conclude that it was not possible to arrive at that end. But that is too simple. There are multiple ways that nature could and did resolve that difficulty.

Let's assume life on earth began close to four billion years ago. The archaeological record clearly supports this timing. Signs of bacteria have shown up in the stones that date back to the earliest geological times. The latest discoveries in South Greenland show evidence of microbes dating back 3.8 billion years. The early bacteria are relatively unchanged from many of those we can identify today, which implies a hardly imaginable continuity over eons.

Evolution continued over this very long time frame, adding to the probabilities of natural advances. The basic building blocks started to appear at the very beginning, which allowed nature room for maneuver. Consider the environment billions of years ago and the life-forms that existed. We know that bacteria, fruit flies, and viruses multiply at fantastic rates today. Richard Dawkins cites the reproduction rate of bacteria as millions per day. We can assume that they accumulated evolutionary advances at a rapid rate as well. We then have a situation akin to the linking of thousands of computers to achieve immense calculating capabilities. Evolution was not on a single-track course, but on a multitrack course in the refinement of both genome and phenome.

Evolution has tended to test change on a continuing basis, but once a solution was arrived at, evolution tended to keep it and to build upon it.

The nearly four billion years saw little waste; nature kept and built on each success and went on building.

A look at humanity's so-called family tree provides a somewhat personal example of how the process works. Archaeologists have unearthed evidence of a good number of our ancient relatives, some of which are our direct forebears and others of which are not. We share genetic similarities with some such as the Neanderthals and the Denisovans, both long gone. We share a phenome likeness with several other hominids, also long gone. Our DNA is very close to that of orangutans. All of this illustrates how the evolutionary process works through trial and error with change and selection applied to many candidates to advance some and to eliminate some yet retain what works in either case. And humans have become what we are in a surprisingly short time.

Lynn Margulis's classic analysis, which postulated the development of symbiotic biological relationships and DNA sharing based on the ingestion of one life-form by another, illustrates another counter to the "not enough time" argument. Margulis's analysis has come under severe criticism. Nevertheless, as more evidence comes to light, more variations on the theme are advanced. Current thinking is that an archeon as host ingested a bacterium, leading to the first eukaryotic cell. Studies have tracked the development of the resultant form toward ever more complex eukaryotes. We see here a shortcut or acceleration of the evolutionary process. Some say it happened only once. It appears to me that, given the environment, the ingestion of one life-form by another had to have happened billions or trillions of times. Some proportion (at least one and maybe only one) of these ingestions would have resulted in the symbiotic DNA-sharing scenario that Margulis proposed.

It should be clear that there has been more than enough time for evolution to have succeeded. Let us not lose sight of the fact that started this chapter's narrative: the process of producing the genome of today advanced over nearly four billion years! And the archaeological evidence is at hand!

The proponents and critics of Darwinian evolution are many, and, in conformance with the basic approach to this work, I do not intend to reinvent the wheel by digging into the original and fundamental investigations that provide the basis for Darwinian or anti-Darwinian arguments. That does not mean that I do not respect the original sources, because I do. But I feel obliged to rest on the revered opinions of the most widely acclaimed experts in the field to make my thesis digestible.

Fossil Findings

Stephen Jay Gould was one of the greatest witnesses for evolution that America has had. He was a significant factor in the incessant American legal and cultural battles between creationists and Darwinians. He was a prolific writer in both journals and professional volumes. Among his most recognized works were: *Wonderful Life, Ever Since Darwin, The Panda's Thumb, Hen's Teeth and Horse's Toes, The Flamingo's Smile, Bully for Brontosaurus*, and *Eight Little Piggies.*

Gould has been criticized by some of his contemporaries as a backslider whose arguments against certain of the Neo-Darwinian theories belayed an inbred philosophical bent toward the involvement of deity in evolution. Be that as it may, Gould has been a great contributor to the Darwinian cause. I am going to concentrate my comments on one of Gould's most recognized works, *Wonderful Life,* because the topic with which Gould deals, the Cambrian explosion, turns out to be one of the favored pieces of supposed evidence for the intelligent design (ID) argument (An intelligent someone or something designed and implanted life on Earth).

Gould's *Wonderful Life* describes the historical and institutional conflicts surrounding the discovery and evaluation of the Burgess shale, a very serendipitous archaeological find in a Canadian park in British Columbia. In effect, the geological discovery amounted to a sudden window into a biological world roughly 550 million years ago. Gould's book concentrates largely on the expert conflicts regarding the reality of the finds and the taxonomy involved with the creatures discovered, and he credits several colleagues with great merit in sorting out the perceived phyla exhibited by the preserved creatures.

One of Gould's fundamental conclusions is that, given the wonderful extremely varied life-forms of that faraway time and the chances of arriving at those life-forms, it is highly unlikely that the evolutionary path could ever be replicated or, perhaps, that *Homo sapiens* would exist today. Christopher Hitchens, in his *god is not Great,* cites a point made by Gould, that the survival of the small *Pikaia gracilens*, the ancestor of today's animal kingdom, is unexplained. Somehow it survived, and that is "just history." If the tape were played again, it would trace a different history and arrive at a different evolutionary result. This concept has been widely challenged.

Gould also challenges the accepted theory that evolution follows a continuous process of increasing diversification. He cites the so-called ladder and cone approaches to evolution in which organisms progress "upward" with increasing diversity toward ever "improved" species. Instead, Gould insists on a process of "massive elimination from an initial large set of forms, with concentration of all future history into a few surviving lineages." He calls this pattern "decimation." Mass extinctions such as that which occurred with the Cambrian fauna present this pattern. Interestingly enough, the end result of this pattern is a reduction of surviving "body types" yet a proliferation of diversity of species based on these body types.

However, it is not the intent of this investigation to argue the existence or not of the creatures in the stones or their taxonomy or the likelihood of their recurrence should the tape be run again or the path to diversity. The debate of interest is more along the lines as to whether the sudden emergence of such a biologically rich slice in geological time represented by the Burgess fauna could be an expected evolutionary development or the intervention of a deity.

The idea that the Cambrian explosion represented a creation by God came even before Darwin published *The Origin of Species*. Darwin expressed frustration with the lack of explanation for the event. Much has transpired since Gould published his book, but the basics remain: roughly 550 million years ago there was an explosion of newly emergent life-forms, some very bizarre, some familiar, and some unbelievable.

Let's start with the facts. The creatures of the Burgess shale did exist. We have their existence in stone. Their physical forms are well preserved. A credible dating system places them roughly 530 to maybe 550 million years ago. They also present a series of invertebrate organisms with an anatomical range exceeding that found in today's oceans, according to Gould. And very few of them can be connected to modern phyla. But then comes the question, why have we this sudden flowering of life-forms? There appears to be no reason for their sudden appearance. There is little direct evidence of their ancestors, although there is somewhat more evidence of their direct descendants within a few millions of years. Most of the evidence, in fact, shows extinction of most of the Burgess fauna. Surely something or someone had to intervene in order to produce this extraordinary event. And that is the argument of the ID community.

Nonsense! There are very plausible reasons why the Cambrian explosion appears to be such an isolated event. To find the Burgess shale in the first place was a truly long shot. This was a once-in-a-lifetime occurrence. Consider also the unusual and unlikely circumstances required to have captured and preserved the imprints of these organisms in sediment. Certain events had to cause them all to be deposited together in the right place at the right time allowing for preservation and proper sedimentation. Then the process of formation of the shale would have to be completed. To duplicate these rare circumstances for the preservation of the immediate ancestors and descendants of the Cambrian organisms would require a lot of luck.

But let's assume we were lucky. There could clearly be rocks millions of years one side or the other of the Burgess shale that could provide a genealogical evolutionary path. But find them! Stones five hundred million years of age that have not been altered by the effects of heat, distorting pressures and tectonic displacement are hard to come by. For example, the ancestors may have been deposited at a different location under different circumstances of sedimentation. The resulting rock, if it, in fact, were ever formed in the first place (sediments may have simply washed away before pressures and other factors created a rock of any strength) would have to survive the same heat and pressures that created them as well as fracturing, weathering, and other threats. Continents have shifted, and seas have come and gone. In short, there are good reasons why there is scant supporting evidence for the Cambrian creatures' appearance.

Gould describes some of the Precambrian paleontology and candidates for ancestors of the Burgess fauna. But there may be no continuity between Burgess and whatever else one might find. The Ediacaran fauna consisting of multicellular animals discovered in Australia are placed, according to Gould, "no more than seven hundred million years old and perhaps younger." Nevertheless, Gould finds that, based on other investigations, the Ediacaran fauna may represent a failed multicellular experiment and not an ancestral link to later creatures with hard parts.

Long after Gould's observations, we now have evidence found in Namibia and Newfoundland in addition to that in South Australia that describe the Ediacaran fauna in some detail. There is still a consensus that that fauna disappeared before or at the beginning of the Cambrian explosion. Worm-like fauna may have contributed to its demise and heralded the Cambrian fauna.

Approximately midway between the Ediacaran and the Burgess fauna we encounter the Tommatian fauna, the "small shelly fauna," found worldwide. The Tommatian fauna possessed a perhaps less developed skeleton and were quite small. Again, we have a fauna that appears to be an experiment that failed.

Finally, lagerstetten, which postdate the Burgess discoveries, also demonstrate another extinction: most of the Burgess fauna.

In sum, we may be stuck with only this one window into the Cambrian/Paleozoic past provided by the Burgess shale. There had to be a workup to the Burgess creatures, and it must be assumed. However, the fact that no links have been established through the archaeological record does not mean that the links were not there. We just have not found them and perhaps never will.

There is recent support for the above arguments, whether pro or con. Peter Von Roy of Yale University and his colleagues placed an article in *Nature* that suggests that there are, in fact, other sites which provide insight into the Cambrian explosion. Their explorations involve an area of the Atlas Mountains of Morocco in which the researchers found a diverse assemblage of soft-bodied organisms from a period after the Burgess shale organisms. This has at least two significant meanings. First, the accepted lack of descendants of the Burgess shale organisms is called into question. Their absence is possibly merely the lack of the circumstances that preserved the organisms to begin with and not a mass extinction of the Burgess shale population. Accepting the fact that most perished does not mean there is no continuity. Second, the evolution of complex life was a continuing uninterrupted process but with fits and starts and difficult to trace.

But, of course, we see no confirmed ancestor of the Burgess fauna, although I find it hard to believe that some organism out of those ahead of the Burgess fauna failed to advance to a later evolutionary stage. Nevertheless, the above fossil findings weave a reasonable enough framework to explain the context of the Cambrian explosion as more or less a continuity and not an insertion from above.

But some still say that a sudden unexplained appearance of the Cambrian creatures means that a supreme being had to be involved. For those who believe in a deity, can they truly think that the Cambrian explosion was an intervention by God in the creation of a series of worms and lobsters, most of which are extinct? This is in my view a total nonargument.

Dawkins, Dennett, and Dembski

Richard Dawkins is one of the strongest advocates of Darwinian evolution. He has held the Charles Simonyi chair of Public Understanding of Science at Oxford University. He is a biologist and one of the leading advocates of evolution in the Darwinian tradition. His most significant works are *The Selfish Gene*, *The Blind Watchmaker*, and recently, *The God Delusion*. Both of the first two remain classics and relevant despite their initial publication in the 1980s. Dawkins declares in his latest printing of *The Blind Watchmaker* (1996) that he finds no major thesis in the chapters that he would withdraw. His message remains intact. It's evolution, pure and simple. Forget God! It is instructive to note that the intelligent design community has in recent times selected themes in *The Blind Watchmaker* for specific and strenuous criticism. The ID community sees his argumentation as very current it seems. His latest tests their mettle even further.

It is, of course, Darwin who stated the basic principles of his theory. However, experts such as Dawkins will and must expand upon the original theory. Dawkins cites some of the other notable proponents of evolution and their works in his preface to the 1996 *The Blind Watchmaker*: Helena Cronin's *The Ant and the Peacock*, Matt Ridley's *The Red Queen*, Daniel Dennett's *Darwin's Dangerous Idea*, Mark Ridley's *Evolution*, and several others. I have found *Darwin's Dangerous Idea* to be particularly convincing. A list of other noteworthy proponents of Darwinian evolution would include Wallace, Asimov, Ruse, Futumaya, and Atkins, to name only a few.

To begin the review of Dawkins's work, I will quote a passage early in *The Blind Watchmaker* and then two at the very end of the book. The central theme is clear.

> A complicated thing is one whose existence we do not feel inclined to take for granted, because it is too "improbable." It could not have come into existence in a single act of chance. We shall explain its coming into existence as a consequence of gradual, cumulative, step-by-step transformations from simpler things, from primordial objects sufficiently simple to have come into being by chance.

And then at the end of the work:

> The essence of life is statistical improbability on a colossal scale. Whatever is the explanation for life, therefore, it cannot be chance. The true explanation for the existence of life must embody the very antithesis of chance. The antithesis of chance is nonrandom survival, properly understood. Nonrandom survival, improperly understood, is not the antithesis of chance, it is chance itself. There is a continuum connecting these two extremes, and it is the continuum from single step selection to cumulative selection. Single step selection is just another way of saying pure chance. This is what I mean by nonrandom survival improperly understood. Cumulative selection, by slow and gradual degrees, is the explanation, the only workable explanation that has ever been proposed, for the existence of life's complex design.

It is worth a further quote to explain the process in more detail.

> The essential difference between single-step selection and cumulative selection is this. In single-step selection the entities selected or sorted, pebbles or whatever they are, are sorted once and for all. In cumulative selection, on the other hand, they "reproduce"; or in some other way

the results of one sieving process are fed into a subsequent sieving, which is fed into … and so on. The entities are subjected to selection or sorting over many "generations" in succession. The end product of one generation of selection is the starting point for the next generation of selection, and so for many generations.

One of Richard Dawkins's most important contributions is his insistence on the above cited process of "cumulative selection." In short, this approach emphasizes the conservative nature and the background knowledge of nature to the effect that the probabilities of evolutionary advances become reasonable and achievable. This is not a statistical trick; it is a viable view of biological and evolutionary reality.

Dawkins, in his books *The Selfish Gene* and *The Blind Watchmaker*, does a magnificent job of describing the gradual but inexorable process whereby evolution creates complex biological organisms. He states, as a subtitle to *The Blind Watchmaker*, that the evidence of evolution reveals a universe without design. I am not sure that that is what he really means, in that design is clearly evident in nature. The ID community emphasizes the terms "intelligent design" and "designated complexity" in a way that infers a designer. I assume that any organism in the environment in which it prospers will exhibit a design that works in that environment. But I attribute such design to the result of evolutionary forces as does Dawkins.

Richard Dawkins lays out several arguments against the proponents of ID who contend that very complex biological structures had to have had a designer since they cannot survive at any reduced complexity due to removal of structures or functions. This they call "irreducible complexity" since the removal of parts or functions from a complex organism results in its failure or demise. Therefore, they say that ancestors of current organisms cannot exist if it means they lack critical parts of today's descendent complex organism. (Which means step-by-step evolution can't work.) More complete organisms or parts thereof with all their complexity would have to be inserted all at once somewhere in time by the designer. This just does not seem to track, and Dawkins responds with a very plausible theory and process whereby evolution could arrive at such complex biosystems as the eye or a bat's echo-locating capability.

Evolution proceeds with a series of steps involving ever more complex and improved organic elements. He reverses the ID scenario. Evolution does not normally reduce or take away capabilities; it enhances them. The key is time—billions of years—and cumulative selection. His argument is convincing in that half an eye is better than none at all until the full eye is available. A long slow process toward the eyes of the creatures of today is reflected in the evolutionary process and supported by many years of research. In fact, we now know that dozens of evolutionary approaches have led to an equal number of different eyes. More on that later.

Dawkins also makes a very valid point that just because we cannot explain something does not mean that it is not true or eventually explainable. This is, of course, a response to the creationists when they contend that evolution has many gaps that are not explainable and is, therefore, not valid in its totality, an infuriating and frustrating argument that totally lacks in logic.

One more note on Richard Dawkins involves his views on the origin of life. Dawkins appears to be very accepting of the fact that life came about billions of years ago through natural chemical/electrical processes (as do many others.) I will pursue this further in a later section.

Richard Dawkins made mention in the last edition of *The Blind Watchmaker* of Daniel C. Dennett's contribution to the case for evolution in Dennett's book *Darwin's Dangerous Idea*. Dennett has been the Distinguished Professor of Arts and Sciences at Tufts University and director of the Center for Cognitive Studies. He is a philosopher, well grounded in other fields, including biology, engineering, and game theory. He is the author of *Brainstorms, Elbow Room, Consciousness Explained*, and *From Bacteria to Bach and Back*, the evolution of minds.

Darwin's Dangerous Idea begins on a philosophical note and quickly expands into more scientifically grounded arguments. The central theme is that Darwin proposed an earth-shaking theory that upended every idea of what life on earth was all about. It challenged the religious and philosophical thinking of the day. New life-forms, including ours, were subject to and the result of a mindless algorithmic process exercised over geologic spaces of time and design opportunity. Here was a statement of a process of natural selection both innovative (chance/mutation) and conservative (build on accumulated design) that acted, in Dennett's words, as a universal acid eating away at the mind-set of generations.

Dennett's work consistently follows the central theme that Darwin was on the right track and that no outside help was needed in the evolution of today's life. He uses a clever analogy to illustrate the difference between the approach taken by the opposing Darwinians and theists. He refers to evolution that uses accumulative design, natural selection, and basic conservatism as a process that employs "cranes." On the other hand, explanations of evolution's progress or explanations of design that depend on something other than natural processes (i.e., a deity or unembodied entity) employ "skyhooks." And Dennett makes no bones about challenging the god-believers. He does so with gusto. Dennett pursues several avenues in his exploration of *Darwin's Dangerous Idea*, and his expositions are extremely persuasive.

It is extremely difficult to boil down many pages of somebody like Daniel Dennett's writings. He has reduced his own inputs to a point that allows a general comprehension. Now we have to compress it even further. But try we must.

The mathematics relative to evolution is a subject of great debate and can be interpreted in very different ways depending on one's basic assumptions and related calculations. Creationists will insist that the odds are so greatly against evolution that it could not, of course, be possible. Dawkins and Dennett and many others of their persuasion are more than ready to cite the vast range of possibilities in design space, and they are also agreed that the probabilities of achieving various biological developments (to begin with, the origin of life) are very, very small.

However, here is where the assumptions mean a lot. Dennett points out that in design space there are uncountable ways of evolutionary development, and, once there is a start point, even though achieved against all odds, something is going to happen. And it will happen according to the rules of evolutionary science. Dennett disagrees with Stephen J. Gould where Gould says that the tape of life cannot be rewound with the same results so far experienced because design space is simply too large. Dennett contends that the processes of evolution force certain moves on development and that evolution would have to basically follow the same paths. It could go either way. In any case, he sees no challenge to the fact that evolution had to be the factual background to our existence today.

But what about arriving at the start point? Dennett has some very convincing arguments regarding the origins of life. They are not unique to the author, as he cites several others for their work, and they are well presented. His discussion of molecular evolution points clearly to the avenues that were likely to have been followed, which include the earliest nonbiological physical building blocks (Cairns-Smith), development of "macros" and viral organisms and the related replicator theories, and the ready availability of the required amino acids and eventually proteins that represent the needed extraordinary catalytic effect for evolutionary advancement. He vehemently defends evolution and the natural origin of life against the god-believers.

As part of the argument, Dennett explores the "Laws of the Game of Life," a two-dimensional game illustrating the self-replicating possibilities inherent in nature. He finds such a process to be viable but expensive. However, the critical point is that, should such gaming be an element in evolution, it would not be the result of design through divine intervention. This is a process that operated without outside direction. We may have discovered it, but it was by no means created. The "Game of Life" and related investigations demonstrate the ways in which pre-biological replicating structures could have been formed following nothing more than the rules of nature based on physics, chemistry, and the rules of probability.

A few more of Dennett's ideas are worth highlighting.

Dennett places a lot of emphasis on adaptionist thinking. To begin with, he makes a strong case for biology as engineering. There is a Darwinian design process. Things are the way they are because that is the best or most acceptable way. Natural selection (fitness) leads in this direction. Therefore, the adaptionist thinker must look at an organism with the challenge to find out why the organism is the way it is. This by no means says that the organisms under scrutiny aimed at a future design. They can't! But natural selection allows an organism to adapt to a changing, threatening, or beneficial environment. The adaptionist shows why, for example, differing species of flat fish are flat, using a reasonable cost-benefit analysis.

Fundamentally, adaptionist thinking is critical to Darwinian evolution. It is not critical that we, the observers, figure out how the bat got to be what it is, but it is critical that the algorithmic process of natural selection through trial and error followed that path to the properly adapted organism. The scientific record shows that nature has, in fact, followed that path. Critics have attacked adaptionist thinking, but it appears very clear to me that evolution has produced the many organisms that it has in the designs that it has for very concrete reasons. Why would it be otherwise? Would nature elect a design that did not match the environment as best as possible? Maybe, but those attempts are extinct!

Dennett makes short shrift of controversies such as Teihard's (evolution strives to achieve humankind), Lemark's inheritance theory (learned abilities can be inherited) and directed mutation (something picks mutations for a purpose). He refutes "irreducible complexity" and makes a very succinct summary to the effect that one cannot rule out outside influence on evolution, but it is not needed and remains unlikely without evidence for such influence.

At this point I feel obliged to note a matter of discomfort that arises from the attacks of the ID community, who have taken advantage of publishing after Gould, Dawkins, Dennett, and other Darwinian writers and have seized upon perceived gaps and contradictions in their presentations to advance the cause of ID. A rising distrust of science in the US population does not help. The Darwinians need to counterattack. The truth of the matter is that there is a great deal of the unknown involved in the presentation of evolution, but that is, as expected, a normal scenario in the conduct of science.

As an example, let us take the evolutionary development of the eye. Darwinians state a very believable scenario whereby today's eyes would logically come about through the gradual process of selection. But the evidence of the evolutionary steps that were taken had been poorly explained, it seems. Michael Behe is said to have conducted an extensive literature search for examples of progression from simple to complex, and he had apparently been unable to find any examples—any! He has been shown to be wrong, however. His was clearly an attempt to undermine evolutionary theory. It has been shown that eyes of many species have evolved by numerous pathways.

Evidence is often difficult to obtain, but it certainly behooves the Darwinian community to come up with far more explanations of the origin of the many complex biological organs and organisms in question such as the eye and to get the details out to the public as widely as possible, the point being that the science must be reduced to language involving concepts, mathematics, and statistics that the public can understand. It would be very helpful if some respected mathematicians could take on the ID community's numbers game.

But maybe things are improving. Victor J. Stenger contends that there has been a lot of peer rebuttal of Dembski and others, and he cites several in his *God the Failed Hypothesis*. TV series such as that of Neil deGrasse Tyson, films on luminaries such as Stephen Hawking, and extensive series of articles and films on science by the National Geographic are a big help. And there are more of this sort of publication.

As for the eye, chapter 9 in Neil Shubin's *Your Inner Fish*, which addresses the eye, is a good example of what needs to be more-often stated. Another: the February 2016 edition of *National Geographic* contains an excellent review of the state of inquiry into the evolution of eyes. It cites a few of today's experts and then summarizes the currently known science. A vast array of eyes evolved independently according to the demands placed upon the various species. Yet all versions of the eye go back to the single ancestor for which the protein opsin provided the earliest versions of sight and continues today as the essential ingredient in all eyes. Evolution works.

In the following section, I spend a great deal of time discussing the arguments of the anti-Darwin community, because the creationists and intelligent designers have seized the initiative and must be engaged, lest the field be conceded to their views. As I stated above, the Darwinians must do more marketing.

The Design Conundrum

The question of design reflected in organisms and their subsystems has become a point of severe contention between the Darwinians and the creationists. In this section I intend to show that design is as pertinent to natural causes as it might be to some unknown special intelligence. Design can be almost anything that shows a pattern that would not ordinarily be expected to occur without some determined process.

Darwinian exponents claim that the natural processes of selection of the most fit in the constant striving for survival account for the design of the species that we now see in the world around us. They agree that this is a gradual process taking place over extended periods of time.

Evolution's critics claim that the odds of arriving at the point at which we are in terms of the Darwinian evolutionary process are not supportable. Some well-known names and organizations of those who support the ID approach are William Paley, Michael Behe, William Dembski, Hugh Ross, Jay Richards, and others. The Discovery Institute in the state of Washington is probably the best known of several institutions pressing the ID cause. In the United States Christian evangelicals constitute a large support base for ID.

William Dembski, Mister ID

William Dembski's arguments appear to summarize those of the ID community. Dembski is clearly an intellectual with a broad academic, experience, and research background and a solid foundation in mathematics. I respect his views and have found his arguments interesting and, on their face, understandable. However, I have real reservations. To be honest, I strongly disagree, as do many others. Start with the fact that Dembski was a professor at Baylor University (he has left Baylor) and was or is also tied in with some of the most known religious organizations in the country such as the Discovery Institute. No researcher can escape his belief community. Dembski is as human as the rest of us, and we are bound to see in his expositions a reflection of his background.

Dembski's arguments have been thoroughly and conclusively countered by the scientific community, so, why am I devoting an entire section to an analysis of his writing? I do because there is a large community of believers, particularly in America, who accept the arguments he supports. This is a never-ending debate.

The ID community has taken pains to propose an intelligent design as being neutral regarding what or who the designer is. The strategy is transparent. Show first that complex design is apparent in all that surrounds us, and once accepted on this basis, introduce God. This is a scam! Should it be determined that there is design for which nature seemingly cannot account, then who the designer is becomes the ID default position. Regardless of how one defines the "unembodied" designer, we have to be referring to God. ID is purely and simply a religious support for god belief.

William Dembski's mathematical address of the questions around Darwinism and Creationism stands out because the probabilities are critical to establishment of the truth. Of all the factors concerning the reality of either Darwinian evolution or ID, the mathematical probabilities of arriving where we are after four billion years is, perhaps, one of the most significant. I have been criticized for dismissing Dembski too easily. I have again gone over Dembski's work, concluding once more that his hypotheses need to be dismissed. I am convinced that, properly reviewed, the ID statistics, like many earlier challenges to Darwin, must be discredited.

The crux of William Dembski's work lies in "specified complexity" and "complex specified information." On these terms hang all that he proposes in support of ID. The origin of the term "specified complexity," according to Dembski, lies with Leslie Orgel in his *Origins of Life* work of 1973. The term seems to be accepted by all sides in the design controversy, but its meaning is much disputed.

On page 35 of *Design Revolution* Dembski says, "An event exhibits specified complexity if it is contingent and therefore not necessary; if it is complex and therefore not readily repeatable by chance; and if it is specified in the sense of exhibiting an independently given pattern."

I get the thrust of his definition, but it leaves me mystified as to what fits the definition. It leaves a great deal of latitude. In the book the author pursues a string of arguments to further define specified complexity and does so by slicing and dicing his arguments to such a degree that it leaves me unsure of where complexity starts or can be called specified. I conclude that almost any complex organism, organ, or organelle can be covered. Period. The choice of a few examples, such as the flagellum, does not help.

There is a very large number of instances where the probability of evolving appears daunting. And we must remember that William Dembski is trying to show that where the evolution of something is dauntingly challenged it can be edged into being by some outside force. He ignores the fact that scientists have been able to show convincingly the evolutionary paths to great complexity.

Worrisome is the choice of the adjective "specified," which implies an entity that makes the specification. If semantics mean anything, the word *specified* presupposes an outcome, a goal, and, of course, a "specifier." Dembski's mathematic underpinning for what is or is not specified is at first glance convincing, except that it appears to exclude the small, hardly discernible complexities that lead to more complexity, those instances in direct conflict with Dembski's "proofs" that nature cannot create complexity.

The friendly critics of Dembski's works state that he decisively refutes the Darwinian underpinnings of evolution in favor of an intelligent designer. Many experts strongly disagree.

Dembski's arguments are generally phrased in mathematical terms buttressed with philosophical inputs. When it comes to a particular argument, an analysis, study, or research program, anyone with experience will tell you that, given the right boundaries, one can often predetermine the outcome by making certain assumptions, inserting limitations, making specific inputs, and using constants.

Here is exactly where I have a problem with the ID arguments. Dembski and others of the same persuasion tend to impose unnecessarily large resource populations and assumptions leading to excessively small probabilities for evolutionary solutions in the equations proposed. In the same vein, they tend to grossly underestimate the power of nature's background knowledge, the bottom-up approach of evolution, cumulative selection, the overwhelming opportunity numbers inherent in the early earth's environment, and the extent of the time evolution has enjoyed.

ID proponents also tend to characterize Darwinism as an exercise in pure chance. Yes, chance is involved, but so is a selection scheme. Chance offers up a large plate of choices from which nature selects one or more winners. Winners will undoubtedly exhibit some sort of design. The design, however, is not due to a specified complexity, complex specified information, or an intelligent designer.

I will take three of William Dembski's arguments as examples. They are the "proof" that specified complexity cannot be created by natural causes, his critique of Richard Dawkins "Methinks it is like a weasel," and the flagellum argument involving irreducible complexity.

In his book *No Free Lunch,* Dembski argues that natural causes cannot produce complexity. His discussions lead me to question whether elements of evolution such as the rise of complexity can be reduced to simple mathematical solutions. I wonder. Some describe statistics and mathematics as very flexible disciplines with many ways to approach a problem such that outcomes can vary greatly. Let's assume that, based on the known inputs, his math seems to work out. Should it be shown, however, that there is incompleteness or an error in the formulation of the mathematical solution, then the entire structure must fall.

In pages 289 through 302 in *N o Free Lunch* Dembski explores the probabilities and their related equations to conclude that the flagellum is highly unlikely to have occurred through natural processes. However, throughout his discussion there is an inference that this unlikelihood applies to a one-time gathering and organization of the developed parts in the finished organ. If this is the basis for his equation, then, yes, the flagellum is not going to appear by natural processes. This would be an erroneous start to a mathematical calculation, since this is not the way evolution works. Evolution involves a step-by-step advance from the simple to the complex end product. It involves time. It involves successes and failures. Nothing comes together all at once. Dembski knows this. In his works he accurately describes the process. He is ignoring it. He is inviting outside help. And innumerable examples of development of complex structures show no evidence of or need of outside help.

The work of Lynn Margulis is another example. Dembski gives short shrift to her work by calling the "idea of symbiosis, where one organism assimilates another to form a more complex organism," "speculative." Margulis' theory has been widely accepted as the process that led to the existence of the eukaryotic cell. Her work has undergone considerable analysis and subsequent restatement but retains its essential thrust. A recent report in the *Los Angeles Times* cites the writing of Noriko Okamoto and Isao Inouye of the University of Tsukuba in Japan in which they describe the ingestion of one single-celled organism by another to use the ingested cell as an energy source. The ingested cell subsequently alters its structure in accommodation. This is purely a thirdhand report, now not corroborated, but there is no reason to doubt that up to the present the process described by Lynn Margulis has support and validity. In fact, over billions of years, this process has possibly contributed to many more advances in biological complexity.

If the ingestion of microbe A by microbe B and the subsequent symbiotic arrangement does not amount to an increase in complexity, I do not know what Dembski is after. He would say that the complexity is no more than that of A and B and that we must trace the complexity all the way back to the origins of both A and B. This is a cop-out. The eukaryotic cell was/is a clear move up in complexity. What Dembski and others fail to factor into their equations are the symbiotic advantages, the increase in mutational possibilities, nature's background knowledge, cumulative selection, and the "sum is greater than its parts" aspect of such a natural happening, all of which lead to greater complexity.

What are we supposed to believe? Has the designer had to step in at every instance of increased complexity? This amounts to an incredibly large number of interventions! Or is the idea that the designer set things up such that nature/evolution does the nitty-gritty work? This would mean, ipso facto, that nature can, in fact, create complexity. On the face of it, to say that the natural combination of two or more complex organisms does not increase complexity is neither sustainable nor believable, regardless of what the math purports to say. I suspect the math may hold up, but the assumptions are wrong. There is something wrong with Dembski's entire analysis.

It is interesting that Dembski in his books makes an appeal to the scientific community to include Intelligent Design as an accepted area of scientific investigation. Is this an admission that ID needs help to survive?

Hamlet, of All Things

"Methinks it is like a weasel" is a statement voiced by Hamlet in Shakespeare's play of the same name. Richard Dawkins uses this phrase to support an evolutionary algorithm in which the phrase is the target sequence in a process of selection. The idea is to spin the wheel to select a letter from the twenty-six-character alphabet to fill each position (initially blank) in the twenty-eight-slot phrase. Dawkins's approach in the exercise of the algorithm is to base the algorithmic calculation on his concept of "cumulative selection." That means that, instead of having to search randomly and repeatedly a space of possibilities at each of the letter spaces in the phrase in order to reach the target sequence, one generates a random first try, but then retains the letters that in this try, by chance, match the target sequence. In the next attempt we have kept the characters that were properly placed the first time around, and if the second random shot manages to properly place more of the characters, we keep those as well. This process continues until the target sequence "METHINKS IT IS LIKE A WEASEL" is reached. Dawkins showed that the target could be reached in as little as forty generations. In other words, evolution is capable of creating complexity in a comparatively reasonable time frame because of cumulative selection.

We should at this point consider the discussion of Manfred Eigen in his *Steps towards Life* on the concept of v-dimensional space of points for binary sequences. At first glance, the possibilities for arriving at a target sequence (a viable mutant or a wild type) are beyond extreme. However, he says, "Guidance is provided by selection, which follows the value topography and thus reduces substantially the freedom of movement." He means that there is a constraint placed on movement, the routes, and directions, through v-dimensional space by the organizational process of selection. Changes that show value will more likely be selected. He concludes the discussion saying, "Thanks to the way in which the system orients itself according to the value criterion, the target sequence appears almost to have been aimed at." There are some differences, but basically this analysis supports Dawkins's Methinks algorithm and Darwin's theories.

William Dembski goes to great length to discredit Dawkins's algorithm and his approach to its solution. His critique, though erudite, is convoluted and, in my view, borders on obfuscation. He ignores Dawkins's cumulative selection and again insists on imposing on the problem the most restrictive probabilities possible. He claims that each pick of a correct letter changes the target and thus the probabilities. I am not sure of that. But that misses the point. Dawkins' point is to show that evolution can progress faster that has been assumed.

I would like to indulge in a bit of my own algorithmic manipulation to try to make the exercise a bit more understandable, and I will use

Dawkins's METHINKS IT IS LIKE A WEASEL as a start point. Richard Dawkins may say no to what I propose (Or he might say, "Dummy, that's what I was saying!"), and William Dembski and others may disagree, but so be it. In any case, I am sticking my neck out.

I will take the twenty-eight characters of METHINKS IT IS A WEASEL to represent twenty-eight attributes of a certain genome that would be the optimum combination of attributes or characteristics to survive and replicate in a given environment. There may be other attributes that would expand the number beyond twenty-eight, and there may be acceptable solutions that fall short of the optimum, but that is not important for the moment. Now, the criticism of the creationists is that the target is one chosen by Dawkins or by me or by some imperative in the algorithm and is not, therefore, valid. This charge has been leveled at Dawkins. But in my vision of the problem, the twenty-eight attributes are purely and simply the most important things a genome could exhibit in the fight for survival and replication, and no one or nothing has designated them. They aren't written. They aren't stated. If the genome wants to survive and replicate, it had best approach those twenty-eight attributes. Nature demands this. Nature defines the target. Very simple.

There comes the question of the fitness function or the fitness measure. The fitness function is quite simply expressed as no more or less than the target itself. In evolutionary terms this means that the survival text can best be achieved by accepting the survival text or optimum configuration as the fitness measure. In other words, if nature demands a certain conformity for survival, then the measure of an organism's survival possibilities is its ability to match its measure of fitness against the target optimum.

Let it be clear that none of the competing candidates has the faintest idea of what the target is or what the fitness factor is. There are millions, if not trillions, of organisms in evolutionary history competing to match a fitness measure with a target. If this is the case, then the search for a statistically supported possibility of achieving a certain biological outcome becomes even less demanding. We spin the mutation wheel. Competitive selection finds an optimum fitness attribute. The attribute is retained. The process repeats itself, and gradually the several attributes for survival are all achieved, in our example the twenty-eight attributes of the target sequence.

Dawkins's (and our) point is that the target can be reached rather quickly, which undermines the ID "not enough time" argument.

The Dembski approach to achieving the twenty-eight-character sequence target appears to be that of a sequential search through the vast space of possibilities to find the completed target. In other words, spin the wheel and observe the outcome. If all the spaces are not properly filled, erase the result and start over again with all blanks. This ignores Dawkins's cumulative selection factor, but it also appears to depict that search as one designer's search or a search emanating from some central perspective.

This is far from evolutionary reality. In Dawkins' analysis, those individuals with one or more of the advantageous attributes will probably survive and replicate at greater rates. The genetic advantages will be carried on through successive generations, adding ever more of the individual twenty-eight attributes. Yes, the probability is 1 of reaching the twenty-eight-character sequence sooner or later, and that is exactly what Dawkins says evolution is all about.

This point needs to be modified a bit. Toynbee's analysis of civilizations argues that stress when appropriately handled by a civilization leads to a bettered civilization. However, if the stress is too strong, the civilization will succumb. Similarly, in evolution, if a population can fall upon enough of the right attributes, it will achieve the required degree of complexity to survive. If the environment is too severe or the environment changes radically or the environment changes too quickly, our population may never come close to the target sequence of attributes to survive. For example, today's climate changes may not allow enough time for species to accumulate the needed new attributes to survive. The species, if that is what we are dealing with, will become extinct. In any case, it will be the natural environment that makes the life and death decisions.

Michael Behe in *Darwin's Black Box* (page 221), completely misses the point. He describes/prescribes extinction and fails to see the gradual nature of evolution. He takes the analogy out of context when he contends that failure to immediately arrive at the required sequence ends in "pushing up daisies." From the evolutionary perspective, the fact that one might pick up only some of the letters in the right place does not lead to sure failure. METH_N_S IT I_ _IKE A WE__EL or some other close approximation might do. And it is reasonable to expect that some of the candidates will have some of the correct letters placed to begin with. Yes, many candidates will fail. But some with half an eye will survive as long as the target environment does not radically change or change too quickly. This is a gradual process.

Dawkins' point is that an organism can reach the target over time and that it can be quicker than expected based on evolutionary conservatism. Behe also asks who is deciding which letters to freeze and why. As we stated above, no one decides. Not Dawkins. Not me. Not Behe. Nature decides. The criteria for meeting a target are what they are. They merely exist, and one meets the criteria or else! If the environment changes, the letters will change. I can only conclude that Michael Behe does not understand the problem or that he tends to ignore it.

I will now direct my comments at a specific section of William Dembski's *No Free Lunch*, the chapter addressing "Irreducible Complexity." Dembski equates "irreducible complexity" with "specified complexity," so he sort of puts it all in one throw of the dice. I chose to speak first to Dembski's analysis instead of that of Michael Behe, who has championed the hypothesis and written most extensively on it, because Dembski expands on Behe's analysis and, in fact, modifies it somewhat. I will return to Behe later.

Dembski invokes the spirit of times past, alchemy, to make the point that there must be a "causal specificity" for any biological development to take place. Since there was no way from here to there for alchemy, alchemy failed. However, he then makes an analogy with "emergence," meaning evolution, insisting that the lack of sufficient data results in a lack of causal specificity for emergence. He does not mention that ID has no scientific evidence of causal specificity. None whatsoever! Dembski himself goes on to say that his analogy could be taken as "misconceived, if not downright churlish." I couldn't agree more. Nevertheless, he goes on to say casually, "If we take seriously the parallel between emergence and alchemy, then ..." and he goes on to negate the Darwinian arguments for emergence. He says they assume too much. There are intractable problems. The evolutionary mechanism can't account for diversity "across all apparent boundaries" The trouble is that evidence for evolution makes the opposite very clear. His remarks are, frankly, far more applicable to ID. His establishment of a parallel between emergence and alchemy is pure rubbish!

Now we get into "irreducible complexity." This means an object has a complexity such that the removal of only one single part leads to the object's collapse or demise. We, of course, are talking primarily about biological organisms. But up comes the mousetrap. It isn't Dembski's fault (others have brought it up), but the analogy of the mousetrap, where the removal of one part makes it nonfunctional, is absurd. First of all, to infer that the mousetrap can be compared with such organic structures as the flagellum is ludicrous. Even taking the mousetrap as analogy is worse than simplistic. The mousetrap was clearly designed by a human all at once so that removal of a part does, in fact, lead to its inoperability. In the larger argument, the mousetrap analogy is a waste of time and a collapse of logic, despite the number of supposed experts who have addressed the point.

The flagellum argument involving irreducible complexity also strikes me as a loser from the very start. The flagellum is only one of millions of complex structures in the biological world. (To me the ATP synthase, a very complex and fascinating structure in cells for producing free energy, is more complex than the flagellum.) Any organism could collapse should one or more critical elements disappear. If a structure were to come into being all at once, yes, the absence of a critical part would be fatal. But we have seen that evolution does not work that way. It builds up to its complexities step-by-step. No designer waved a wand to introduce a finished complex structure.

It is true that once the evolutionary process arrives at a complex state the process will not work in reverse. However, evolution seldom starts removing parts; it moves them around, allows new ones to appear, and rarely gets rid of old ones. I am surprised that the argument to date (as far as I know) has not addressed the human genome in its entirety. For example, let's remove the mitochondria! Not only would the *Homo sapiens* cease to exist; most of the existent species would vanish. To say that this means that an undetermined entity designed and, of course, created these complex organisms is very far-fetched

In *The God Delusion*, Richard Dawkins does an excellent job of countering the ID flagellum argument. He cites Kenneth Miller and his book *Finding Darwin's God*. In short, there are biological antecedents comprising the critical elements of the flagellar motor. Evolution clearly can produce the flagellum, and, although all of the questions may not have been answered, to attribute the design to God is premature at best, and most certainly unwarranted.

Dembski does mention "cumulative complexity," which somewhat approaches one of Richard Dawkins' main points, but he gives it short shrift. He now cuts to the bone and says that selection can lead to irreducible complexity as long as there is a god.

And, since selection has no goal, it cannot exhibit complexity. He cites Behe in saying that irreducible systems must be produced all at once, since precursors would also fail if parts were absent. The flagellum is too complex; all of the myriad proteins must be there in the beginning as in the final version. Therefore, irreducibly complex systems are so complex that they are improbable and therefore indicate intelligence.

Dembski then goes on to discredit several of the counterarguments from the evolutionists, including scaffolding/Roman arches co-optation/ patchwork/bricolage, reducible complexity, incremental indispensability, and redundant complexity. These are all analogies and arguments that the proponents of evolution have employed in this great debate, and I do not want to get into a detailed explanation for each of them. Suffice it to say they are generally engineering analogies that show how organic structures can move toward greater complexity. Although analogies lend themselves to criticism, I read Dembski's attacking statements as assertions and his rebuttals as rather weak. Causal specificity is the main basis of his arguments, and their essence is that, because natural selection has not got all the answers, it has to be wrong. And ID?

Dembski does not accept the computer programming analogy, which makes the point that development of a program cannot always be traced, and, similarly, development of a biological system also may not be traceable. Yet he plays on the mousetrap, alchemy, and prisoner analogies without a second thought. You can't have it both ways, Dr. Dembski!

In summary, first Dembski tries to show that, because evolution cannot account for all the causal specificity and emergence, the transformation of the simple to complex is not possible. He claims to have proved this in *No Free Lunch*. Further, one cannot backtrack from a system of irreducible complexity. Evolution could by his calculations in no case create nature's complex biological systems. We would, in fact, fall below his universal probability bound (10 to the 150th). He claims to demonstrate this. Clearly then, the ID analysis means that God did it! This is all very suspect!

Manfred Eigen in his *Steps towards Life* shows convincingly throughout the book that complex does, in fact, flow from simplicity. It can be argued that the complex that does exist cannot be broken down without greatly negating the function of the complex structure. In other words, we can't go backward. But this is not "irreducible complexity" in the ID sense. It does not deny that in arriving at the complex one passed through less complex forms. If one accepts this as the case, then Dembski's mentioned mathematical/statistical analysis is a waste of time.

Here I will cite Daniel C. Dennett's discussion of the Baldwin effect in his book *Consciousness Explained*. The central idea is plasticity in the nervous system of an organism, say *Homo sapiens*, which means that the brain of an individual is capable of reorganizing itself in response to the challenges of the environment. Some have the trick, and some don't. It is *not* inherited, but it gives organisms an edge over the competition and thus leads to a better chance of reproduction and faster evolution. Both plasticity and cumulative selection tend to undermine the mathematical/statistical and biological arguments of the ID community. Evolution may involve severe challenges over great expanses of time, but it is nowhere near the impossibility that they claim.

Another area of consequential meaning in the evolution vs ID debate involves the very recent developments in epigenetics and the horizontal transfer of genes among and between species. This ever-expanding body of research implies a greatly expanded set of options for increasing complexity and advancing evolution to contend with environmental change. I recommend *The Tangled Tree* by David Quammen.

William Dembski has made his mark and now seems less active in support of ID. Why do I address his work? Answer: his arguments continue in some form to today, and America's religious right is more energetic than ever. The old arguments never seem to go away. This applies to Michael Behe as well.

Behe Misfires

Michael Behe in *Darwin's Black Box* argues in favor of the evidence for design of biological complex systems. In truth, almost all of his well-known book is devoted to showing that biological systems are very complex and that many show clear signs of design. I, for one, am not in any way won over by Behe's argumentation for intelligent design, and I am joined by many scientists with far more background and credibility than I have. Design there may be, but it was arrived at by other means than some undefined intelligence.

Yes, biological systems are extremely complex. At the molecular level the complexity seems to defy all comprehension. However, Michael Behe's argumentation leaves a few serious gaps. Behe cites several chemical-biological complexities involving the complex chemical cascades necessary to achieve blood clotting, optic nerve sensory transmission, and the mind-boggling immunity system. I certainly understand the complexity involved. But I can see that there is no statistical argument against such cascades occurring. And they occur instantly.

Is Behe saying that it is not possible to get the right chemicals together? It has occurred to me in my research that biological systems employ an amazingly limited palette. Getting the right ones should not be impossible if this occurs over time step-by-step from simple to complex. If the required chemicals and enzymes are present, is it not probable that cascades will automatically occur? Certain elements and molecules will by their very nature react with each other. Is there a need to take step one and say, stop, now take step two? Or is it probable that steps one, two, and those beyond happen extremely quickly? I feel assured that the latter is strictly the case. A designer is not necessary, once the basics are in place.

Behe relies on a series of analogies to bolster his arguments. I must again state my personal hesitation in the use of analogies, although I note that, no matter what side of the argument one is on, the tendency is to use analogies to help explain difficult theories, thoughts, processes, etc. When an author's readers are expected to be among the uninitiated, I agree they can sometimes be useful. But they can be extremely misleading as well.

I am uncomfortable with Behe's contention that certain things are irreducibly complex while other things are not. All things biological are complex to some degree. Where do we draw the line? And if some things do not require intelligent design, how do we explain the remainder? Do we leave the certain percent of non-irreducibly complex developments to something like, perhaps, evolution? You can't have your cake and eat it too. Either an intelligent designer put it all together, or he didn't do it at all!

The very concept of irreducible complexity, whether it be mousetraps, watches, Boeing 747s, immunity systems, the cilium, the flagellum, or the clotting system, is suspect. Okay, remove a part. This is what evolution is all about! It's called extinction. When an organism or system is denied use of one or more of its critical components, it dies, and millions upon millions of species have disappeared because critical elements in their survival kit were denied. However, the fact that a system's complexity renders it vulnerable to catastrophe does not show that it got to its final state, bingo, all at once.

The ID community is looking at the process from the top down and is ignoring the process as it proceeds from bottom up. There is no valid rationale for claiming that a complex system had to be designed, as is, without any development leading step-by-step to the contemporary system. The immune system, for example, as complicated as it is, can surely trace its roots to earlier simpler cellular attempts to fight off intruders. Even the astoundingly large numbers of antibodies that the system can generate are the result of the presence of a small number of molecules whose effect is mathematically greatly enhanced by interaction. Improbable? No. Does anyone know what the evolutionary progression was exactly? No. But that does not mean it did not happen. There is just too much evidence to show that complex systems were built up over time even if we cannot demonstrate the molecular pathways followed in the evolutionary process.

Christopher Hitchens cites a 2006 study at the University of Oregon, published in *Science*, which by reconstructing ancient genes of extinct animals shows that the non-theory of "irreducible complexity" is a "joke" (Hitchens's term).

It is interesting that Behe, despite being an accomplished molecular biologist, has made no attempt on his own to show how evolution at the molecular level might have proceeded. His research into the efforts of others is also interesting. Behe conducted what supposedly was a very comprehensive review of all available credible scientific contributions to the question of how biologically complex systems could have been achieved at the molecular level. He found that little if any real research has demonstrated how evolution may have produced the complex molecular processes necessary to the existence of complex systems. How can this be? I have already referred to Manfred Eigen among others, and he in turn refers to numerous respected investigators in the field of molecular biology and related disciplines. I have come across even more.

There may, in fact, be some arm-waving and glossing over of some real theoretical problems by some investigators. But that does not mean that research has not been done or that evolution has not done its work toward complexity. Behe's conclusion is just as shaky as any of the arm-waving and supposedly unsubstantiated theories that he says he confronts.

There may be some valid reasons for a supposed lack of solid demonstrations of molecular evolutionary paths toward what are identified as "irreducibly complex" biological systems. To begin with, the scientific community may have informally come to the conclusion that a demonstration of the molecular evolutionary paths is impossible. Looking back over billions of years and the trillions upon trillions of organisms actively pursuing survival and replication, how could one determine at the molecular level the zillions of attempts, failures, and incremental successes that led to today's complex biological systems? I have to imagine that innumerable paths were explored and that any evidence of what those paths were has long ago been erased. As Behe himself expresses it, "When a question is too difficult for science to deal with immediately, it is happily forgotten while other, more accessible questions are investigated." Or one brings in God!

There is a counterpoint brought out clearly by Neil Shubin in his *Your Inner Fish*. Through advances in paleontology, genetic research, massive computer capabilities, and other disciplines, we are, in fact, discovering the many evolutionary attempts, failures, and successes that lead to today's complex systems. Ever more rapidly we are uncovering what was once considered impossible to find. I think this is the correct view. Looking back over the past several years it seems to me that there has been an exploding amount of research and commentary in this field, and much has been uncovered.

That leads to another reason for perceived lack of scientific contribution to the subject. Before any design can exist there must be a plan, and there must be a way to proceed from plan to execution of the design. It appears that the scientific community that Behe criticizes, having recognized that the way to get from plan to execution of the design is difficult to describe at best, has decided to seek first a viable plan. That is what Behe sees as a series of inconsequential and superficial explanations of the evolutionary process. If I recall correctly, Dawkins calls it a narrative approach or something similar.

Given that almost all of what we know about molecular biology is very new (decades mean nothing), and, given the unknowns on the pathways sought, it is to be expected that the community would come up with a surfeit of sometimes off-the-wall ideas (plans) on how to get from the simple to the complex. Until such time that a peer-recognized plan of how the simple to complex problem can be solved, do not expect the molecular details to come to light. That may lie far in the future. The first order of the day is to speculate (yes, a needed element in the scientific approach) as to what might or might not work, and that is where I think we are. It is still early in the game, although the pace at which molecular research is proceeding at the moment is breathtaking, and these doubts may be unwarranted.

There may be one more reason for the dearth of demonstrations of how evolution can account for the molecular complexity present in biological systems. Follow the money! How many aspiring biologists, geneticists, or chemists today are going to invest an entire career in the pursuit of solutions to an unpopular conundrum when the pharma industry and other interests are willing to pay big bucks to join their teams? I really do not know, but I suspect, not enough.

I cannot challenge Michael Behe on the basis of molecular biology. That is his field, not mine. But I can challenge his assumptions and inputs to his argumentation. It is clear to me that he greatly underestimates several fundamental factors: the billions of years that life has been developing, the trillions upon trillions upon trillions of organisms that have been competing over these times, the rapidity with which organisms interact and replicate, the fact that all this interaction was proceeding simultaneously (highly multiple tracks), and cumulative selection. The resultant numbers tell me that evolution certainly had a good chance of producing complex systems.

It is worth commenting on another point brought up by Michael Behe, that being that combining systems (symbiosis) (Lynn Margulis) does not account for the complexity of the combined systems but rather only passes the buck to earlier unknown origins and therefore shows nothing gained. As stated earlier, I think this is a real dodge. In effect it says that not only does symbiosis fail to contribute directly to complexity, but, since you can't explain some earlier unknown, then you can't explain what is in hand. Wrong!

I composed a little ditty to illustrate the point.

X plus Y plus Z plus A plus B plus C equals D
This we all can plainly see.
But just how came we to Z?
On this we cannot agree.
So, all therefore cannot equal D.

Silly poem. Even more silly logic! If we can show experimentally and conclusively that $X+Y+Z+A+B+C=D$, then how Z came to be is irrelevant despite being a valid question. Z can be an emergent factor. Wrong poetic conclusion.

Both William Dembski and Michael Behe have been severely discredited over recent years, but that does not mean that their arguments have gone away. They are still alive and endorsed by many among the religious right and institutions such as the Discovery Institute. It is apparent to me that Behe and his supporters have followed the age-old habit of referring something they do not understand to God's doing.

MORE ID CRITIQUE

In support of evolution and its approach to design we should listen to Manfred Eigen as brought out in his *Steps towards Life*. Eigen's work is totally secular: it shows no signs of any religious intent, one way or the other (He expressly states that he avoided the issue). The book itself is obviously only the tip of the iceberg, so to speak, of the great amount of research and analysis that backs it up. And it shows a serious presentation of the probable optimization and organization displayed by life's early organisms.

The evidence of evolution is overwhelming! The genes of today could not have arisen randomly. There was a process of optimization, and Eigen defends this by mathematical analyses. Manfred Eigen goes back to the very beginning of life—three to four thousand million years ago—and describes a genealogical sequence that leads, logically, to the genotypes that we can recognize today. That means that a genetic code originated around four thousand million years ago. Evidence suggests that evolution proceeds at incredibly fast rates.

He emphasizes the role of information in the compounds/acids that form the building blocks of life's foundation. In effect there is an order in biological systems. Information arises from noninformation. Complexity builds upon simplicity. Evolution is the steady generation of information. And this is written down in the genes of organisms. Eigen's work is principally based on his deep understanding of nucleic acids and genetic processes. His work is a must reference.

To add emphasis to Eigen's work, one must recognize his deep understanding of the chemical processes involved in the production and actions of the building blocks of life, DNA (deoxyribonucleic acid) and RNA (ribonucleic acid). There is a verifiable trail. There is chemical certainty. Evolution follows a path in total harmony with physical and chemical laws. Go through his explanations of the chemical processes that gird the genealogical progression, and one must appreciate the solid fundamentals upon which current molecular biology is based.

Of critical note for our search for the "beginning" of life, it is well worth mentioning Manfred Eigen's belief that the early monomers leading to more complex systems could have come about relatively easily, meaning that conditions on primordial Earth could easily have led to production of the basic ingredients for life as we know it.

Through a series of logical/mathematical/statistical analyses, Eigen shows that Darwin's interpretation of selection is far more complex than first envisioned. Selection can proceed in different ways. He does not dispute the Darwinian basics. But he makes a very reasonable argument that mutant populations form a so-called quasi species that occupies the upper regions of the optimization/value landscape and, in fact, defines the selection process. Survival of the fittest, in other words, is not that simple. The one-off single mutant, despite any significant advantages, does not necessarily succeed; it takes more than one.

What is Manfred Eigen's contribution to the debate? Primarily, he proposes a scientifically solid explanation of genetic evolution all the way back to the very beginning. Evolution is a fact, and more than that, it is based on a verifiable physical and chemical empirical history.

I may be criticized for citing too much of Richard Dawkins's work, but he is a leader in atheist thinking, and his recent publication *The God Delusion* contains many superb arguments for a disbelief in God. In his chapter "Why there is certainly no God," he debunks ID rather convincingly. He begins with a few comments on the Boeing 747 argument from improbability. It has been suggested that evolution is like tossing a junkyard in the air and having it come down as a 747.

Dawkins breezes right by the point, and, I believe, misses a great opportunity. As one who has spent considerable time in the electronics industry closely associated with the aircraft industry, it is crystal clear to me that the Boeing 747 and the Airbus 380 are perfect examples of evolution. Even before the Wright brothers accomplished their historical feat, there were literally centuries of investigation into the nature of flight. After Kitty Hawk, air structures went through decade after decade of development. The airframes, the engines, the communications, the radars, and any number of flight systems went through a very competitive process and many failures to finally achieve success after success. This is evolution in a nutshell! A storm in the junkyard? In no way! How dumb to take this as an example of ID!

Nevertheless, I received a very pertinent critique from a respected reviewer to the effect that the 747 development was clearly guided by human intelligence, the implication being that some intelligence was behind evolution. This is a reasonable objection, and I am generally critical of analogies, but I believe there is sufficient support for my interpretation. First of all, the 747 story is not about one entity prescribing outcomes. As in nature and evolution, the 747 was a result of millions of attempts, failures, and successes in the fields of physics and chemistry that led to a viable thing. And there was a target that the thing had to reach: to fly and to fly competitively better. There was no central direction beyond obvious commercial, economic decisions at numerous levels of research, development, and production to achieve the target. Humans made decisions based on survivability/success and then stopped or advanced. Are these like God's interventions at certain stages? Not really. Such efforts like natural constraints merely push the evolution. The 747 evolved, not by central direction, but by trial and error. If it works, you win!

Dawkins proceeds to discredit "irreducible complexity" as a fallacy based on the argument from improbability and addresses the eye and wing as structures, he himself has investigated in detail and has shown to be perfectly aligned with evolutionary theory. He has found no example of any complex organ that "could not possibly have been formed by numerous successive slight modifications." Further on, Dawkins cites the work of Kenneth Miller of Brown University in providing an explanation of various biological components that can explain the supposedly irreducibly complex flagellum. There is also a body of research into the evolution of the immune system, another ID favorite. Miller's conclusion: ID is a lazy default. The gap in our knowledge on many things biological is no excuse for giving up and saying God did it.

Richard Dawkins also mentions the famous Dover, Pennsylvania, 2005 court case challenging decisions in which the directors of the school board imposed a statement of policy to students regarding the teaching of ID in parallel with the teaching of evolution. The court decided against the school board. I have the entire court decision in hand. We must be careful in evaluating this decision when it comes to its pertinence to the existence or not of God. It does not. The entire case involved constitutional law and in particular the Establishment Clause.

The court concluded that ID is not science but rather an "untestable alternative hypothesis grounded in religion." Since it is not science, it should not be imposed as such by a public institution. The court did not challenge religious belief or the right to belief, but it did deliver a body blow to the ID community. The court's appraisal of Michael Behe's testimony was devastating. It is interesting to me that, although William Dembski's name came up in the proceedings, nothing seems to have been introduced relative to his mathematical propositions, which are, to my view, more convincing than Michael Behe's microbiological ID arguments. Again, I contend that both are fatally flawed.

I feel obliged to cite a book review of Michael Behe's second book, *The Edge of Evolution*, the review appearing in the *New York Times* on July 1, 2007. Unfortunately, or fortunately, the reviewer was Richard Dawkins, whom I have cited, perhaps in excess. But the review is devastating to Michael Behe's theses, and Dawkins cites a review by Jerry Coyne in the *New Republic* (which I could not access) that is also termed "devastating."

Among other things, Behe challenges the viability of an approach in which random mutations will lead to an evolutionary outcome. He contends there cannot be enough mutations. Dawkins provides some very convincing evidence to the contrary and refers to a solid body of expert evidence in support.

It is worth noting that Manfred Eigen sees an absolute surfeit of mutation possibilities. To support that view there is evidence that Galapagos finches' bills change back and forth in response to weather cycles even over a short time span. They mutate a lot, get selected, and survive. Right out of Darwin's neighborhood!

Victor J. Stenger in his *God, the Failed Hypothesis* devotes a chapter to what he calls "The Illusion of Design." He reiterates many of the arguments that we have already seen, but he adds some very cogent thoughts and citations. He refers to the "Wedge of Intelligent Design," which we have all seen for what it is, a clever attempt to appeal to the supposed religious intellectuals. He cites several books and publications by serious critics of the works and views of the ID community, and adding his own criticism, judges their views to be totally erroneous.

Stenger claims to have disproved Dembski's "Law of Conservation of Information." He contends that Dembski bases his hypothesis on an approach involving negative entropy, and that being the case along with the fact that living systems are "open" systems, which may exhibit an increase or a decrease in entropy, it makes Dembski's hypothesis false. It is the closed system that inevitably show an entropy increase with time.

Stenger's discussion of "Self Organization" is worth reviewing. In short he says that natural biological systems reproduce what the physical world produces/repeats/demonstrates.

The fact that many patterns observed in biological systems are also present in nonliving systems and can be understood in terms of elementary, reductionist physics also should provide an antidote for those who still labor under the delusion that special holistic or non-reductive processes are needed to account for the complexity of life. Simplicity easily begets complexity in the world of locally interacting particles.

Stenger, in short, dismisses the intelligent design hypothesis, again, because there is no evidence where it would logically be expected. Where things seem to show bad design, that is nothing more than a part of the process, he says, and is, in this writer's view, evidence that the designer does not exist. Surely not if the designer is supposed to be omniscient!

Adding to the debate, we have John H. Hick in his *Philosophy of Religion*. In the chapter presenting "Arguments for the Existence of God," Hick provides a brief background involving William Paley's argument. Paley (1743–1805) published his *Natural Theology,* in which he lays out the design or teleological argument. Hick then goes on to cite what he calls the classic critique of the design argument by David Hume in his *Dialogues Concerning Natural Religion*. It's worth repeating here. Hume says that "any universe is bound to have the appearance of being designed." Hick quotes him further:

> The universe consists of a finite number of particles in random motion. In unlimited time these go through every combination that is possible to them. If one of these combinations constitutes a stable order (whether temporary or permanent), this order will in due course be realized and may be the orderly cosmos in which we now find ourselves.

Hume continues to show that the analogies presented by advocates of divine design are rather weak. Hick concludes this section by stating:

It has, therefore, seemed to most philosophers that the design argument, considered as a proof of the existence of God, is fatally weakened by Hume's criticisms.

For our purposes we must agree that life is truly very complex! We have been asking how it is that we got to where we are. If the idea that an intelligent designer just dropped complex things in place has been discredited, the only way a designer could come up with the complex world and life as we know it is to establish a system to execute the "vision." In other words, God should have a scheme, a plan. But if the scheme amounts to the natural universe that we see, which seems to do quite well on its own, thank you, why do we need God?

Moot point says the theist. God's will is not to be interpreted by us. We know not what God desires. We only see the wonders he has created. Could this then mean that God is nature? Does this mean that God merely sets things in motion, lets nature take its course, and accepts human thanks for the wonders he has created? But again, why should we concede that some spiritual thing created these wonders and complexities when it's unnecessary? And why should these wonders be taken as proof of that spirit?

Evolution Copycat

Let me introduce Neil Shubin's *Your Inner Fish* (although I have referred to it several times already). In my view this work is one of the best of all that I have reviewed for encapsulating the up-to-date and convincing research in several areas that proves that evolution is a fact and dispenses completely with any serious acceptance of ID.

Neil Shubin is a paleontologist and leading member of the team that in 2004 unearthed in the arctic and identified Tiktaalik, a clear intermediate between fish and land-living animals, for which he has received much acclaim. The importance of this discovery is the role Tiktaalik plays in illustrating the major theme of *Your Inner Fish*. Through the employment of several scientific disciplines, we are able to construct the histories of living things from the earliest times to today. Every living thing has/had a parent, and by placing the changes in ancestors and descendants in the proper time frame by scientific analyses, we thus construct those histories. There emerges a pattern, or several patterns, showing without a doubt that incremental changes over time lead from one's ancestors to their descendants and their descendants, and on and on. Shared characteristics help us place each living thing in its proper time and place.

Of course, such analyses contradict any claim for the imposition of any specific design anywhere in the history of a living thing. The slow but incremental advance from the early forms to later versions provides a continuum in which a one-time insertion of a design is neither reasonable nor logical.

Shubin summarizes several biological tendencies that demonstrate the themes emphasized in his book. The first involves the limbs found in most animals. He discusses the subject initially in essentially two research areas: paleontology and genealogy. Later discussion involving embryology adds to the theme. Not wishing to attempt a summary of a summary, I will quickly outline the meaning of the fossil record that Shubin and others have managed to document.

With regard to the limbs of animals, there is a remarkable similarity across the entire kingdom, which can only be attributed to evolution's conservative nature. Structures came about in the earliest bodies. Nature liked the design, and thereupon over millions of years and incremental changes passed on a pattern that shows up literally everywhere. An exciting example is the limb pattern, which demonstrates the upper one-bone, the middle two-bone, the multibone wrist areas, and the five-digit finger pattern. It's all over the animal kingdom. We have truly inherited much or most of our bodies from ancient life-forms!

Genealogy adds critical support to the fossil record. Genes have been identified that are responsible for building and later operating parts of bodies such as the limbs. Certain genes are switched on and off to develop specific parts. There are so-called organizer genes and other genes that work in teams, communicating through exchanges of molecules. It turns out that, like similar fossilized body parts found across a wide and diverse animal kingdom, similar genes are present in widely differing species. A fascinating example is the sonic hedgehog gene. This gene is present in all limbed animals. No matter where it is found, it performs the same function. When turned on or off at the right times, it sculpts the limbs. Sonic hedgehog has been found to act the same in very distant species such as sharks and humans. Shubin concludes that this evolutionary development did not involve new DNA but evolved using ancient DNA in new ways to make limbs of varying structure. Evolution is very conservative. Shubin relates a similar theme in the evolutionary development of teeth, mammary glands, and feathers.

I mentioned embryology earlier. Again, the emphasis is on the surprisingly similar characteristics and development of embryos in widely differing animal species. There are so-called arches, blobs, and creases in the embryo of every animal with a head, and these forms are responsible for the development of the head. The process may lead to different structures in the head, but the process or pattern remains the same, and we must conclude that the functions involving the arches of ancient animal embryos have been passed on to animals with heads today.

Going further, Shubin found that embryos in mammals, birds, amphibians, and fish are amazingly similar in all their fundamentals. Citing a number of researchers and their work, he summarizes the functions of embryos and the responsible genes, and as an example, he describes the research involving fly embryos. A pattern was found in the DNA that reflects the front to rear development in the embryo. All then led to the discovery of the Hox genes, which appear in every animal with a body. Hox genes cause the making of body parts and their proportions according to their code and DNA positions. The lesson is that these and other stretches of DNA perform similar tasks and that these processes not only take us far back in animal history but involve the entire animal kingdom.

Shubin also addresses the sense of smell and the development of eyes and ears. In each case the theme is the same. Over many millions of years, we are able to trace the development of biological systems and patterns that appear across the entire animal kingdom and that lead progressively to animals present today.

Throughout his work, Neil Shubin refers to the many researchers and associates who have contributed to our knowledge in his area of interest. There appears to be more than adequate support for his observations and conclusions.

And what are the conclusions Shubin arrives at?

First, he points out that, through the labor in a number of scientific disciplines, we are able to construct the history of the animals on earth past and present because we are able to identify changes (mutations), patterns and related animal characteristics of parents and descendants and are able, therefore, to place individuals in their appropriate time and place. And we can trace relationships among the many disparate members of the kingdom.

Next, the historical record shows that animals (humans among them) may not be rationally designed, which leads to faults resulting from adaptations and new uses of older parts and processes.

There are a number of subordinate conclusions reached in his book, of course, but the final one, in my mind, contains the very essence of Shubin's work. He contends that everything that we see in life past and present is "old stuff that has been recycled, recombined, repurposed, or otherwise modified for new uses."

And "Our bodies and minds have emerged from parts common to other living creatures."

It is interesting that Shubin does not address selection. Nor does he address the processes in terms of mutation populations. I assume he takes such considerations to be givens and the task of others such as Manfred Eigen. Nor does he directly address the ID controversy. He does not need to. My conclusion is that, although he does not state it or directly infer it, his work and book clearly put a seal of authenticity on evolution and a stake in the heart of intelligent design.

Musings on Design

Having debated the hypothesis of specified and irreducible complexity and other related concepts, let us see where the ID approach truly leads us. It must mean, of course, that given ID, there must be an intelligent designer!

Let us first dispense with the notion that anything other than God is the intelligent designer. What else or who other than God could the designer be? Does ID mean that a Merlin arose in some form billions of years ago? Should we assume that extraterrestrials visited earth and designed its inhabitants? Or maybe we should blame the Wizard of Oz. To speak about ID while intentionally dropping any reference to God is a deceptive maneuver or façade intended to advance the hypothesis in such a way as to avoid a political vulnerability. Should the ID hypothesis gain acceptance, then the strategy is crystal clear; insert God as the designer. In recent years the ID community has become bolder and has clearly proclaimed God as the designer and maker.

Now the question is: What did God supposedly design? The ID community has highlighted several complex biological systems/organs/capabilities as irreducibly complex, such that they must have been created all at once: otherwise, they could never have gotten to their existing state, particularly not through the accepted theory of evolution.

But all of the biological universe is complex! The simplest cell is complex. So where do we draw the line? With complexity throughout the biological kingdoms, where did the intelligent designer have to intervene? Everywhere? Only 80 percent of the time? If not always, what process would be devoted to the development of the other 20 percent, or 30 percent, or 50 percent? Would God take care of the really tough problems and leave the rest to something else (like evolution)? Naturally, one could argue that God set up a system of evolution but programmed certain solutions into the system. This, of course, is the very opposite of what evolution does. Future forms are never predicted.

Genetic change and selection result in success for some, the degree of complexity being perhaps one of the drivers in that success. And how would the tough designs be inserted into the system, whatever system that might be? God could have simply set evolution in motion, but the ID community insists that that would not do the job. Not only that, but the need for God would disappear! How God placed his designs is therefore a true mystery because, to the best of my knowledge, there is no evidence of such placement.

This leads me to another question. Why would/should God be so interested in creating complex forms? Just for the fun of it? Why could he not have let physics and chemistry take their course as the Darwinians insist is the case? According to the sacred texts of Judaism, Islam, and Christianity (apologies to the other great religions, but here is where the debate is the hottest), all of whom share belief in many passages of the Old Testament, God created man in his own image. Therefore, the creation of Man is one of God's goals, and he would lay the groundwork for that creation.

Homo sapiens is an extremely complex organism, one in which are incorporated the very "irreducibly complex" subsystems that Michael Behe addresses in his *Darwin's Black Box*. Two of them are the cilium and the flagellum, and without them *Homo sapiens* would have a hard time surviving, to say the least. They are critical in sexual reproduction, breathing, and hearing among other processes. The believer could insist that God designed and implemented these and other complex subsystems in order to be able to create humans. This is a real stretch! The idea is pure faith and still leaves the question as to why God would be in the complex design business in the first place, not to mention the question as to when he decided to intervene: with our ancestors a million years ago, during the competition between Neanderthal and Sapiens, or some other opportune moment in the geological past?

Should the above difficulties be explained away by the ID community, there is still that interesting question about timing referred to above. When would God impose his designs and upon whom and what? At what particular points in time would a certain design be introduced? Despite the best efforts of the ID community to deny evolution, there is just too much evidence showing biological change over time. Selection works.

Did God insert the design for the eye a million years ago so that humans could see? Probably not. Our predecessors existed long before then, and there is no doubt in my mind that their sight was different from ours. Perhaps better! The dinosaurs could also see. Did God give the falcon his incredible vision? Why are there eyes that see in the depths of the oceans? In short, where did the eye come in? Why have there been so many versions over geologic time. What did God supposedly do? Did he start with a simple model and then upgrade to a point that was, voilà, the right solution? The answer is evolution. And, of course, the eye is only one of an incredible number of systems and subsystems that apply.

The above discussion of what God would have or could have or should have done regarding complex systems makes it clear that the idea of an intelligent designer has far more challenges than does the theory of evolution. Darwinians have been criticized as portraying fantasies; the ID community spins the greatest fantasy of all.

An early critique of my book claimed that I tended to dismiss out-of-hand the arguments of those of opposing views. I do not believe that is the case, and I have since reviewed my sources, including those of Dembski and Behe. I see no reason to change my conclusions.

Finally, a note regarding evolution in the very near term, say a mere fifty thousand years or more in our past. Nicholas Wade in his 2009 book, *The Faith Instinct* claims that there is genetic tendency for human adherence to religion. There were benefits in religious behavior or belief in the supernatural that accrued to the group and the individual. Is god belief in our genes? We address this in the next chapter.

CHAPTER 3

The Brain

It Can Make You a Believer

This chapter will show that the brain and its development are in complete harmony with the evolutionary process, and it will also show that the human brain tends to support belief in a supernatural being and the establishment of religious philosophy.

The chapter title is "The Brain" rather than "The Human Brain" for a good reason. Let us start with the fact that there have long been and now are many species with brains. Some are reasonably well advanced, like the primates. There are many with much reduced capabilities, and some exhibit extraordinary capabilities. Examples of the latter are bats, whales, and migratory birds, all of which demonstrate awesome sensory and computational traits beyond those of the human being. Acknowledging the existence of the many "brain" systems that nature has provided helps to understand that evolution has been the true instrument whereby we have arrived at our human brains. Brains can be large or small, or they can be more "advanced," or they may be very specialized. Evolution has followed many tracks. Genetic variations occurred, and natural selection has determined what brain was to succeed in what niche.

And what is our niche? It appears to be that of the only genome/phenome capable of conscious thought, although that fact is somewhat in doubt because of recent investigations into the capabilities of brains of several other species. Nevertheless, our brains have allowed humankind to accomplish as much as it has in the last many millennia. There are, of course, a number of questions to be answered while addressing the fundamental thesis of this book—that being that God was not needed in getting to where we are and, in fact, that God does not exist at all.

How did the human brain come about?

What is consciousness and what are its religious implications?

What is it that makes a brain act as it does when dealing with belief?

Does the evolution of or the current state of the brain/mind and consciousness lead to god belief, and if so, why?

The Physical Brain

The human brain exists today as a result of evolutionary differentiation and selection for the *Homo sapiens* genome. The archaeological record clearly shows that hominid ancestors existed millions of years ago, and despite all sorts of disputes as to the details, the facts support an evolutionary approach to the manner of how we got here. There is archaeological evidence regarding mammalian presence as far back as the age of the dinosaurs. There were brains then, perhaps less complex than today, but brains nonetheless. Many investigations have been conducted over the years into the evolution of the brain, leading to the human brain of today. The body of research supports a causal response to environmental condition that led to the evolution of our highly developed cerebral cortex and other brain functional centers.

One of the most eye-opening books I have read is *Mammoths, Sabre Tooths, and Homonids*, by Agusti and Anton, which is an account of life in the last sixty-five million years in Europe. In this geological blink of an eye, changes in species, populations, continents, climates, and oceans were amazingly extreme. This is an example of how fast things can change. It also infers that a few million years are more than enough to produce *Homo sapiens* and his brain.

If that is the case, then the evolution of *Homo sapiens* must continue today, and, in fact, there is evidence that genetic change in *Homo sapiens* can occur over several generations, the conclusion of studies involving Jewish mental proclivities and genetic disorders in European communities. Also consider the inhabitants of the high Andes and the Himalayas who show an inherited lung ability to efficiently process the reduced oxygen levels at high altitudes. This is not a matter of the brain specifically, but it illustrates that evolution continues as we speak, and that the brain may very well be evolving as well, albeit at rates that we cannot detect.

Many of the great thinkers have questioned how something as complex as the human brain could have come about by "chance." Chance plays a role only in providing candidates for success. Natural selection, on the other hand, is anything but chance; it is a rigorous elimination from the race of the weak and a bestowal of success on the strong. The brain along with its phenotype is surely a result of this struggle for survival. There does not appear to be any valid argument to say that the brain came about other than through the evolutionary process.

In his widely acclaimed book *Consciousness Explained*, Daniel C. Dennett devotes a very demanding chapter to evolution. His argument is persuasive. He describes the early hominid brain as one primarily oriented to reaction, meaning either "scram or go-for-it." His argumentation progresses to a point where functions in the brain assume multiple tasks over time. The idea is that certain capabilities of the brain, though not selected for some functions, can, in fact, fulfill other functions and do. As evolution proceeded, the primitive alarm systems began to serve other needs and functions. And the physical brain built upon and adapted in accordance with these altered functions. We eventually arrive at a stage in the evolution of the brain that Dennett calls a major innovation: plasticity.

Although there are a number of other factors, plasticity goes a long way toward explaining how and why the human brain developed as fast as it did. Plasticity means the phenotype gains an evolutionary advantage through its use of its brain power. In effect, the ability of the brain to learn and to bestow a competitive advantage on the phenotype becomes a positive evolutionary factor leading to greater genetic success.

Dennett assures us that this is not Lamarckism. Lamarckism is named after the French biologist Jean-Baptiste Lamarck (1744–1829). Lamarckism relies on the notions of "use and non-use" and "acquired characteristics," both of which combined propose that what humans (animals) develop in their lifetimes is passed on as hereditary traits. This has been disproved. Over time characteristics may be passed on only genetically through the process of selection, a process distinctly different from the immediacy of Lamarckism. Nevertheless, the plasticity of the brain allows the individual to supplement the advantages that may reside in the genes, a phenomenon known as the Baldwin effect. I quote from page 190 of Dennett's *Consciousness Explained:*

> So the tremendous advance of Homo sapiens in the last 10,000 years must almost all be due to harnessing the plasticity of that brain in radically new ways by creating something like software to enhance its underlying powers.

At this point it is worth mentioning that recent studies in the field of epigenetics suggest the possibility of inheritance of acquired traits. More research is needed to confirm such hypotheses.

Dennett goes on to discuss auto-stimulation and then memes and cultural evolution, which he calls "The Third Evolutionary Process." (His latest book, *From Bacteria to Bach and Back*, is devoted entirely to words, memes, language, and cultural evolution.) He then proceeds to a description of the human brain as a virtual machine as in Turing and von Neumann. He likens human consciousness to software.

My short summary may seem to downgrade Dennett's most emphatic declarations, but that is not my intent. If his thesis is to depict the brain/mind as a virtual machine or perhaps a series of computers in parallel, then we are on track.

What is consciousness, and what does it imply? Human consciousness is to this day an area of intense debate. It is extremely complex. How could the consciousness of the human being possibly exist without help from somewhere? The creationists have their answer, and I cite the Judeo-Christian testaments as well as a vast series of other theological publications. Many others of the scientific community, however, think otherwise, and I begin here by again citing Dennett. In *Consciousness Explained*, he starts out by discrediting the so-called Cartesian Theatre or the idea that somewhere in the brain there is a central something that directs the brain as would a conductor of a symphony orchestra. He cites several authorities in his support, and recent investigations attest to the fact that the brain functions as a multicentered cooperative (not coordinated!) system.

The central argument that is extremely convincing is that the brain and the mind are one and the same. Dennett is among many who reject dualism. That means, in my words, that there is no designated self or soul that oversees and directs the activities of the brain that governs our existence. A self may develop as the brain matures and accumulates experience in the form of the many inputs that life offers, but that self is something that merely encapsulates the brain's sensing, processing, and subsequent signaling for action. What the phenotype senses and lodges in the myriad synapses of the brain defines a tendency to observe and to act in a way in accordance with experience and genetic influences. That becomes a self.

According to Dennett's analysis and his multiple drafts model, the brain processes all that it experiences in a centrally uncoordinated but well -connected architecture with each part of the brain acting on specific inputs and functions while sharing its activity with other parts of the brain. He equates the brain to a virtual machine.

The December 23, 2006, *Economist* presented a set of articles that summarized very well the centers of various activities in the brain and the work that has been and is being done in the related research. I judge that the reported research fully supports Dennett in his interpretation of the mind in a "Multiple Drafts" sense and as a virtual machine.

How do we interpret Daniel Dennett's *Consciousness Explained*? First, he provides numerous insights as to how the brain processes and expresses its many sensory inputs in a way that is completely in tune with natural selection. One may dispute the presented hypotheses as far as detail or various intermediate conclusions, and a number of respected scientists disagree with him, but there does not appear to be any vacuum to be filled by the supernatural. Dennett provides a very logical progression for the development of mind and consciousness. He cites many supporting researchers to reinforce his views, and it becomes clear that the evolutionary path from millions of years ago up until today is perfectly supportable. Our minds got here by natural selection.

What is it that makes the brain act as it does? How does the brain accomplish the task that it has acquired?

The brain is a complex structure, which according to general consensus, involves roughly one hundred billion nerve cells, many thousands of cell types, trillions of neural interconnections, and an interacting incrementally developed chemical/electrical system of multidirectional interconnections.

The brain is dependent on support from the biological body in which it resides. It is also dependent on experience input to supplement its genetic computational and conceptual capabilities. It is affected by the phenotype reaction to hunger, pain, sex, exertion, trauma, etc. It is becoming apparent with time that the human brain during life develops in fantastic fits and starts as outside inputs increase and body rhythms adjust. The teenager benefits or perhaps suffers from this phenomenon.

But of all the factors involved, it is clear that chemicals exert the most if not almost all the influence on the performance of the brain. Genetic influence on the brain involves DNA, which is a chemical, an acid. Once the genetic imprint is reflected in an individual's brain, chemicals again dominate. The efforts and studies of the pharmaceutical industry and academia continuously show the critical, almost singular, part that chemical reactions have on the brain. Much or most of what humans imagine and act upon is therefore a matter of the influence of the many chemicals that work the brain's functions and the sensory inputs, which in turn are "burned" into the brain's databank through chemical/electrical reactions.

An insight as to the dominance of chemicals on the performance of the brain is shown by the following examples, and these are only the tip of the iceberg.

- DNA, as mentioned, carries the recipe of the genome. The makeup of the DNA strand is comprised of amino acids cobbled together in long series.
- Where the dendrites and axons of brain cells meet (synapse), information is passed by chemical messengers called neurotransmitters.
- Neurons in various portions of the brain release chemicals specific to a certain stimulation response.
- Dopamine controls the expression of pleasure.
- The serotonin system (chemical) has reportedly an effect on belief systems in the brain. Serotonin also affects an individual's romantic feelings.

- Oxytocin may help in trusting a stranger. This hormone and vasopressin (both chemicals) affect sexual preferences among some mammals and perhaps humans.
- Alcohol affects the brain, and so do caffeine and nicotine as each of them interacts with other chemicals to produce the physical and biological reactions familiar to all of us.
- Opioids/endorphins tend to reduce pain signals and to contribute to a more pleasurable mental reaction.
- Consider the tremendous number of medications developed by the pharmaceutical industry. Most, if not all, of these medications are chemicals. Many, such as the statins, target organs other than the brain, but many such as the antidepressants clearly target the brain.
- Drugs, as in abuse, have the effects they do because they affect or mimic chemicals that the brain normally employs.

It has been said many times that the human body (other biosystems as well) is nothing more than a bag of water with a lot of chemicals. This could not be closer to the truth, and it applies equally to the brain as to the body. Humans are far more organisms obeying the imperatives of the physical-chemical existence than the free thinking and acting life-form that we like to imagine.

I mentioned dualism earlier with respect to Dennett's work. My interpretation of the facts tells me that there is no way that a mind separate from the brain can exist. Dualism is a nonstarter. There is absolutely no evidence to support it. The brain is the conscious me! There is no other soul or entity apart from the brain. Any other interpretation just does not make sense and, again, cannot be scientifically proved. Whatever we beings think or calculate has to be a product of the brain and its overwhelmingly chemical processes. Most of the scientific community concurs with this view.

So, what does this discussion conclude? It means that we have brains that are what they are because of evolutionary processes, and that has been largely, if not completely, a matter of chemical developments, whether they are those associated with DNA or those involved in the operation of the brain/phenotype. There is clearly a challenge to be recognized in the ID community based on their argument that the brain is too complex to have come about by natural means, but the evidence and the logic of a slow but sure process of differentiation and natural selection are too persuasive. There are no facts to support an alternative. The theist community's belief in dualism, or the existence of a soul apart from the operating brain, lacks any factual support.

The Brain and God Belief

Does the evolution of or the current state of the brain/mind and consciousness lead to god belief, and if so, why?

I start with a quote from an article in *Time*, October 25, 2004, that neatly cites work investigating the genetic basis for god belief.

> The need for God may be a crucial trait stamped deeper and deeper into our genome with every passing generation. Humans who developed a spiritual sense thrived and bequeathed that trait to their offspring. Those who didn't risked dying out in chaos and killing. The evolutionary equation is a simple but powerful one.
>
> Nowhere has that idea received a more intriguing going-over than in the recently published book *The God Gene: How Faith Is Hardwired into Our Genes* (Doubleday; 256 pages), by molecular biologist Dean Hamer, chief of gene structure at the National Cancer Institute. Hamer not only claims that human spirituality is an adaptive trait, but he also says he has located one of the genes responsible, a gene that just happens to also code for production of the neurotransmitters that regulate our moods.

In response, I can only say that there may be an evolutionary tendency (genes) developed through the Darwinian societal and power competitions that cause chemical actions in the brain relative to spiritual beliefs. This is a reasonable hypothesis, but it remains a hypothesis yet to be proved. Should it be shown that there is solid evidence for a genetic tendency toward god belief, the evidence would have to establish what gain or benefit the genome/phenotype enjoys. For instance, peace of mind or the "feel good" aspect is a benefit of belief for many. But it is not clear to me how to connect feeling good with the advancement of a gene's competitive advantage due to god belief. In any case being able to fall back on God for peace of mind is not a valid reason to say that He must exist.

There are other factors that might be instrumental in the evolution of a genetic god bias, and I will mention one here. If over the millennia societies remove individuals who will not or do not exhibit the accepted and mandatory religious beliefs, would this not give believers an evolutionary advantage that would eventually show up in the genes? It seems possible, but a good story line and some strong evidence would have to be presented.

I place the blame for belief on the brain/mind limitations. The brain handles best that which relates to its input or experience. If experience provides no basis for an explanation of events, the brain is in unexplored territory. Doubt can lead to a search for a reason or explanation of events, and this could be a belief in some other power.

Further, the blame resides in part with the anthropocentric egotism of the human race. We are masters of the universe, it seems. On the other hand, as good as we are, there remain innumerable unanswered questions regarding the universe and the development of our genome among other things. For instance, what came before the big bang? And now that the numbers and the complexity involved in the DNA double helix are known, how did it originate? Many unknowns are beyond the ken of humans, at least for the foreseeable future. The human response to the challenge of these concepts and immensities, particularly in ancient times, has been to declare, bluntly put, that since I do not understand despite being so wonderfully smart, the solution must reside in a superhuman entity: God!

But why can't nature and the laws of physics and chemistry be trusted to work as they are known to work? No, only God can understand these complexities.

It is not only complexity that baffles the human mind. Catastrophic events bring the same emotions. Witness the reactions of those who lived through the 2004 tsunami in the Indian Ocean. Since the reason (as opposed to the scientific explanation) for such an event is beyond the ken of humans, the event must be the result of "bad karma." It is not, apparently, human inclination to accept that nature has its ways and that some win and some lose. The conclusion here is that where the human mind is overwhelmed, there is an innate tendency to make the excuse that a supreme power is in charge.

The brain is an extremely complex melding of biological processes. The brain's cells, like all other cells in the body, require nourishment and oxygen to survive. Those cells also carry the capability to exchange electrical impulses within regions of the brain and between regions. This activity is generally controlled or influenced through chemical catalysts or chemical reactions. The net effect of this biological strategy is a system that functions superbly under normal and beneficial circumstances. However, when nutritional and chemical imbalances occur under stress or bodily malfunctions, the brain can cause the individual to experience sensations that are unusual. It has been said that the mystics' sayings were induced by periods of hunger or physical pain and that religious figures were inspired by meditation under stressful circumstances.

There are numerous situations cited for the emergence of overwhelming religious feeling in individuals. One of the best-known researchers in this field is Dr. Michael A. Persinger, a pioneer in the science of the human brain's impact on religious experiences. Persinger has his critics and his detractors, as would be expected, but his conclusions are persuasive.

Persinger attributes many of the cases of the god experience to "normal, transient electrical perturbations of the human temporal lobe." He calls these perturbations "temporal lobe transients" or TLT. According to Persinger, the god experience takes place when the individual reacts to certain stresses. He says, "The God experience exists for a few seconds or minutes at any given time. Multiple experiences can occur in quick succession. During this period, the person feels that the 'self,' or some reference indicating 'the thinking entity' becomes united with or 'at one' with the symbolic form of all space-time. It may be called Allah, God, Cosmic Consciousness, or even some idiosyncratic label." TLT may lead to a number of different experiences and levels of intensity, but Persinger has said that most, in his analysis, involve religion.

My take on the work is to reduce a complex analysis to maybe simplistic terms—that is, the chemical and electrical activities of the human brain are primary sources of human reverence for the gods or God.

Since Persinger published his theses, research into the brain's functioning has accelerated at an exponential rate. We are now able to trace or locate brain activity as it relates to sensory input to a very exact degree. The result is a view of the brain's activities that is more complex than originally thought. Any number of the locations in the physical brain may light up as the senses are stimulated. Yes, there may be a dominant center of activity, but several other portions of the brain may participate. This does not mean that the temporal lobe emphasis explored by Persinger is wrong; it only means the analysis is more complicated. Several recent projects challenge the thesis that god belief originates or is centered in certain areas of the brain. But that does not exclude brain activity in general as a source or stimulus for god belief.

In his book *God, the Failed Hypothesis*, Victor J. Stenger cites Persinger but also his critics, specifically P. Granquist, who with others claim that mystical experiences are results of suggestibility.

Stenger's explanation of the brain versus soul controversy is instructing. It is difficult, if not impossible, to prove that that which does not exist, does, in fact, not exist. It is equally difficult to prove that that which does exist, though not humanly identifiable, does, in fact, exist. Stenger contends that by scientific standards one should be able to cite empirical evidence of God's existence and God's works. We should be able to find unique circumstances that confirm prophetic predictions. We should be able to find credible evidence of biblical accounts. We should be able to find evidence of the efficacy of prayer. Stenger basically concludes across several areas of investigation that there is no scientifically acceptable evidence that God exists.

In particular, he finds no scientific evidence for dualism (soul apart from brain), the efficacy of prayer, the so-called vital forces, and extra sensory perception (ESP). Nor does the scientific basis for immortality stand up. Overall, he contends, the experiments that have been conducted in support of the mentioned phenomena do not subscribe to scientific standards. In sum, Victor Stenger finds no scientific evidence in the examination of the brain for God's existence!

As an indicator of some of the trends and thoughts currently in vogue, I cite a summary that appeared in the *Economist*, March 22, 2008. The review addressed the emerging scientific exploration of religion. It is titled "Religion cries out for a biological explanation." This statement could betray the mind-set of the researchers (i.e., there is a biological explanation). In the summary, one of the theses is the belief in the biological tendency to select on the basis of group cooperation and thus survival, as opposed to Darwinian survival based on the individual. Religion or belief in the supernatural seems to fall into this group survival category. Several mentioned studies seem to support the thesis that religious belief does in fact favor the individual by favoring the group. Religious commitment appears to give a signal that the individual is committed to the group. Other studies proclaim an individual as well as group advantage to god belief.

In his *The Faith Instinct*, Nicholas Wade promotes group selection. He concentrates on the early hunter-gatherer communities. In his view the evolutionary advantage lay with those who adhered to a communal benefit. There is a binding force in the morals of the group. Morality helps the individual in the eyes of the group. What is better for the group becomes better for the individual. Wade places emphasis on the role of dance and music in the aboriginal origins of religion. In other words, there is a communal meaning in the trance-induced states that introduce the supernatural. Leaders then co-opt the trance-induced states and the original and inherent moral imperatives to institute religion. Religious leaders set the standards and then enlist the gods to support them. Religion is communal and, ultimately, political.

Wade argues that religion has a critical and fundamental influence on human behavior and concludes that religious behavior is so universal across humanity's many cultural societies that religion must be genetic. He states that all religions have the concept of the supernatural. He, interestingly, does not engage in any description of the genetic basis for such a conclusion. What genes? Where in the brain is a defined god belief processed?

Richard Dawkins seems to prefer to see religion and god belief as a by-product of other biological imperatives, perhaps in the realm of the meme. It may be that fifty thousand years are not enough to have produced a human genetic tendency toward god belief; cultural and political, yes, but genetic, not yet demonstrated.

Worth mentioning is Richard Dawkins's discussion of "The Root of Morality" and specifically the evolutionary basis for altruism. In essence

Dawkins's analysis backs up the advantages to be gained by the individual through his favors to others and his adherence to group principle and sensitivities. Perhaps the parallel is not perfect, but the advantages of being religious and being altruistic appear to achieve a better chance of survival in a similar way. I quote Dawkins here on altruism.

> We now have four good Darwinian reasons for individuals to be altruistic, generous or "moral" towards each other. First, there is the special case of genetic kinship. Second, there is reciprocation: the repayment of favors given, and the giving of favors in "anticipation" of payback. Following on from this there is, third, the Darwinian benefit of acquiring a reputation for generosity and kindness. And fourth, if Zahavi is right, there is the particular additional benefit of conspicuous generosity as a way of buying unfakeably authentic advertising.

Andrew Neuberg, Eugene D'Aguili, and Vince Rause provide an intriguing analysis in their book *Why God Won't Go Away*. The key theme of their work is the human brain's ability and tendency to engage in or support mysticism, which evolution has hardwired into our brains and leads an individual to naturally seek union with God or "the all" or the so-called "Absolute Unitary Being." Mysticism runs through this entire book. Based on their experiments and research they state the following:

> Gradually we shaped a hypothesis that suggests that spiritual experience, at its very root, is intimately interwoven with human biology. That biology, in some way, compels the spiritual urge.

And then:

> We saw evidence of a neurological process that has evolved to allow us humans to transcend material existence and acknowledge and connect with a deeper, more spiritual part of ourselves perceived of as an absolute, universal reality that connects us to all that is.

Why God Won't Go Away begins with a layman's review of the human brain. The brain and its neural networks developed from the bottom up involving genetic fine-tuning through nearly a million years of evolution. The result is a machinery that incorporates neural networks of great complexity that are capable of interpreting sensory information and then providing the human being the impulses needed to act within his environment. The authors describe a long series of brain centers: primary receptive areas, secondary receptive areas, the orientation association area, the attention association area, the visual association area, the verbal conceptual association area, the amygdala, the hippocampus, the hypothalamus, the arousal system, the quiescent system, and the limbic system. There are also several operators.

I do not know if or how much of this breakdown is accepted by the scientific community, although most of what I have encountered in the literature seems to be in basic agreement. In this work the descriptions of mental activities assume an almost mechanistic engagement of these brain centers as the human being assesses and acts on sensory and memory inputs.

As it pertains to god belief, the authors state: "Neurology makes it clear: there's no other way for God to get into your head except through the brain's neural pathways." Further they say, "Correspondingly, God cannot exist as a concept or as a reality anyplace else but in your mind." Note that the authors conclude that the brain can lead one to experience the divine, in whatever form, to be real. Concluding the discussion of brain architecture, the authors' state:

> Every event that happens to us or any action that we take can be associated with activity in one or more specific regions of the brain. This includes, necessarily, all religious and spiritual experiences. The evidence further compels us to believe that if God does indeed exist, the only place he can manifest his existence would be in the tangled neural pathways and physiological structures of the brain.

Are the authors describing God as a virtual reality?

The authors then proceed to expound upon the human compulsion to create myths and beliefs upon which all religions are founded. They again conclude that these creations are the result of "the fundamental neurological processes through which the brain makes sense of the world."

And further, ritual is reported to be a reflection of a primordial inclination, now wired into the brain, to respond to rhythms and music in such a way that the individual feels a bond with others in a group or eventually perhaps with a divinity. In accord with most of the scientific community's thinking regarding nature's tendency to adopt systems for other than their original uses, Newberg et al. accept that evolution may have co-opted the neural circuitry of mating and sexual experience for the spiritual aspect. The brain has utilized those neural networks for other purposes, to include religious belief.

I find the views of the authors to be instructive and often convincing, particularly as they describe the mechanisms of the brain and how one would expect the brain to resolve its many inputs and then order appropriate responses. However, woven throughout the text, and particularly in the later chapters, there is an inference that the envisioned mystic unions that the brain supports are more than mental constructions and are, in fact, reflections of reality. Here I am very doubtful. Some of this seems to be based on less than scientific input. Virtual reality? Maybe.

Despite the fact that *Why God Won't Go Away* places so much emphasis on the mystical (as opposed to several other reasonable and differing explanations of human visions), the book's bias toward the philosophies of the Eastern religions, and the inference that God does, in fact, exist, I believe the authors have made a clear case for the fact that God is a vision arrived at through a brain mechanism that is a biological result of evolution. I am going to enjoy the luxury of cherry-picking; I will discard the more ethereal aspects of their hypothesis and accept the more substantiated elements to the effect that God is a human (brain's) creation!

In Karen Armstrong's book, *The Lost Art of Scripture,* the author dismisses the modern approach to scripture and makes the case for the historical and early emphasis on ritual, oral recitation, and the stimulus of voice, sound, and body language. Scripture was always changing with the times and culture. It often involved master-student relationships. Activity led at times to a perceived unity with nature and with gods. And, significantly, this was in large part attributed to the influence of the right side of the human brain. Armstrong makes this point numerous times in her book. I draw the conclusion that much of scripture and religion therefore is essentially the product of the brain. Can this also mean that humans visualized the reality of the supernatural? That is an inference too far in my view. It all comes from our heads.

I am a bit skeptical of studies on god belief that rely heavily on the use of "economic games," which some of the above cited studies did. Valid approach? Maybe. Maybe not. Valid conclusions? Maybe. Maybe not. Nevertheless, I can accept the investigations and their conclusions as evidence for the determination of the eventual truth.

Regardless of the specific outcome of all these studies, my thesis is upheld. Whether for the individual or for the group, there is evidence that god belief and religious behavior contribute to survival and competitive selection. Our brains may be wired to appeal to the spiritual. This would certainly support the view that god belief is anchored in our genes. None of this proves the existence or not of God; it only testifies to the human tendency to create gods.

Philosophy, an Exercise of the Brain

Richard Dawkins in his book *The God Delusion*, has included a chapter titled "Arguments for God's Existence." Although Dawkins is a biologist, this chapter is almost exclusively philosophical. He starts with Thomas Aquinas's arguments and those of St. Anselm of Canterbury and proceeds through David Hume, Immanuel Kant, and many others, even citing Sam Harris. He marshals the arguments against those favoring God's existence and wastes no words in rejecting and ridiculing them. He undermines the so-called "argument from beauty," the "argument from personal 'experience'," the "argument from scripture," the "argument from admired religious scientists," "Pascal's Wager," and the "Bayesian arguments." The reader must go to Dawkins's book for the details, and it is well worth the time. He does a superb job of stating them. Dawkins does us a service in presenting the material in his own enviable style.

Let's now consider a respected scholar's review of the philosophy of religion contained in John H. Hick's *Philosophy of Religion*. Hick's book is a treasure when it comes to appreciating the philosophy and logic behind the great debates of Judaic-Christian religious history. It merely manages to scratch the surface of an immense field of study, but it does so very adequately. Although he discusses Muslim, Hindu, and Buddhist philosophy at the end of his book, the emphasis throughout is on the Judaic-Christian tradition. He acknowledges this. In fact, Hick is a Christian, and even though he generally presents a very balanced presentation of the arguments, there is some evidence of a god-believing and Christian bias in his discussions.

Let me introduce one of my biases. I have found it extremely hard to follow, much less understand, many of the philosophical arguments that I have encountered. Quite bluntly, I find many such arguments to be absolute rubbish. The philosophical presenter may provide analogies that are far-fetched and unsupported. He may invent new words. He may twist phrases to lead us to a presupposed conclusion. He may make assertions that do not stand the light of day. He may conclude that which his own argument does not support. He may take as a starting point something without any basis whatsoever. I willingly apply this criticism to many of the great thinkers of the past centuries. Yes, they may have sparked valid controversies. Yes, they may have arrived at some of the truisms of science, religious fundamentals, and philosophical argumentation, but they have also widely missed the mark, I would say, much of the time. I believe John Hick's summary has avoided these problems.

Let me repeat that Hick's book is a splendid review of religious philosophy, which presents a balanced evaluation of the many arguments presented. The chapters that I will discuss the most address the central themes of this book: "Grounds for Belief in God" and "Grounds for Disbelief in God," chapters 2 and 3.

Grounds for belief are based here on six or more arguments: the ontological argument, the first cause and cosmological arguments, the design (or teleological) argument, theism and probability, the moral argument, and the argument from special events and experiences. Richard Dawkins's down-and-dirty critique of some of these arguments was mentioned earlier. I would like to add some further thoughts.

The argument that gives me the most heartburn is the ontological argument, and I am not alone in this reaction. The first to state the argument in 1078 was Anselm, the archbishop of Canterbury. Anselm bases his beginning argument regarding the existence of God on the phrase: "a being-than-which-nothing-greater-can-be-conceived." Through a series of suppositions (assertions) and contradictions the argument concludes that God not only exists in the mind but exists in reality. Quite frankly, the logic escapes me entirely. One might argue that I am too dense or something. But I say, it does not compute!

The argument has been debated and rephrased over many centuries, which leads me to conclude that many great minds (Descartes for example) saw the flaws in the original argument and then attempted to correct the flaws in order to keep the argument alive. But, simply put, at the very beginning, to claim a relationship between the imaginations of the human mind relative to God with God's reality is a gross violation of logic and reason. It does not hold up to any decent scrutiny. You may try linguistic sleights of hand, but I am a linguist, and I know better than to fall for word tricks. The ontological argument is a very overrated nonargument. When Anselm himself out of the blue later inserts or asserts that the idea of God involves "necessary existence," we have a classic example of defining oneself out of an argumentative predicament. The great Descartes adds his twist to the argument, but that effort is no more satisfying.

To begin with, there is an implicit start point that God exists, and the argument is intended to prove it. Of equal concern is the idea that what humankind can or cannot imagine has anything to do with God's existence. Why should we care what we humans can imagine? God would be beyond belief in any case, no matter what our extremes of thought may be. The "a being-than-which-a-greater-cannot-be-conceived" thought as a central point of an argument is a nonstarter.

In an effort to stay somewhat within the boundaries of the centuries-old debate, I must certainly side with John Hick's statement on page 19 of his *Philosophy of Religion* regarding the predicate nature of existence, even though I am very suspicious of arguments that hinge on a grammatical nuance. Nevertheless, note the last sentence.

> But if existence, although it appears grammatically in the role of a predicate, has the quite different logical function of asserting that a description applies to something in reality, then the ontological argument, considered as a

proof of God's existence, fails. For if existence is not a predicate, it cannot be a defining predicate of God, and the question whether anything in reality corresponds to the concept of the most perfect conceivable being remains open to inquiry. A definition of God describes one's concept of God but cannot prove the actual existence of any such being.

The ontological argument is very adequately critiqued by Richard Dawkins in his *The God Delusion*.

The first-cause and cosmological arguments must be similarly debunked, and Hick does so.

The design argument is dealt with elsewhere in this book, but it is interesting to note that as far back as the eighteenth century, David Hume provided a telling argument against intelligent design even before William Paley published his famous argument for design.

Theism based on probability is dependent on wishful thinking, by my calculation, and, based on his own critique, Hick also dismisses the argument.

The moral argument in addition leads nowhere.

Finally, the review of special events (read miracles?) and experiences leads us to no proof of God's existence.

In fact, John Hick states that his conclusion regarding the theistic proofs is negative. I could not agree more. He then goes on to the grounds for disbelief and concludes the same. The sociological theory of religion, the Freudian theory, and the challenge of modern science from a philosophical point of view do not disprove God's existence. Since we are dealing with philosophy, this should not be a surprise.

We must find evidence elsewhere, and it is there in abundance. Even in his critique of the sociological theory, Hick provides an interpretation to the effect that "it is the human animal who has created God in order to preserve its own social existence." Voilà! The theme of this book! Maybe this cannot be philosophically proved, but evidence elsewhere certainly supports the thought. (See discussions regarding the thinking of J. H. Randall Jr., pp. 83–85, and Wilfred Cantwell, p. 112 in *Philosophy of Religion*).

Hick continues. The Freudian interpretation of God as a father figure with which humankind would find a familiar and satisfying relationship cannot of itself disprove God's existence either, but it can qualify as evidence.

Finally, perhaps science has not been able to disprove the existence of an unembodied, non-sensed entity, but it has certainly provided a vast library of theory and data to suggest strongly that much of what has been attributed to God is not true and that God is not only not needed for the realization of the universe and the world as we know it, but has been created by we humans to fulfill certain of our immediate corporal needs. Again, voilà!

The Philosophy of Religion goes on to address evil. For purposes of this book, the topic is of no great importance as I mention toward the end of chapter 1. Human beings being what they are (i.e., biological creatures with sociological underpinnings), we can expect aberrant behavior on the part of some of them as a matter of course. Evil there will be! And count on nature to represent "evil" from time to time. Evil may be evidence but not proof that God or the supernatural do not exist.

In subsequent chapters Hick explores a number of intellectual challenges, most of which are addressed by known theists throughout history, which to me is merely internecine warfare, albeit honest philosophical debate. The initial premise, however, always seems to be that God exists, and the argument must proceed from there.

Hick concludes with chapters that address immortality, resurrection, Karma, and reincarnation. I believe he treats all of these subjects with the respect they deserve from the perspective of a philosopher, and the result is a reference to the very Old Testament texts as a possible basis for the Judaic-Christian beliefs in immortality and resurrection, and a moral, ethical basis for the faith in reincarnation. He does not affirm the truth or the untruth of any of these beliefs. Philosophy is apparently incapable of doing so.

To bring us up to date, let me quote a phrase or two from, of all places, J. K. Rowling's final book in the Harry Potter series, *Harry Potter and the Deathly Hallows* (p. 411). The quotation restates what has oft been said, but I like its simplicity.

You could claim that anything's real if the only basis for believing in it is that nobody's proved it doesn't exist.

We Conclude

The brain is a complex organ that can lend itself to belief in God or the supernatural, largely because it functions as it does, based on not only its inherited characteristics and chemistry, but on experience gained through the body's senses.

We do not know if there is a genetic basis for god belief. Life's experience tends to encourage god belief. Some experiences can force belief. In fact, considering the way the brain acts, it is almost exclusively the reaction to experience external to the brain that explains humankind's god belief.

There are centers in the brain that might amplify god belief, but there is no central control, the organ employing a cooperative structure, and there exists no duality involving a "soul." All of this does not prove that God does not exist, but it leaves no room to say that he does.

Philosophy is helpful in deconstructing theistic arguments but as a discipline cannot conclude whether God exists or not.

All of this does not prove that God does not exist, but it leaves no room to say that He does. Based on the preponderance of the evidence, we conclude that God exists only in the brain.

CHAPTER 4

Society, Culture, and Power Politics

Believe or Suffer the Consequences

In this chapter I will show how several cultural factors have a significant effect on human perceptions and acceptance of God. Belief in God is not entirely something that comes naturally, although there may be evidence that god belief could be passed on genetically. There are a number of other factors that must be considered, among them: parental influence, a child's learning capability, the allure of sensory attractions, fear and coercion, societal rules of good conduct, health and nutrition, and political/power manipulations of beliefs.

In this discussion we should distinguish between those fundamental factors that influence an individual's acceptance of the existence of God as opposed to the reinforcing effects of certain singular events that have convulsed humankind's history such as natural catastrophes, wars, crusades, and more. Such events do have an effect on peoples' beliefs, but there are more fundamental forces at work.

Nevertheless, let's first look at that reinforcing effect. Throughout ancient history we find a multitude of kingdoms and dynasties, each with its particular endorsement of certain gods. Subjects universally adhered to the rulers' beliefs. This began with hunter-gatherer bands and went on for millennia. During the period of the Greek and Roman empires, the advance of Muhammad's Islam, and the earlier Hindu, Buddhist, and Eastern religious expansions there is little to be said of the effect of the consequent invasions, conversions, and flowering of new ministries other than to say that they merely reinforced the already existing human perceptions of ancient times. Earlier beliefs continued to be enforced.

Alexander the Great through his invasions did not invent God or gods; he merely made the required god substitutions and supported them.

The fact that Buddhism suddenly sprang from its Hindu roots does not mean that the Buddhists invented God or a central divine entity; this societal force merely made such beliefs dominant in much of Asia. Gods were already accepted.

Constantine led the adoption of Christianity, but that does not mean he suddenly made his constituents believers in God; they already believed in gods or a god. His decision was surely partly political.

The Thirty Years War was a horrific conflict between believers of different sects. It forced certain religious practices on large portions of the Germanic region. The war had more to do with power politics. God belief was already there.

The reinforcing function goes on and on. The point is that these historical events and institutions had a strong role in human belief in a supreme being. They are truly significant and influential in the support for belief, but they are, again, a reinforcing factor. Great events do have a way of making everyone conform to beliefs.

Capture the Young Mind

A child is uniquely adapted to the process of learning from the time it is born. Perhaps before it is born. The child learns faces and sounds—meaning language—exceptionally fast. In my field as a linguist, it has long been accepted that a child's ability to learn a language is amazingly strong at least through the age of six. I do not believe there is any discipline that does not accord the early years with an extraordinary ability to learn. And what does the young child learn? It can only be what the child perceives. The young brain absorbs what it sees, hears, smells, feels, and tastes. As it develops the synapses between the brain cells, it begins to develop a view of what is "out there."

This view is, of course, highly influenced by the mother, the provider of all that the infant needs. The father may fill some of this space. In any case, the parents occupy the center of the infant's small universe. The young child under most circumstances will develop a fundamental trust in his or her parents. When puberty approaches and the teen years begin, trust and allegiance may be thrown up for grabs, but it has been substantiated by any number of investigations that the earlier formative years establish a solid base for the future, and the parents occupy center stage.

I doubt that there are any societies, incorporating religion as part of the social fabric, in which the parents do not urge upon their offspring the beliefs and precepts of the religion common to themselves and to their society. This applies equally to atheists as well as all others. A child will unerringly pick up on the views of the parents. The observance of ideas and rites may be forced but need not be. The child is already in a learning mode. Therefore, the religious beliefs of a child are certainly going to mirror those of its parents, at least in the formative years. Accompanying the parents to the temple, church, or mosque surely imprints God's authority on the young mind. If the society is liberal in its approach to religion, adolescents may stray from the fold. Adolescence can lead to a backlash and general resistance to parental guidance. But let there be no doubt, where a society is uniformly and strongly tied to specific religious beliefs and practices, straying from the fold is not possible other than under unusual circumstances.

In effect, humans believe in God or gods because they were taught to so believe, and their early years cast this belief in concrete. In liberal societies beliefs may change somewhat with age and education, but in other societies that is not always the case. Most are forcibly kept in a belief. Today we have examples of Muslims threatened with death for apostasy. The Malaysian Supreme Court ruled in early 2007 that a woman who had years ago decided to convert from Islam to Christianity may not do so without facing and receiving sanction from a sharia court. Militants today in the Middle East go to extremes to enforce their religious views. Once learned, beliefs are hard to drop.

Richard Dawkins theorizes (*The God Delusion*) that the propensity for religious belief is a by-product of several evolutionary developments. He applies this thesis to the religious upbringing of children. One factor that favors religious belief among youth is the evolutionary advantage of undisputed obedience to the demands of parents. This obedience may have become a genetic disposition for other reasons, but it supports (as a by-product) adoption of the beliefs of the parents and other figures of authority. Dawkins cites the activities of religious leaders from Augustine to today's religious right as examples of the recognition by those leaders of the vulnerability of a child/adolescent to manipulation. The madrassas found throughout the Islamic world as well as Christian schools and Buddhist monasteries are complicit in this respect.

I am unnerved by the activities of the Falwells, the Dobsons, and the preachers in the megachurches in America. The leaders involved know well how to use mass psychology, peer pressure, and seduction to advance their purposes. In America the employment of modern music, sports, and other popular activities as attractions linked to god belief appears to take full advantage of youth's generally open and gullible nature to mold minds to religion. All of this is a curse on the human mind; it limits and inhibits freedom of thought and investigation and the search for truth. It also leads in all too many cases to minds that adopt and act upon bizarre religious fringe theories.

As a young person advances in age, a support system for religious belief becomes operative. Ceremonies, many of them joyous in nature, provide an attraction. One meets with others of the society in a temple, a church, a mosque, a synagogue, a monastery, at weddings, at burials, and at many more communal gatherings. Friendships develop, organizations flourish, leaderships are defined, webs of influence emerge, etc. An individual is hard-pressed to resist this inexorable move toward religious belief. In fact, why should one? Has it not been the belief of all the family and all those around the individual? Who and what would advise otherwise?

After Childhood

After childhood a human being begins to face the fact that one is not immortal. One begins to understand that life does not go on forever. Humans then enter a state of denial in which they accept the temporary state of corporal existence while hoping fervently that a life after death is possible. Do not deny this assertion; it is a very fundamental dream in most cultures and religions. Humans hope and expect that they can, given certain conditions, exist forever. There exists a vast amount of archaeological evidence that demonstrates a long held human belief in the afterlife and a clear dread of the finality of death. The religious hierarchy plays on this expectation with venomous force, and it uses every means to take advantage of this fundamental longing.

There is an interesting statistic found in the field of education. Reportedly the more one is educated, the more one becomes secular. The less one is educated, the more one is likely to accept religious myths. Dawkins states this and presents some figures. Susan Jacoby in her recent book *The Age of American Unreason* argues strongly the point that less-educated individuals are statistically inclined to place belief in the literal truth of the Bible and the Bible as a basis for law. In my research I have encountered corroborating statistics.

The Siren Song

Religious powers have from the beginning used the sensual to validate and to substantiate the existence and power of the gods. What one senses does not necessarily provide a direct message to the effect that something such as God exists, but the sensory effects can induce a state or a general feeling that reinforces suggested and supposedly related themes. I do not know which of the senses have the most effect on the human psyche, but I am certain that they all have a role to play.

What humans hear is surely one of the most influential of the sensorial factors. The evidence has shown up throughout history and is with us in abundance. The effect of music on the human psyche has been a fundamental part of the human consciousness from the beginning of time. Rhythmic chants and drum sequences have been essential elements in the cultures of primitive peoples and are to this day very current in most places in our contemporary world. The chants of the monks throughout the world have attracted the masses since time immemorial. There is a clear appeal in the celestial intonations of a medieval choir. Bach champions the spiritual in his incomparable compositions revolving around Christian themes. Bach clearly devoted his considerable talent explicitly to the furthering of the Christian message. There is no accident here. And the wonderful rhythms and choral elaborations of the black churches of the American South are acclaimed as spiritually stimulating.

When the human attraction for rhythm and tone are linked to belief systems, then the belief systems benefit immensely. Beautiful music as a lure and a benefit of subscription to a faith is hard to deny, and it must be accepted as a pressure on humankind to believe. I admit to a personal strong attachment to monastic chants and Negro spirituals, among others, and I am convinced of the strong pull that this sensory element exerts on belief. Music for me is a stimulating experience. Am I any different than the mass of humanity? I doubt it. Powerful religious figures have used this element to further belief.

Newberg, D'Aguili, and Rause in their book *Why God Won't Go Away* place music in the field of ritual. They contend that it involves repetitive rhythmic stimulation that can drive the limbic and autonomic systems. Music is wired into the mind through the evolutionary process and involves the mystic association of the individual with a group or the "all," providing a visceral experience that can be religious. Thus, music enlists the brain's inherent ability in support of mystical experience.

Nicholas Wade in his *The Faith Instinct* makes a very strong pitch for the force of music and dance in the history of religion. Starting with the hunter-gatherer societies of roughly fifty thousand years and more ago, he spells out a human tendency to sing and dance such that states of trance through communal pressures or just plain exhaustion led to experience with the supernatural. The singer and dancer seem to touch something or somebody in an ethereal sense or state that evokes awe, acceptance, binding, and, perhaps, an erotic feeling. This is a very individual experience, yet he places it in the context of a communal rite and meaning. An inflicted feeling of ecstasy appeals to the individual and the group. God or something similar becomes a very direct and personal and communal contact. Wade places great emphasis on this relationship.

It is very instructive that once religions became organized and autocratic, the priests or clergy often sought to downplay or ban music and dance because these activities conflicted with the priesthood's supposed exclusive claim on communication with God.

Observe the Greatness of My Kingdom

A human's visual perception of his or her environment must be a strong influence on whatever that person thinks and does. How can it be otherwise? Should the visual palette be attractive and linked to a belief system, as music has been so associated, then the belief system benefits. Enter a temple with its awesome figures of mythical spirits. The art itself is awe-inspiring. Look at the opulence of so many temples and churches with their treasures of gold and silver and vaulted ceilings with priceless paintings. With such wonderful works on display in cathedrals, temples, and monasteries, it is surely meant to show that there must be some divine presence behind their existence. The cathedrals of the West are breathtaking. Islam is not off the hook here either. Although statuary and depictions of the holy ones are forbidden, the beauty of its myriad mosques must inspire the faithful.

Combine the visual with the olfactory—the universal employment of incense—and the religious experience is further magnified. Taken altogether, the serenity of a temple, mosque, monastery, or church with the sensory surrounding that many seek from time to time is powerful. It works on the human need for acceptance and relief from the stresses of life and the fears of death.

Watch Your Stomach

I mentioned earlier the factors of health and nutrition in religion. Why does the Jew eschew shellfish? Why does the Catholic elect fish on Friday? Why does the Hindu not eat beef? Why is the pig reviled in Islam? And there are more examples of religious dos and don'ts when it comes to what one should or should not eat. However you put it, there are historical reasons for these practices. Experience led leaders to proclaim a god's prohibition of certain foods to protect the populace from certain hazards like fish that goes quickly bad. There was apparently a perception that pork can quickly go bad and that pigs cleaned up the mess of excrement and bodies that towns dumped into the alleys. Perhaps economics led religious leaders to favor one thing over another. In any case, we find religions defining the culinary habits of their constituents by claiming a god's mandate, one more way of coercing the fold to adhere to the faith.

Escape!

Let me throw in another factor—the yearning for the imaginary world where one can realize his or her dreams and can avoid the burdens of life's reality. I, for one, am a great fan of *Dune, Star Wars, The Hobbitt*, the Ring trilogy, Harry Potter, and the Chinese martial arts mythologies. I know that this is all fantasy, but it provides an escape, a chance to release the pressures on the mind—a form of relaxation. There is a sort of force that pulls one into these imaginary worlds. I see the same pull being exerted by god belief. I wish it were so! It must be so! I can escape to the arms of God! God will protect me and give me everlasting life! Religious myths and stories provide the fantasy for escape.

Believe or Suffer the Consequences

Now let us go beyond childhood's vulnerability, the fears of mortality, and the sensory reinforcements of belief. Power, exercised either by individuals or by groups, is a very significant factor. Humans are not alone in the animal kingdom when it comes to the exercise of power of individuals or groups over other individuals and groups. The alpha male and the alpha female of a pack are examples, as are the hierarchies found in communities of birds, cattle, seals, and many other species.

In the case of the human, however, this exercise of power involves not only that associated with reproduction and survival, but also the realm of ideas, self-esteem, and accumulation of wealth. The belief in God or gods and how this belief is exercised is a significant power factor. One can seek and exert power to advance the prospects of religious beliefs because one does, in fact, believe. One can also exploit religious beliefs for the purpose of acquiring dominance over communities, territory, and wealth. Once in power, religion is used to keep one in power. We might say religion is nothing more than politics in another form.

History is loaded with examples: Egyptian dynasties, kings, emperors, warlords, religious hierarchies, popes, the Inquisition, monastic organizations, and more.

Today conflict in India, attitudes in the Middle East, and even the politics of presidents of the United States bear witness to the political, social, and organizational efforts to impose religious views on society and individuals. In all cases there is the striving for dominance by ruling elites over peoples and lands and over the beliefs of their subjects. In almost all historical examples the individual citizen had little or no choice as to his or her religious beliefs. The rulers defined that belief, and it was necessary to follow that lead or else. In other words, most of humankind has grown up adhering logically to the beliefs of the parents but then conforming under duress to the religious beliefs of the society.

The United States today is not an exception. The religious right and its core constituency are clearly trying to impose their religious beliefs on all the population. The religious have a receptive population and society in America, and god belief is as strong or stronger here as it is in any developed Western nation.

In a *Los Angeles Times* op-ed contribution on March 8, 2007, Timothy Garton Ash traced an interesting sequence of gods throughout Egypt's history. He starts with the sun god Ra, Isis, Osiris, and Horus, goes on to Amun Ra, Serapis, Jesus, and Mary, and enters the merger of religion and politics represented by socialism, democracy, and Islam. The following quote is telling:

> Politics, seen from this perspective of 5,000 years of Egyptian history, is something very different from what you find in American civics textbooks. It's not about the installation of this or that logically and legally constructed political system, based on this or that ideology. It's about rulers borrowing, bending and merging gods, ideologies and legal systems, adapting to internal and external forces, mixing coercion and patronage, sharing some of the spoils where necessary, but always with the goal of maximizing your own power and wealth and hanging on to it for as long as possible—for yourself, and your children, and your children's children. Those who take the legitimating religion or ideology too seriously—be it Osiris or socialism—are missing the point. The gods come and go, and what endures over the millennia is men's lust for power and wealth and their vain quest for immortality.

Early humans envisioned gods with the power to provide benefits in the way of harvests, fertility, protection, and power over rivals. If things went well, the gods were thanked and acclaimed. If things went bad, the gods were perhaps blamed, but they were asked to exert their power and set things right again. Somewhere in this narrative certain dominant individuals coopted this supposed god power and declared themselves as gods or speakers for the gods. Two realms were fused: gods and the god-like on earth. This paradigm persisted up to the pre-industrial era and even touches some of today's religious institutions. It's all about power.

Now let's get down to bare knuckles conflict! As a start, let's name the world's most long-lasting and prosperous corporate entity. It has to be the Roman Catholic Church. Most lasting should not be a problem. Prosperous? I cannot believe that the Catholic Church, which includes not only the Vatican, but the bishoprics, the various related religious organizations, and its millions of parishes accounts for less than a multiple of the world's most capitalized corporations. We have an extremely successful organization that has a strong interest in the belief in and dependence on God. It has the muscle to force belief! Who pays for this effort and its vast bureaucracy? The believer, of course. Who benefits? The pope. The cardinals. The priests. These persons have a strong incentive to keep God alive.

I do not want to castigate solely the Catholic Church. Islam and its network of mosques, madrassas, clerics, and holy sites enjoys the same incentives. Jewish synagogues traditionally expect hefty donations from synagogue adherents to support their faith and its activities. Temples and organizations across Asia solicit the same "tax" on believing populations. The authorities in these organizations have a vested interest in making sure the believers (and their pocketbooks) remain true to the faith.

GENETICS

The pressures of society and power structures have plausibly resulted in an evolutionary development toward human acceptance of gods or god. After all, the person who did not accept the prevailing views regarding the gods was most likely expelled from the community or eliminated. The ability to procreate of those whose views were not in accord with the community was severely limited. The believers, on the other hand, would enjoy all the privileges needed to pass on their genes to the successive generations. There should be an effect derived from this process. If and how supportive genes may have come about, which genes they are, how they gave a selection advantage, and how they would be activated is not clear.

Molecular biologist Dean Hamer, chief of Gene Structures at the National Cancer Institute, published his *The God Gene: How Faith Is Hardwired into Our Genes*, in which he claims that there are genes in the human genome that control production of neurotransmitters that control mood. The resulting chemical reactions may influence human feelings of spirituality. This thesis has, of course, met opposition, but the argument for an evolutionary response to society's insistence on god belief cannot be easily dismissed. Richard Dawkins proposes a thesis that there is a genetic propensity to believe in a god or gods but that this propensity is a by-product of other genetic imperatives.

Other studies and reports/books purport to claim a genetic tendency for god belief. I cannot take any of them as proof of such a tendency. However, it seems to me to be very logical that the societal/political pressures of the last many millennia may have resulted in a selection process that rewards the believers.

Morals

With few if any exceptions, all religions proclaim adherence to some or all the basic human interpersonal/societal norms beneficial to its members. Call them morals, society's rules of good conduct. The modern version of the Ten Commandments is an example, as is the Noble Eightfold Path of Siddhartha Gautama, the Buddha. The religions of China have through the centuries stood for harmony and the doing of good. The Jewish religion emphasizes living a good life on earth.

The fact that many individuals in humankind's history have identified certain rules of good conduct should not be surprising. It had to be obvious to some that humankind could best prosper if certain norms were established and followed. And it would not be uncustomary for some powerful individuals to claim support of the gods in enforcing the rules.

However, the claim by any religious community that their laws—the laws of good conduct—derive from the sublime is an affront to humanity and nothing more than a grab for power. Furthermore, to then claim that moral conduct is the exclusive domain of the theists is a cruel insult and simply false. To directly associate belief in God with the proper conduct of the individual in human society is a failure of logic and a blatant assertion in favor of God's existence. The gods are invoked for a reason: power and credibility. In this sense I cite Augustine, *City of God*, chapter 4, book III, in which he, in turn, cites Varros ("learned heathen") regarding how useful it is to falsely state descent from the gods. He claims that many of the religions and sacred legends would be feigned when judged profitable. Very insightful!

After millions of years of evolution and thousands of years of exercise of the modern human brain, it should come as no surprise that humanity would figure out to a *T* the desirable norms of conduct within the society. Humans are social animals. There must be rules of proper behavior, and there must be ways of recognizing good and bad behavior as well as ways of rewarding or punishing behavior. Humans have done this throughout history, using numerous solutions to the problems presented. Other primates do this.

It is an absurdity when the theist damns the atheist as being immoral and being less than the "good" theist simply because one does not believe in God. Any half-smart individual could have long ago codified proper behavior in human society. Many have done so, yet many have claimed godliness or god's relationship in codifying and justifying the right behavior. Nonsense!

Spelling out how we ought to live together in no way justifies a claim that God defined the rules of morality. For the religious power-seekers it is more a matter of codifying, legislating, and enforcing views felt to be in accord with that individual's views of society and their dominance. Those views may be beneficial to harmony within the society, but they in no way honestly imply the existence of God or his definition of morality. Evoking the presence of God clearly is very convenient since it adds an aura of invincibility to the proclaimer.

Summation

Simply put, familial, sensual, societal, political, and economic, and perhaps genetic influences implant on most of us a belief in God or the supernatural. Regardless of the thoughts that we as individuals may have, the pressures for god belief are strong. Few can resist the pressures. God is pushed on us. We as humans appear doomed to bow down to a power in the sky that will protect us and ensure our survival into perpetuity, as unrealistic as this may be. This is not necessarily a given, however. The more open society becomes, the more the god belief pressures can be reduced and the more one can decide one's personal beliefs. This is a work in progress!

CHAPTER 5

Cosmic Continuity

The Cosmos Shows There Is
No Beginning or End

This chapter involves a series of very controversial arguments and a number of competing theories that impact a central theme of this book—that being the belief that there was no beginning and no involvement of a supernatural being in such a beginning. I will begin with a general view of the arguments from my perspective and will then cite several respected sources as support for my views. Some will be of an opposing view.

How the universe came to be, what it is, and from what it may have been born are critical elements of the argument behind the thesis of this book. Simply put, the reality of evolution is confirmed, the history tells us why and how humankind created gods, the biology of the human brain and cultural and societal pressures make us believers. But we do not as yet have conclusive answers as to the establishment of life and the beginning or infinite nature of the universe. Since these questions have not yet been conclusively answered by the scientific community, the theist community has seized the opportunity to claim that God created the universe and then the life on earth that we know. If we cannot provide a reasonable explanation of the life of the universe and of life's origins on earth, then we must concede advantage to the theists. I do not believe we must do that. We are going to see that their claims are unfounded.

This writer, after years of research, believes that there never was a beginning of the universe, nor of life. What we have today arises from what already existed and will continue to exist forever, whatever form it may take. Who am I to state such a definitive declaration? No one of great repute. But I will cite some good evidence brought out by others more well-known than I in support of my thinking. I am a believer in the multiverse. In this chapter, I will explore the beginning or not of the universe. The following chapter will deal with the origins of life.

The Source of the Universe

Scientists have been able to mathematically describe the big bang and inflation that occurred roughly fourteen billion years ago leading to the expanding universe we can observe (and theorize) today. The facts are there to support the big bang theory, but a host of unanswered or partially answered questions remain, and some challenge the theory in its entirety. The uniformity of the many galaxies across the universe (and why), black holes, wormholes, the mass of the universe and whether it is a critical mass or not (leading to eventual collapse or to infinite expansion); the existence and nature of dark matter; the existence of other planets and possible life on those planets are all areas of research loaded with questions, few of which we have been able to answer definitively. What about the implications of the string and M theories and other theories claiming to describe a universal theory and a beginning or lack thereof?

Some of the most intractable questions involve what existed and occurred in the first few nanoseconds after the big bang event and, of course, what came before. Was there something before? If so, what? What was its state? How did it get there? So far there is largely a body of mathematical work on which to base the current theories, and there are a number of hypotheses that remain purely in the speculative domain. The identification of gravitational waves, which Einstein predicted, could add to evidence for the first few nanoseconds of the universe. But the math and the evidence stop abruptly at that point. What came before is a scientific complete unknown. A true singularity.

The theist may question the big bang theory in its entirety and fall back on the written word's description of creation. Theist critics claim that scientific explanations of the big bang and the universe are so full of questions that the theory is invalid and the only explanation for creation is that contained in the holy scriptures or the idea that God set it all in motion. This view does not in any way stand up to scrutiny and is, in fact, pure rubbish. Any theory may have gaps that need to be filled, but to abandon it in favor of an alternative with no hard facts and fraught with more fundamental questions is utter nonsense.

Nevertheless, some theists today might accept the big bang theory while trying to reconcile the theory with a less literal interpretation of the scriptures. They could, for example, argue that God began his creation at the point of the big bang, since there is no evidence of anything existing prior to that instant. Victor Stenger and many others would contend just the opposite: there is no scientific evidence of God's intervention either after or before the "beginning of the universe." To be honest, there are credible theorists who believe that the big bang plus inflation cannot stand up to plausible analysis, but that does not mean therefore that God made the universe.

The striking aspect of this discussion is the appearance of what I call anthropocentric egotism (others have different terms). This says, I cannot comprehend the big bang, the universe, and ultimately evolution; but since I am so awesomely smart and would understand it all if it were humanly possible, there must be a god or gods who are responsible. This god is like me, but just a lot smarter and more capable. This is a manner of thought that goes back to prehistoric thinking. The mysteries that cannot be explained must have gods behind them.

One thing that has amazed me as I read about discoveries in science and specifically the study of the universe is the oft-repeated expression of surprise at the nature of a new discovery. It comes across as follows: a celestial body has been identified that turns to the left, and the community is numbed by the discovery, since, up until now, all like bodies turned to the right, as substantiated by all calculations on the phenomenon. But, of course, there might be an exception. I had long thought exceptions should really be the standard. It was with absolute glee to read an article in the *Los Angeles Times* of April 14, 2010, entitled "These planets go one way, theories go another."

>   European researchers reported Tuesday that some
>   of the recently observed extra-solar planets are revolving

around their stars in the opposite direction from the stars spin. That finding is inconsistent with the view that planets are formed by the condensation of dust from a disk surrounding a newly formed star. Some other planets were found to have highly tilted orbits that are also at odds with conventional theory. "This is a real bomb we are dropping into the field of exoplanets," said one of the authors of the report.

To me, anything goes out there! The universe is so vast and so complex that we should expect to find a violation of almost any of the rules. I, therefore, feel no guilt in speculating about the birth and death of the universe. It turns out that others have come up with the same or similar hypotheses to those that I will describe. I also have no inhibitions in considering even the wildest hypotheses. Anything is possible!

Back to the biography of the universe. Underlying my speculation is the thesis that there never was a beginning, much less a creation. The energy and matter that we observe today has always existed, albeit in differing forms, combinations, and concentrations unknown to us. A universe such as ours might suddenly appear out of nowhere. It appears intuitively impossible that so much appears out of nothing, yet calculations of some of the greatest figures in the field of physics have the nascent universe coming from a state of essentially nothing. I would tend to believe that in the postulated "nothing" there would have been some latent form of neutralized energy just waiting for a trigger.

There are conditions placed on this "nothing." Some like Stephen Hawking assert that the arrow of time could work backward from the initial state of the universe, and that, of course, assumes a "something" existed before the "nothing" of the nascent universe. That means it all began with nothing, but there was something before the nothing! Time would have started at the big bang, yet, if I understand Stephen Hawking, time could have reflected back—in a sense, negative time before the big bang. What that means is that there may have been a previous universe of sorts that led to the entity that went through the big bang to become our universe.

Hawking also makes the point that, since there was nothing at the beginning, there was no chance for God to have existed either. Do we see a conflict in views or a case of speculative musings?

It seems to me that the makings of our universe were always there, or the factors of physics were there to produce this particular universe. Although it is speculative, it also appears logical that our universe before the big bang could have been preceded by a collapse of a previous universe or was an event triggered by a space-time anomaly, a massive black hole, a collision of universes, or some other event. Roger Penrose proposed a concept in this line that we will discuss later. What would this mean for the then very small dense body that they say existed before the big bang? What would this mean for the subsequent inflation? In any case, I see no logical explanation for a God-given creation or a need for one. Things might have progressed as one would expect under scenarios researchers have proposed or scenarios as yet unstated. I propose a scenario of my own at the end of this chapter.

Although there seems to be a consensus in favor of an unlimited expansion of our universe, the jury is still out on whether the mass of our universe will lead to an eventual big rip or to a collapse into a supremely dense center that might again inflate and expand into another universe. I, by the way, do not find the energy arguments against a bouncing universe to be convincing. A continued bouncing violates the laws of thermodynamics (a scientific sin and showstopper). What we see may be a one-time event, however, meaning it bounced only once or twice.

Other factors could well have led to what we now experience. An accretion of another universe's matter and energy? Should our universe continue to expand at what is now seen to be an accelerating rate, as seems to be the consensus of the scientific community, then it may end up as a dust of subatomic particles/energies surging through space. It could very well be that these remnants of our universe would be swept up by a neighboring universe. What then transpires is a matter of further deep speculation. Despite all the unknowns, this writer is inclined to believe that the universe or its dust will continue to exist in perpetuity in some form or other. Therefore, why need there be a God to oversee a creation that never happened or a reality that will never end? Obviously, there is no need.

There Must Be Evidence

I cite Victor Stenger and his book *God, the Failed Hypothesis*. His title is worth highlighting. Two chapters in the book apply to our discussion in this chapter. The first is entitled "Cosmic Evidence" and the second "The Uncongenial Universe." Much of what Stenger writes in both chapters supports my contentions in this chapter, and I recommend that the reader review Stenger's overview of early and contemporary analyses on the issues in this chapter. It is a summary of many very deep investigations, and it does them justice. Stenger's analysis concludes that there was no beginning.

I have mentioned Victor Stenger several times already in this book. I owe the reader a brief review of who Victor Stenger really is. Stenger has a Master of Science degree in physics and a PhD in physics from UCLA. He has served on the faculty of the University of Hawaii and the University of Colorado. He has held visiting positions on the faculties of the University of Heidelberg and Oxford and has been a visiting researcher at Rutherford Laboratory in England, the National Nuclear Physics Laboratory in Italy, and the University of Florence in Italy. He has participated in several leading research projects and is a voice well worth listening to.

First, we will address Stenger's cosmic evidence, and it needs restating that Stenger's premise is that there should be evidence of God's intrusions into the origin of the universe where evidence would be expected. He sees no such evidence. The laws of physics and the accumulated mathematical support for those laws show no need for intervention by God or any other power. Nor is there evidence that, needed or not, intervention, in fact, took place.

Stenger discusses creating matter and concludes that "the existence of matter and energy in the universe did not require the violation of energy conservation at the assumed creation." No God needed!

Stenger addresses order, and that means basically a change in entropy. He infers that the initial state of the universe was so small that, although entropy was at a maximum because of the total chaos, it was essentially close to zero. This appears to be a conflict with the entropy model, since the initial utterly chaotic state, the magnitude of particles present, and the supposed extremely high temperatures would call for an extremely high entropy. But again, we are talking about a very small volume, and Stenger probably has it right. Remember, entropy is a man-made measure. Suffice it to say that the total chaos present in the nascent universe and the question of entropy show no sign of design, which should have been evident should God have existed and intervened.

Stenger tackles the ultimate debate regarding the beginning (or not) of the universe and cites William Lane Craig as a principal proponent of God's influence. Craig basically asserts that God had to have had a hand in creating the universe. According to Stenger, with support from and citing several respected sources, there is no evidence, nor is there need for any effort by God. Stenger cites an oft-quoted statement of Hawking.

> So long as the universe had a beginning, we could suppose it had a creator. But if the universe is really completely self-contained, having no boundary or edge, it would have neither beginning nor end; it would simply be. What place then for a creator?

There are many factual and theoretical points that undermine any assertion that a supernatural entity has ever been involved. If we take the calculations and conclusions of Albert Einstein, Edwin Hubble, Max Planck, Roger Penrose, Frank Wilczek, Stephen Hawking, and other luminaries in the world of physics micro and macro, the universe as we know it is as we would expect it to be. No need for intervention.

My understanding that the universe had no beginning is again well supported in a few paragraphs in Stenger's *Failed Hypothesis*, "Cosmic Evidence" chapter (p. 126). Here he presents the conclusion of his work in his book, *The Comprehensible Cosmos*. In effect our universe "tunneled" through the chaos at the Planck time from a prior universe that existed for all previous time. He based his calculations on the "no-boundary model" of James Hartle and Stephen Hawking. And it appears that Hawking's earlier mentioned statement that there is "no singularity at the beginning of the universe" would be a significant factor in Stenger's calculations. We have already seen Hawking's famous statement cited above regarding "What place then for a creator?" In sum, Stenger concludes, based on his own work and that of others, that there was something there before the "nothing" that became our universe. Space-time went back endlessly before then.

Stenger also makes the point that nothing is less stable than something. Nothing is, in fact, unstable. Spontaneous transitions of nothing-to-something are natural. I am not certain that I am convinced by the argument. But he claims that explaining our universe as derived from nothing involves a natural tendency. This "nothing" would have to do something and become something. This led to a small space at "infinitely" high temperature, with an "infinitely" dense chaos of subatomic particles, almost zero entropy, zero mass, and zero energy. Stenger gives such an occurrence a 60 percent probability. He cites Nobel Laureate physicist Frank Wilczek for support.

I cannot challenge the analysis or the computations, but I am confused by the theoretical conflicts that I perceive. I am at a loss to explain the belief that the universe sprang from nothing when the same experts espouse the existence of the initial high temperature dense chaos of subatomic particles. And no time infers no movement or temperature. How do we get there from here? I do believe that the experts should have a way to reconcile these differences.

The question, however, reinforces my belief that at the so-called beginning there had to be something stretching back in space-time as Stenger concludes in the previous paragraph. I may be way off the mark in my thinking, but in any case, natural not divine laws are the determinants.

In his chapter "The Uncongenial Universe," Stenger addresses primarily the so-called "fine tuning" of the universe that would permit the existence of our Earth and eventually humanity. He contends that there is no evidence that the state of the universe involves fine-tuning and that, therefore, there was no involvement by a supernatural being. Fine-tuning refers to the thirty-something factors that must be exactly as they are in order to arrive at the universe that can support an Earth and the life on it as we know it. A designer might have played with these factors to come out as they did—that designer being God. But as demanding as the parameters required for earthly conditions are, the cards were merely dealt that way, and Earth and its conditions followed so that as a result here we are. The anthropic principle!

Richard Dawkins among many others addresses the anthropic

principle in his book *The God Delusion* and applies it to the universe as an alternative to the design hypothesis. The odds of a universe friendly to the existence of Earth and life on Earth are very slim. For things to develop to what they are today, the universe had to exhibit a very specific state. Any, even minor, deviation from this state could deny the existence of a life-friendly Earth. Yet here we are on this planet. With all the possibilities for a different universe, however improbable, the right one exists. One could say that God set it up that way. But a design-free explanation is simply that the universe is as it is: among a myriad of possibilities, one was suited to lead to a planet like Earth. There are innumerable possible universes and galaxies, and we just happen to be in one that fills the bill. It's statistically possible, and the proof is here to see.

But there is more in play than just the anthropic principle. The odds for an earth-like situation may not be as slim as Dawkins and others claim. An article in the *Los Angeles Times* of February 3, 2011, adds a thought to the debate. NASA has found dozens of "just right" planets, and the article states that there are more than fifty exoplanets that reside in the Goldilocks range that would allow for life. These exoplanets inhabit areas in the universe between five hundred and three thousand light years away. The data are the result of the space-based Kepler mission at NASA. Some of the data involving exoplanets roughly two thousand light years away are said to have been reported in the journal *Nature*. That was only a start point. Since early 2011 we have been apprised of more accounts of the discovery of even more exoplanets. Considering the size of the universe there should be, statistically, billions of these planets and many that could support life. As we know it? Maybe. As we don't know it? Maybe. The general point is that the universe is not fine-tuned to lead to good old Earth. We are only one of lots of possibilities in the universe. If the universe were "tuned" otherwise, we might have a different presence with no Earth-like planets. But so what? That proves nothing.

Space and The Multiverse

There are schools of thought in the scientific community that support a multiple, even infinite, number of universes (multiverse). Those other universes may respond to different rules of physics, and they may emerge, dissipate, or collide with one another in accordance with the constraints of space and time.

The debate on the existence, definition, and meaning of space has been going on for centuries. Brian Greene's book *The Fabric of the Cosmos* does justice to the debate on the meaning of space, and it is worth the reader's time to review it. That meaning is not easy to define, and the great physicists have all taken shots at it. Brian Greene is a professor of physics and mathematics at Columbia University. He has published several illuminating books addressing the themes of astrophysics.

I am well aware that the theory of relativity may postulate that there is no space or time beyond or before our universe. Einstein's theory is a rock of Gibraltar in the realm of science. To challenge it is to commit the unpardonable. Nevertheless, there have been many interpretations and alterations to his basic theory, and his equations, in fact, take us only to the first instants of the big bang. I submit that there should be a way to extend current theories to include what lies beyond our universe. Philosophically it appears impossible to me that our universe floats majestically through an enclosed bubble of space and time with a total blank outside the bubble. Now, there may be nothing else out there, but there is a chance that there is another universe, and as Stenger contends, nothing begets something.

There are some who conclude that, since space within our universe is itself expanding, there is not or cannot be any space into which the universe would expand. But does that prove that there isn't space out there? I would think not. Should our universe continue to inflate forever, its remnants would occupy some of that space. From all that I have explored, there is reason to believe that space and thus space-time are infinite. The thought stated earlier that there was no creation depends on a universe whose matter and energy in some form exist forever—that is, infinitely into the past as well as into the future. Would that not include other universes? Even if our universe were curved such that it connects without boundaries, this view, which proposes that one would travel forever through our universe, does not prove that there is neither something nor nothing outside our universe. It would just not be observed.

I have recently read that there are some clues to the source of the dark energy and dark matter in our universe, but my understanding is that we are far, far away from a definitive answer. Maybe the Large Hadron

Collider will give us a clue. However, could it be that the dark matter and energy came from a dissipating universe with different rules of existence and were swept up as flotsam and jetsam somewhere in the process of the birth and death cycle of our universe? Pure fantasy? Maybe. But who knows? Roger Penrose comes close to the idea with his concept of conformal cyclic cosmology. Recent research into the behavior of neutrinos and their transformations may provide clues to the existence of dark matter and may kill such wild speculations as to sources outside our universe. But, again, who really knows?

When it comes to an evaluation of the concept of the multiverse, Brian Greene's *The Hidden Reality* provides one of the best guides. This particular book covers multiverses from cover to cover. Multiverse for Brian Greene means infinite variations on the theme. His book's chapters progress through Einstein's theories, parallel worlds, infinite space, inflationary theory and an eternal spawning of ballooning universes, the string theory's brane-worlds, the cosmological constant and its consequences and controversies, quantum mechanics with its "many worlds" version of parallel universes, quantum measurement and the quantum multiverse, the holographic universe, and the artificial universe. That's quite a list! This is a daunting amount of investigation. The best that I can say is that there exists an enormous number of possibilities for what comes out at the end of the tube.

I have no intent to go over Greene's arguments. However, an underlying theme for all that he discusses is that there is an almost infinite number of possible universes, regardless of what model one pursues. In support of the book you are now reading (mine), there is in Greene's work evidence and argumentation that generally concludes that space-time should be infinite, that multiple and parallel universes exist throughout eternity, and that there was no beginning to it all nor a perceived ending. This, of course, requires no need for a guiding hand other than that of physics, even though the rules of physics may be bent or changed depending on universe variants.

As for Greene's views on holographic and imagined universes, I am very skeptical, as I am with Brian Clegg's similar views that follow.

Brian Clegg, a Skeptic on Many Points

Brian Clegg has a physics degree from Cambridge and has written several books in the area of cosmology. He came out with *Before the Big Bang*, in August 2009. This book is largely a historical review of the many scientific minds and the theories they have proposed starting as far back as the early Greeks and Augustine of Hippo. In fact, most of the text involves explanation of the fundamentals, the experiments, the research, and the basics of past and current theories. One of the principal impressions gained from his book is that no theory—none—is without some serious holes. His final comments conclude that we have yet to find the answer(s) and maybe never will.

Clegg was a fan of the steady state—meaning the universe was in a steady state of continuous creation and expansion. As the universe expanded, more matter came into being, there being no beginning and no end. This theory was supposedly an answer to the problems seen in the big bang. However, improved data and certain other reasons led to the demise of the steady state model. According to Clegg, the majority of the scientific community now backs the big bang plus inflation theory. But Clegg is a real doubter. He sees too much that is lacking in data and experience in support of the theory. Something is wrong with it. Among other things, in order to fill in the holes and make the big bang work, a series of BAND-AIDs had to be applied.

Dark energy and dark matter are examples. We have not identified them to this date. They are merely a useful construct. And, of course, there is the question of how something could come out of a point of zero size (or maybe just a tiny space) with infinite temperature and energy. How can this be explained? Clegg argues the reasons are no better explained than they are by Genesis. And then, why did inflation occur when it did, and why did it stop when it did? Inflation suffers from other theoretical problems beyond the question of when.

On the other hand, the cosmic background radiation does support the big bang plus inflation, while the lack of evidence of a gravitational wave that should have resulted from the big bang takes support away. Clegg claims several times that, should no evidence of the gravitational wave be found, this could kill the big bang theory. Gravitational waves have now been detected, although they emanated from events involving collisions of black holes and of neutron stars. Will we detect waves from the big bang? Who knows?

So, where does that leave us? With a somewhat shaky foundation! *Before the Big Bang* continues with a series of hypotheses that appear to avoid the problems of the big bang but have their own difficulties. String theory and M theory avoid the debate on a beginning, which appeals to me. Both, however, began with the mathematics rather than empirical observations of nature that ask for proof, and the result is theories that, so far, cannot be tested empirically. In each theory we are dealing with more than the four dimensions with which we are familiar—ten and eleven dimensions respectively. This leads to the possible existence of parallel universes in other dimensions as well as branes.

Clegg goes on to discuss the big bounce or big crunch and bang, which are challenged by the impossibility of perpetual motion due to thermodynamic constraints. (At this point I must again question the very idea of multiple crunches. Who says it has to be a recurring phenomenon? Many other influences may have been exerted.) He addresses the universe in a black hole, the collision of branes, parallel universes, a bubble universe, the multiverse, and more. Most of these theories lead to the conclusion that there never was a beginning or a need for a beginning.

Clegg goes off the deep end later in the book when he gives equal time to a matrix world, a computer simulated universe, a holographic universe, and the views of the universe usually associated with Eastern religions. I see no evidence that such constructs are at all plausible, which leads me to a couple of objections to today's trends. Why, for instance, must we deal with an established physical statement of a conservative nature when dealing with evolution and then entertain exotic solutions in the realm of cosmology? Multiple dimensions? Parallel universes? Whether evolution or cosmology, should we not expect the same adherence to fundamental, essentially straight-forward physics? Why does the interpretation of the universe have to be so convoluted, bordering on fantasy? Yes, scientifically speaking, we cannot exclude something because it is only remotely possible. It is still possible. And math can prove lots of things if we make certain assumptions and interpretations. But is the king naked?

Maybe not. Brian Greene's *The Elegant Universe* lays out a very credible argument for the superstring theory. He among many others has been working on the theory for many years. It appears that the math works out conclusively and in accord with most other accepted theories to date. However, the hard empirical data are yet to be identified. The Large Hadron Collider? Maybe.

Back to Brian Clegg's *Before the Big Bang*. It is a wonderful read and an exceptionally instructive book. It places lots of things in doubt. And that is good. As for the purpose of my book, it is to be noted that Brian Clegg presents no support for the God thesis. Yes, he mentions that the big bang theory could introduce God when all was nothing, and he gets into the Eastern religions' belief in "the all" of everything, but there is no stated argument in his work in favor of God's influence whatsoever. The main thing that I would retain from his work is that there is sufficient evidence to sustain the view that there was, in fact, no beginning of the universe, and, of course, therefore, no requirement for involvement of a god or gods.

I feel obliged to note another spokesman for the opposition before concluding this section. Robert L. Piccioni published in 2010 a short but densely packed booklet entitled *Can Life Be Merely an Accident?* Piccioni is a PhD, author, and lecturer worth listening to. In his booklet, Piccioni focuses on the extreme numbers and probabilities involved in arriving at the conditions that were necessary for the universe to have become what it is and that are necessary for the existence of Earth and life as we know it. The numbers and statistical probabilities are, in fact, mind-boggling. He goes on to address the biological numbers and probabilities that apply to, among other things, the creation and evolution of the replicating process involving DNA. Again, the numbers and probabilities are eye-opening. His conclusion is that there is no way that all this has come about without some outside intervention. This is much like William Dembski. Both Piccioni and Dembski are respected scientists, and they have presented their conclusions based on the science they understand. Why should I even mention Piccioni? Because he represents an intellectually endowed number of individuals who are not the stars in the great debate but must be taken into account in that debate.

I believe, nonetheless, that there are fatal flaws in their arguments. One would have to show conclusively that specific physical and chemical actions could not be completed in the time in which such actions have, in fact, occurred. I do not see that that analysis has been presented. And we can turn the numbers gambit upside down. The incredible numbers of courses of action over an incredible amount of time had to make a difference. Earth's conditions and evolution came about at rates far greater than first expected. And our existence today is merely what results from parameters which existed irrespective of the likelihood of those parameters. Exactly where should this be impossible?

I object to the use of the word *accident*. This must be the preferred terminology of that institute up there in Seattle, and it is inappropriate. The state of the universe and the fact of evolution do not result from accident. They obey the laws of physics and chemistry. Yes, there is an element of chance when choices are to be made. But solutions, celestial or biological, are based on universal rules. There is seldom an accident.

As to the numbers, it is not clear why extreme figures must mean an outside intelligence is needed. As I said, one has to consider the extreme numbers on the other side of the argument. The universe has existed for roughly fourteen billion years. And the unexpected and unusual Earth came about around four billion years ago. In the biological sphere, over these billions of years, reproductive rates were often in the millions per day range. Evolution had to proceed at a very rapid pace. One can conclude that the celestial and evolutionary numbers more than counterbalance the extreme numbers of the doubters. Because we are here! The anthropic principle! If the constants, numbers, and probabilities were different, then we might have had life-as-we-don't-know-it!

The last point is pertinent because we must question why our being here must drive all the factors involved. Piccioni and others of his belief are saying that we are so special that the universe had to be designed for us. Talk about egotism! We humans are the result of an element of chance, all right, but not an accident in the sense that Piccioni intends. The universe and Earth came about, and, as an afterthought, here we are.

Stephen Hawking: Time Is of the Essence

Stephen Hawking was perhaps the preeminent figure in astrophysics and cosmology of his day. He will figure in the historical pantheon. In his publications and discourses, many of which have turned up on the internet, he has postulated an origin of the universe that has to be respected. Hawking examines space and time, the uncertainty principle, black holes, wormholes, and much more. His published views are easily understood. His backup mathematical underpinnings are something else again and surely far more demanding. Hawking has, of course, been challenged in certain areas—witness the controversy with Leonard Susskind over theory related to information and black holes. Hawking did not always win.

Hawking is always obedient to the precepts of Albert Einstein, and, in particular, to the concept of time based on the theory of relativity. Time is not a constant. Time changes—slower or faster—depending on space-time influences, gravity, velocities, the observer, and other factors. It is postulated that time began at the occurrence of the big bang. Since there are no data whatsoever to support existence before the big bang, scientifically, one would have to say there was nothing. Nothing! No time! Since we are dealing with the so-called singularity of the initial state of the universe, literally everything, including time, space, and matter are cast into the unknown. Time is lost in a clouded past.

Enter here my view of time. I tend to agree with the group that contends that time does not exist! Only space and intervals between events large and small exist. We humans have developed a system based on the rotation of the Earth and its orbit around the sun to measure what we call time. But you can't touch, smell, taste, see, hear, or capture time. Space is clearly there. Not time. Depending on conditions and the observer, time can vary considerably. While measuring events and movements in the universe, time can show significant contortions.

The physics community was clever in instituting the term space-time. I would think they knew space was the only true thing being measured. But, of course, time as a measurement tool is absolutely essential in our calculations involving nearly all of the phenomena related to our universe. Does that mean that it exists?

How did we get to the prenatal conditions of the universe if there was no time and basically nothing else to begin with? (I repeat here some of the argumentation brought up earlier merely to add emphasis.) There was no mass. Matter and antimatter canceled each other out. There was no energy. The negative force of gravity in such an assumed initial very limited space was very strong, and it canceled out the positive electromagnetic and strong and weak energy forces. Supposedly entropy was near zero since the total chaos at the beginning in the small space postulated was maximum but low simply because of the extremely small space involved. There are apparently technical and mathematical explanations for these phenomena, but I, like Brian Clegg, see possible contradictions coming out of the scientific community. And nothing yet satisfies my craving for an answer to what was there (or not there) before our universe came into being.

I have read repeatedly that the universe started with nothing. Three cheers from the theist community. God did it!.

Stephen Hawking, among others, envisioned a universe that appeared from nothing and a so-called initial state involving chaos, infinitely high density, and infinitely high temperature resulting from a singularity. It seems that these several views are in conflict. I am not sure I interpret his views correctly, but it all still leads me to the question as to how a universe could come out of nothing.

Was the intensely packed preuniverse a gigantic black hole? Stenger says it amounted to a black hole. According to Hawking's investigations, this does not seem likely. Black holes, at least the primordial ones, display temperatures at their core only a few degrees above zero Kelvin. This does not accord with the "infinitely" high temperature of the prenatal universe. So, what other possibilities are there? There are several. Interpretations of the M theory and the related string theory could lead to the conclusion that there was no beginning. The theory of colliding branes also can assume no beginning. These theories postulate our universe as a continuity over past, present, and future space-time. Hawking has endorsed M theory.

There is what appears to be a popular belief that the universe would go through a cycle of expansion, collapse, expansion, collapse, and on forever. It does not appear that our universe is headed for a collapse. Just the opposite—it looks to be expanding without limit. Collapse and bounce over and over does not appear to be thermodynamically supportable. Eventually a limit is reached, and then how would one explain where it all came from? We mentioned this earlier.

Let's leave Hawking for a while and consider some ideas from his sometimes collaborator Roger Penrose. Professor Sir Roger Penrose was Emeritus Rouse Ball Professor of Mathematics at the University of Oxford.

In a report published in the December 4, 2010, *Economist* (for me thirdhand sourcing), it is stated that Penrose believes that the big bang was not the beginning of everything. The report focuses on the claim that the cosmic microwave background might show signs of a preceding universe, in this case concentric circular marks representing spherical ripples in the fabric of space-time in the form of gravitational waves resulting from black hole collisions in the preceding universe. The search for such evidence has been performed by Dr. Gurzadyan of the Yerevan Physics Institute in Armenia, and there appears to be evidence that the circles are there. The jury is still out.

But Roger Penrose carries out his thoughts and calculations in an enhanced form in his *Cycles of Time*. He proposes a concept in which there is no beginning or end in an infinite sequence of universes, each one going through a life cycle that progresses through a phase of expansion (inflation?), of black hole accumulation, black hole evaporation (my term), loss of entropy (due to loss of black hole information), eventual loss of particle mass across the universe, and a resulting infinitely small space-time, all of which match the conditions prior to a big bang. The sequence, whether going forward in space-time or back, goes on and on.

His concept, which he terms the conformal cyclic cosmology (CCC), relies heavily on the treatment of entropy as applied to the universe. Entropy is a man-made measure of disorder in a system. There are equations that calculate its value. This measure is a derivative of the second law of thermodynamics, which mandates that in a closed system entropy must remain constant or increase in value. It should never decrease. A violation of the second law in a concept is a showstopper. Yet Penrose does propose a decrease in entropy across the entire universe as it fades into the remote future, while claiming that his solution does not violate the second law.

In his CCC concept, he follows the universe into the remote future as space-time continues to expand until we have what could be called an ever-thinning cloud of dust (subatomic particles). During this process the many black holes in the universe go from an accumulation phase (today's situation) to an evaporation (my term) phase in which the black holes are slowly reduced by emitting radiation, leading eventually to their disappearance. The key here is that the entropy of the universe, which has been constantly increasing, can be attributed mainly to the existence of the black holes, and as they disappear entropy is reduced.

The birth and death of black holes, according to Penrose, involves a significant loss of information. The accretion of matter and energy by the black hole and its emission of radiation results in this loss. This then leads to a vast reduction of entropy across the universe. The result is a remote future dust universe with the low level of entropy that matches that of the supposed pre-big-bang conditions. Critical to his analysis is also the idea that the subatomic particles in the remote future would somehow or other lose their mass. Should this happen, then these mass-less particles moving at the speed of light would create an infinitely small space-time, again in accord with what would precede a big bang for a future universe. Penrose goes so far as to say that the state of the universe in the remote future, in fact, constitutes the inflationary phase of the reborn universe.

To put it all together, Penrose proposes that as a universe progresses through space-time it lays the foundations for a subsequent universe. He proposes a series of universes progressing from one eon through a crossover to the next eon, meaning universe after universe after universe on and on.

Roger Penrose's development of his CCC concept is complex, and I am certain that a host of experts challenge him. I, as a nonexpert, have my own questions. Could there, in fact, be a reduction of entropy? How does a cloud of dust cross over to become an infinitely dense and hot early universe? What about a cold nothing? If the cloud of dust is the inflationary stage of the reborn universe, do we skip over a big bang? Could it be possible that our cloud of dust runs into another active or decaying universe rather than becoming the cloned universe envisaged by the CCC concept? What happens then?

There is an even more serious challenge to his hypothesis resulting from the Susskind/Hawking debate concerning the supposed loss of information as a black hole accretes and then dissipates. Hawking had endorsed the view that information could be lost. Susskind energetically contested this view. Susskind is the reported winner of the debate, claiming that by the fundamental laws of physics, information can never be lost. It survives somewhere in some form or other. If this, in fact, is the case, then Roger Penrose's concept is built on a house of cards. No loss of information means no loss of entropy.

I consulted a professorial expert on things like entropy, and his view was that a loss of information would, in fact, increase entropy. What then?

Has Penrose found some loophole in the laws? When he refers to the "remote future," does he expect that the temperature of the universe would approach zero degrees Kelvin, allowing the black holes to dissipate and to lose information and then, supposedly, entropy? I cannot say. Perhaps Hawking, Susskind, and Penrose are all somewhat right. Perhaps there is another solution.

In any case, Roger Penrose has proposed a concept that supports the thesis of my book. CCC or some variant thereof predicts no beginning or end to space-time. Whether or not Penrose's concept gains acceptance, the very feeling that there was no beginning and that there is no end permeates the discourse. There are, of course, other concepts proposing no beginning and no end. I believe that one or some of them should be correct. Nothing was created. Something has always been here.

What then are we to believe? What would have led to the dense and hot beginning? What was the something before? I have a highly speculative yet, to me, attractive scenario. Our sun is a second- or third-generation star. That means it was created by the recurring process across the universe of stars developing from the gases and detritus of burned out and exploding earlier stars as well as whatever else might be swept up. Why should we not apply this process to the greater realm of the multiverse? Suppose our universe was preceded by a universe that collapsed. It then resides in that very small, dense, and hot state of "nothing." Why should it all of a sudden decide to go bang? Could it be that during or after the collapse a significant amount from a neighboring but extinct universe was absorbed by our nascent universe, the effect being an overload that could only be relieved explosively? Preposterous? Maybe. Maybe not. Or could one of the two (or more) be an active maturing universe?

Suppose the energy and matter of that other universe behaved totally differently from that that we know? Suppose it does not vibrate. Light would not, for instance, be able to reflect from such matter. Everything that we see and rely upon in our world and our universe depends on vibrations or frequencies and wave lengths. What do you know that does not have that dependency? Nothing! If the dark energy and dark matter that we calculate should be out there is not identifiable through our only known sensory systems because it does not vibrate, then that provides at least part of an answer to the question regarding the unexplainable mass in our expanding universe. It also provides a reason for the big bang.

And then, why should I have to register a reminder that Richard Feynman's multiple histories can be expanded to cover all sorts of possible scenarios? Feynman postulated, and it is now generally accepted, that the universe must have every possible history, each with its own probability. Feynman formulated a mathematical expression called the Feynman "sum over histories" that is an integral part of the theory of quantum physics. In effect, things like quantum particles take all possible paths and do so simultaneously. His equations might possibly be applied to the universe or universes as well. Stephen J. Gould's views on the vast possible number of histories for evolutionary development are, in my view, in parallel with the number and probabilities of universe histories that derive from Feynman's ideas.

Let's get back to Stephen Hawking. What is his take on God? To be frank, I am not sure. Maybe he was not sure. Hawking makes frequent references to God in his discussions. I detect somewhat of a tongue-in-cheek flavor in these references. But he may be downright serious. On the other hand, he could be using God as a foil to emphasize the scientific validity of his arguments. On September 7, 2010, at 9:00 a.m. I was watching ABC-TV. There was an interview with Stephen Hawking. He was shown in his mobile chair, no body movement, and only slight facial movements. His statements came through his voice synthesizer. A series of questions was posed, but the one statement that means something for our purposes involved God. Hawking said very clearly that science shows that God is not necessary. He says that he has devoted twenty years to adjusting his thinking on this matter and arrives at that conclusion. This does not say that God does not exist, but it comes close.

In his latest and last book Hawking is clear.

> You can't get to a time before the Big Bang because there was no time before the Big Bang. We have finally found something that doesn't have a cause, because there was no time for a cause to exist in. For me this means that there is no possibility of a creator, because there is no time for a creator to have existed in.

It must be remembered that Einstein made his God statements, most of which have been misinterpreted or taken out of context. Let Hawking have his say. In both cases there is some support for the thesis that humans default to God when explanations do not suffice. There is an element of Pascal's wager here. Einstein, Hawking, and other scientists know the immensity of meaning that lies behind the origin of the universe and the origin of life. They, being human and preeminent scientists, are going to keep their options open, and I cannot fault them for that. In support of this point, I refer to an interview via video of Richard Dawkins by Bill Maher on April 11, 2008. Maher asked Dawkins why he ranked himself only 6 instead of the maximum 7 for atheist thinking. Dawkins responded that no true scientist could or would commit himself to 100 percent. He said he might go for 6.99.

There is also the celebrity factor. Any famous person can be quoted on his or her views, but the truth or not behind those views is dependent on more than the expertise of the famous person in mind and may not be in accord. Or that person may not want to express his or her real views in order to avoid controversy.

Stephen Hawking in *The Universe in a Nutshell* gets into early macromolecules, evolution, DNA, and the development of intelligence among other things. It is very interesting that he does not give credit to the underlying simplicity and conservative nature of evolution, and I find this interesting because he and others do not appear willing to apply nature's tendencies to the greater cosmological world. Branes? Really? M and string theory? Really?

Stephen Hawking and Leonard Mlodinow in their recent *The Grand Design* might help with some of our questions. They start by stating that philosophy is dead, which I consider a stupid thing to say. The entire book that follows is full of scientific philosophy including the *why* questions toward the end of the book. So be it!

There are several dominant themes in the H and M book. The origin or "beginning" of the universe is a quantum event. Time did not then exist. Time behaves like space. Time is a dimension that can be warped, as are the other dimensions. Feynman's sum-over-histories concept leads to innumerable histories for a universe: we are in one of them. Fine-tuning of the universe and the earthly environment is not acceptable. The anthropic principles apply. Finally, M theory is it! I mention here only quick statements of very complex thoughts and theories. The reader will have to pursue these themes on his or her own.

What is truly significant in Hawking's book is the support for the M theory. The M theory is described as a network of theories each of which describes certain phenomena within a certain range. They overlap. H and M do a lousy job of laying out exactly what falls within the M theory. The string theory is a subset thereof. But how many of the theories that H and M discuss are formally part of the M theory? At the very end, the authors suddenly say the M theory is the grand design. Oh, really?! Show me! The best I can say is that all the M theory family of sub theories apparently shows no need for a beginning and, specifically, no need for a grand designer—a god.

I, for one, find the M theory idea that universes in the form of "bouncing branes" in different dimensions collide and thus lead to a universe such as ours to be suspect because of the dimensions aspect. Nevertheless, it gives me some satisfaction to say that I have for years thought that the event that brought our universe into being could have been the result of the collision or combination of a collapsed universe and the gravitational accretion of the debris from an expanded and defunct universe followed by a triggering quantum event.

I do have a problem with the mathematicians' conclusion that colliding branes do the job in differing dimensions. Why must we accept M theory assumptions for universe collisions in different dimensions? If all that falls into the realm of statistical possibility while reality is something else, then maybe okay. But nature has generally shown itself to be very conservative; the exotic is not the norm.

However, in their book there are several passages that state that the scientific facts preclude any need for God. The point is that physics, nature's law, explains everything. As far as God as a designer (for universe and environment), this, according to H and M, is "not the answer of modern science."

To support the purpose of this book we need to derive meaning from Stephen Hawking's arguments. Some, such as Russell Stannard in his *The End of Discovery*, take on the task of explaining and yet circumscribing them to the extent that many questions remain unanswered and may never be answered. Stannard praises the extent to which science has gone but says we may be reaching its limits. Science is unlikely to resolve many basic problems. He is said to be critical of a stance that makes God unnecessary.

Russell Stannard represents a very necessary community of critics, and he does point out areas of scientific endeavor where doubt is needed. Yet, in the case of Steven Hawking, the thinking and data that Hawking has produced, based on earlier great advances, act as a rock-solid foundation for the principles that underlie the existence of the universe and the world in which we live. There are doubters, but the progression of science appears to be on course.

Brian Greene covers many relevant topics in his *The Elegant Universe*. He argues a need for a new theory as he runs through space-time, his so-called microscopic weirdness, among other topics, and the essentials of the superstring theory. In other words, this book is all about supporting the superstring theory. He admits that there is much needed in the way of empirical evidence and data to support the theory, and he places some hope on the results of the Large Hadron Collider. But, in the end, his idea is to embrace a theory that unites all that we know of astrophysics and quantum mechanics in one calculation. A tall task!

From the perspective of my book, there is throughout the argumentation for the superstring theory a clear inference that there was no beginning and that there will be no ending. There were strings, and there will always be strings!

Of course, there is always the other opposing view. On January 6, 2011, an item based on a report from *Technology and Science* appeared on the internet. The pope was quoted as saying, "God's mind was behind complex scientific theories such as the big bang, and Christians should reject the idea that the universe came into being by accident." This quote was reported by Reuters, Yahoo News, and several more syndicates. I am amused by the church's adoption of not only evolution but the big bang as proofs for God's existence. It is their only and final line of defense. Now they will have to accommodate the probability that there was no beginning.

At this time, after discussing a good number of sources and ideas, I would like to propose my own solution to the question of the source of our universe. I give some specifics, but that does not mean that variations on the theme are out of the question. The reader will hopefully pardon me for some amount of repetition of my earlier text. The argument must be rounded out.

An Emerging Universe

The big bang theory is the accepted story of our universe from its beginning and then its evolution. Inflation has been added to the theory or, perhaps, should be considered as an adjunct to the central theory. Through the years much research has been accomplished, and considerable data has been accumulated, all of which provides support for the theory. For example, the discovery of the cosmic microwave background has proved to be of immense help in defining the early stages in the life of the universe. Recent research has detected the gravitational waves produced through galactic collisions. But the waves that have been predicted as a necessary result of the big bang have not yet been detected. Nevertheless, the big bang theory is the one and only accepted story of the emergence of our universe.

There are some doubters, however. I have read of several notable individuals expressing some degree of doubt. I for one have several questions dealing mainly with the first nanoseconds of the birth of the universe and what preceded that event. Whatever it was that went bang was supposedly the size of a pea and even much smaller—perhaps the size of a single atom. The birthing nugget was extremely dense and extremely hot. But was that density and heat enough to provide the needed amount of energy for our universe? Energy cannot be created, nor can it be destroyed. It can take a different form, but, whatever the form, it must come from somewhere. Where did the nugget and its energy content come from? What conditions and what impulse brought it into existence? Why would nature behave so? Did the nugget emerge from a tunnel? Was the appearance of the nugget spontaneous such as quantum level particles that appear and disappear (having met the antiparticle)?

And, of course, was there nothing?

In any of these and other cases we need to explain where the energy originally came from. If a nugget appears only once, this leads to a serious criticism of any scenario, since the infinite space in which our universe floats would preclude a once-only event. If nature is wont to provide multiple nuggets, that would imply a process that goes well beyond the emergence of the universe we know. In short, why, and how did the conditions and an entity that would lead to the big bang come together?

To answer these questions, we need to hypothesize a background for the big bang or whatever alternative we come up with. For the alternative we must engage in some deep speculation, something I believe is absolutely essential in most scientific endeavors. A hypothesis or a theory does not suddenly pop up. Someone has to do some thinking first, followed by testing, dissemination of the results, peer review, and so forth. So, I will not apologize for speculating, regardless of how extreme it may be.

Our universe is large and getting larger at an exponential rate of expansion such that we will never be able to detect the farthest bodies at its edges. However, despite this size, there must be something even larger, that being the space into which our universe emerged and is still resident. Going back in time we encounter very early speculation on the part of gifted individuals such as Copernicus, thinking that when we look toward the heavens we are looking into eternity. It would have been difficult for earlier savants to understand fully the context of this thinking because their knowledge of the cosmos was very limited. However, the idea was that beyond what they saw, space went on forever. And I among many others see it exactly that way. After all, once one gets past the last galaxies of our universe, do we expect to encounter a brick wall? Would there be some sort of mysterious barrier? Even if we answer yes, what will lie on the other side of the barrier? Another barrier? And we could go on forever. Beyond our universe there stretches infinity. And what does this infinity display? A multiverse, certainly, because to contend that our universe is unique in an infinite space is a contradiction in terms. I refer to this infinite space as interuniverse space.

With the above in mind, let's see if we can surmise why and how the situation that led to the big bang came together. The *why* is not a problem. In an infinite and timeless interuniverse space, if something can happen, it will happen, and it did once for sure. There is no reason why. It was statistically bound to happen. The real question is *how*, and I propose here a scenario that leads to the condition that sparked the emergence of our universe.

Interuniverse space would be anything but a vast calm void. Innumerable universes would be in the process of emergence, expansion, collapse, explosion, dissipation, or collision, much as the galaxies in our universe behave. There could be other more exotic events, and there could be innumerable forms that any particular universe would assume. Interuniverse space would be more chaos than calm with universes in various life phases located among energy fields and energy waves, which are both the result of universe activity and the spawning grounds of nascent universes, reflecting a never-ending cycle. Time would not exist in interuniverse space, although in any given universe a clock expression might apply as it does in our universe.

The above-mentioned universe spawning grounds would consist of energy fields and waves of energy, the fields akin to the fields encountered in our universe and waves similar to solar flares or the intense and massive radiation emitted by our galaxies from time to time, only orders of magnitude greater. What form would all this energy take? I do not know. X-rays, gamma rays, photons, neutrinos, and many other forms in some state or other are candidates. And there is the question of the presence of subatomic particles as envisioned by quantum mechanics or the superstring and M theories in the energy mix. I cannot say, and I certainly have no mathematical model to rely upon. Nevertheless, I contend that in infinite interuniverse space it is inevitable that a number of these pools of energy come together and through gravitational forces form a concentration of extreme density and high temperature much as predicted in the big bang theory. Yes, gravity would probably be a factor beyond our known experience. At this point I propose that a quantum-level event embedded in the energy concentration and propelled by the extreme conditions would cause something like crystallization or inflation to occur.

Under the circumstances, I suggest that a large number of quantum-level events could have triggered almost simultaneously or in an ultrafast cascade. This would define the bang and inflation of our universe, and I am partial to such a scenario because it provides an explanation for the immense amount of energy it contains. It can also explain away the mystery of the origin of that very small nugget in the big bang theory. If one insists that the math points the arrow of time back to the small entity just prior to the big bang, then I contend that the small something could have been the quantum-level particle or particles that triggered the bang and the excitation of the surrounding energy field.

I believe it is reasonable to assume that parts of the above-mentioned concentration of energy came from regions and entities in interuniverse space with differing laws of physics. This could account for the presence of dark energy and mass in our universe. I am not sure how one would figure the start point for a calculation of entropy, given the assumption that space beyond our universe is infinite and that my scenario infers an infinite cycle of events. Are we dealing here with an open or closed system? I do not know. Finally, my scenario shows that our universe was not created but emerged from that timeless cycle of events. As a counter to my thoughts, current thinking shows the arrow of time pointing back to an infinitely dense and infinitely hot small entity. But, as I just said, could not the arrow of time point to a quantum event in a large, dense, and hot field?

Beginning or Continuity?

Continuity, of course! I have only touched on a few sources, but they are backed by an army of researchers and experts. I am well aware of the rock-solid status of current theories and their mathematical underpinnings. Yet it seems to me that variations on the theme could certainly be entertained if they can be somehow accommodated by current theory. Certainly, the room before the big bang should be wide open for speculation. In this chapter I have bent a few of the rules, but that should not detract from the central conclusion that pops out from the evidence.

Despite the need for more clarity in some areas, it is clear to me that the universe as we know it is governed by defined rules needing of no outside help. It is also clear to me that there are very plausible explanations for what came before, based on the same rules, despite the paucity of hard data. I conclude there was no beginning. As with many other experts, I see no evidence or need for a god. He or it did not begin or create anything, and all moves along by itself, thank you.

CHAPTER 6

Life's Continuity

It Was a Natural from the Start

Is there such a thing as life? Or is it all a matter of physics and chemistry? The term *life* is one invented by humans, and its definition is not all that clear. It appears to apply to anything that has a means of reproduction and shows the means for independent reaction to its surroundings, albeit perhaps limited by its environment as to its actions. Biologists have some very specific points that must be met to qualify something as a form of life. An early reference to life by the ancients probably meant something that moved and multiplied. In whatever language they used, the usage meant to reflect these attributes. Life must be that which we see and experience. Thus, the term *life* must be considered a subjective human definition of a lasting and pervasive idea—a meme. It's a matter of semantics. If you have a definition for life, then that's what life is for you. But in the end, life boils down to a matter of physics and chemistry.

At this point, I would like to insert a thought that has to do with the emergence of life but is also pertinent to the existence of the universe and consistent with the idea that "anything is possible." I believe the scientific community has too cavalierly dismissed the possibility of some sort of life apart from the "life as we know it" syndrome. If on earth we find creatures that live and procreate under the most incredible conditions, why can't such life exist elsewhere? I am talking about the example of bacteria and archaea that exist in extreme heat and cold conditions and others that appear to live incredibly long lives. Beyond that, why must replicating entities be restricted to water-based environments? Why could there not be beings out there that depend on a totally different physics and chemical circumstances? Why do we continually dismiss the fact that nature has always come up with the solutions that defy our imagination?

The search for life *not* as we know it but based on alternate biologies is not being ignored. The *National Geographic* July 2014 issue, in an article titled "The Hunt for Life Beyond Earth," cites a group at Harvard led by Dimitar Sasselov, an astronomer, that is looking at alternate biologies— lifeforms unlike ours.

A very interesting article addressing this thought appeared in *The Economist* dated May 28th 2022. Essentially, there are distinct possibilities for inorganic replicating entities involving certain elements under certain conditions. The conditions can be extreme. The elements and some molecules serve to substitute for earth's building blocks under these differing environmental conditions. For instance, substitute silicon for carbon. Employ ammonia as the needed liquid. Or better: formaldehyde. And there are some such as the polyoxymetalates that exhibit the ability to form membranes and even a possible replicating code like DNA. There are sure to be more possibilities. We use only 20 amino acids for our organisms. But a larger number exist. The article reports on the growing effort to research the possibilities and to incorporate these new characteristics in our search for exoplanets.

We need, therefore, to examine carefully what we mean by life as we know it, and if we consider *life* that which we see on earth, then we must appreciate the physics and the chemistry that created it. They, physics and chemistry, appear more than adequate to handle the challenge. Exactly how life came about we do not know. But it appears to have been a certainty. Of the billions and billions of possibilities in the universe, there had to be one circumstance that would create an Earth as it exists with its physics and chemistry leading to life as we know it—the anthropic principle.

I propose that there is no beginning for life and that life as we know it is a natural result of physical and chemical laws. Simple, yet basic elements and a myriad of nonorganic substances such as acids and crystalline compounds have been around ever since the earth formed. Under the appropriate circumstances, these elements and substances combined in such a way as to produce life. There was no clear boundary.

Replication would have been a major challenge, yet game theory as well as elemental behavior suggests that this was eventually bound to be overcome. We then have a linear perhaps hyperbolic though sometimes rocky progression from the universe's basic elements toward what we humans call life. I claim that life had no definable beginning. It was already here, just in its earliest building blocks.

Bacteria and Archea are life-forms—among the first. A virus is a life-form, though some may dispute this. In any case these forms appear relatively simple. Yet they display the generic foundations of today's species and an astounding complexity for such supposedly simple organisms.

What happened between the time that the earth was a boiling pot of elements and compounds and the appearance of these life-forms? The boundary between the original raw ingredients and a *life* is very fuzzy. As stated above, it is my contention that there is no boundary. Given the conditions and the elements and compounds present on the earth's surface, it seems probable that forms would develop that would display the characteristics of so-called *life*. There had to be a steady and unbroken progression from the basic elements to a replicating form, accepting also that the process may have advanced in fits and starts. Experiments have been carried out to investigate this transition, and a number of them support the thesis that natural nonorganic processes resulted in the creation of forms that displayed the characteristics of *life*.

There are a number of hypotheses describing the environmental conditions that led to the origin of life. Primordial pools is one of them. Thermal vents in the bottom of the oceans is another. Crystalline forms of clays and muds is another. Seeding from some object in space or the solar system has been suggested, and I am sure there are additional theses worth investigating.

I mentioned these "origin of life" scenarios earlier, and the reader can get into the details as much as desired. Suffice it to say that many experts believe there is a reasonable probability that life emerged as a result of physical/chemical/electrical processes early in Earth's history.

There is no more challenging question in science today than the explanation of the origin of life, and several reputable organizations are undertaking the task of finding the answers. I suspect that life may have emerged in each and every one of the hypothesized pathways and that evolutionary selection picked the winner and got us to where we are today.

Start with the primordial soup. What was the environment on Earth four-plus billion years ago? By most accounts, it was a tumultuous world of bombardments from space, violent storms, humid and electric, volcanic activity, surging seas, vast areas of warm and chemically rich pools/seas (primordial soup), and an unforgiving blazing sun, with, unfortunately, lots of unshielded UV. It should be here that the required amino acids and other compounds necessary to life would occur. What about UV exposure? There was no oxygen in the atmosphere. And how could the hundreds of needed acids come together as required? The odds appear too high. Really? Isn't it likely that the "soup" that produces one compound would produce others as well, maybe most of them despite the seemingly killer constants?

It would seem that the violent world of that time would have brought together many or most of the elements needed. It is not too far-fetched to say that the conditions for the required chemical reactions would at some time or other exist. The human genome only requires twenty specific amino acids among hundreds. At the beginning, however, the different acids and other pre-organic compounds were certain to have come into being, and evolutionary time has appropriately sorted them out. I suspect that not only was the coming together of all the needed acids and related organic building blocks a given at some time or other but that it had to occur very early on. The path to development of the needed proteins and eventually the complexity of the nucleotides, critical to the replicating code, was surely more difficult, but the environment and the vast timeframe involved meant that certain proteins and replicating systems should somehow result.

The complexity of organic compounds and the demanding chemical reactions and conditions needed to produce them introduce a great deal of doubt for this pathway to life. The primordial soup thesis is also suspect because, among other things, the atmospheric oxygen content was too low to provide the needed CHON (carbon, hydrogen, oxygen, nitrogen) combinations typical of known life-forms, and the UV intensity would have had a fatal effect for emerging life-forms.

However, it must be remembered that microbes early on figured out how to avoid the hazards by forming colonies called stromatolites. Earlier proto lifeforms may well have arrived at similar solutions. In the tradition of science, things can change, new thoughts and evidence can arise, and the primordial soup thesis should remain a possibility, particularly if it is combined with other speculations. I would not toss it out yet.

The processes that occur at the thermal vents deep in the oceans are considered viable candidates for the creation of those molecules necessary for life. These vents are the result of tectonic movements and the circulating subsurface flows of liquid material that result in infusions of heated mineral-rich solutions into the deep cold waters, an environment that supposedly is conducive to the formation of organic building blocks.

Understanding the extreme nature of the conditions for this pathway to life leads me to suspect that, should this be viable, we should be looking at other extreme environmental conditions as well. Recent investigations are revealing more and more life-forms that exist under the most demanding circumstances and some that live at metabolic rates so slow as to presume a life span in the millions of years. Anything appears possible!

Richard Dawkins, along with others such as Daniel C. Dennett, appears to be very accepting of the fact that life came about billions of years ago through natural chemical/electrical processes. He follows the primordial soup theory in his book *The Selfish Gene*. In *The Blind Watchmaker*, he pursues the "inorganic mineral" theory of the Glasgow chemist Graham Cairns-Smith, according to which we have:

> A speculative picture of mineral crystals on the primeval Earth showing some of the properties of replication, multiplication, heredity and mutation that would have been necessary in order for a form of cumulative selection to get started.

Graham Cairns-Smith espouses the theory that the crystalline properties of clays and muds can lead to self-replicating entities that eventually lead to biological organisms. His view is that a simpler replicator preceded DNA, the latter winning out in the Darwinian struggle. In his book *Seven Clues to the Origin of Life*, he begins his argumentation by demonstrating the great complexity and workings of biological organisms. His conclusion from such an analysis is a strong rejection of "chemical evolution," meaning primordial soup, etc. There is, he says, simply too much to be done to produce organic matter to be anywhere possible through this popularly accepted process for life's beginning. The statistical probability of the production of a replicating mechanism is, he says, beyond astronomical.

Manfred Eigen appears to disagree here. Eigen seems to believe that the early necessary monomers came about with some ease. I use "appears" and "seems" because he infers rather than categorically states certain conditions and outcomes. Nevertheless, his is a modifying viewpoint.

Cairns-Smith makes a case for inorganic clay crystals being the first replicators leading eventually to organic evolution. He describes a surprisingly complex clay-crystal world in which minerals in and of themselves, in combination with other minerals and under certain environmental conditions, can produce structures that can reproduce themselves. They have to be simple, and they are. They represent the first step toward the far more complex organic compounds, which could not have arisen without the help of less complex predecessors. The author describes how it would be possible for organic material to develop from the favorable conditions brought by the inorganic first entities. Certain light-sensitive properties of minerals and the more developed photosynthesis play a part. These physical/chemical reactions and certain resulting organic building blocks could have assisted the crystal structures in surviving and replicating. Eventually organic structures developed to the point that their superiority allowed them to take over supremacy in an evolutionary sense, leading to the nucleotides, RNA, and DNA that we see today.

Cairns-Smith contributes a telling argument. I find his speculation on the bridge from the mineral replicator to the organic winner to be just that: speculation. Nevertheless, everything starts with speculation. We go on from there, and this is one reason why I believe his dismissal of "chemical evolution" to be premature. He himself envisages some organic giant steps aided and abetted by the mineral "organisms." Why could not some other radical conditions have similarly supported the proper chemical processes needed to create biological organisms? Let me quote Cairns-Smith on page 109 of the *Seven Clues to the Origin of Life*.

> When natural selection is in operation—when there is, in effect, a continuing memory of past successes—then

such games of chance are radically transformed. Expertise can be gradually built up. The impossible may become highly feasible.

Interestingly, Stephen Hawking rather casually addresses in *The Universe in a Nutshell* his view that perhaps random collisions of atoms in the primordial oceans built up macromolecules that "could reproduce themselves and assemble themselves into more complicated structures." This is a physicist of some renown who apparently sees no great impediment to such a process.

A large community believes in the chemical-biological creation of life as we know it. In his work *Steps towards Life*, Manfred Eigen demonstrates the biological and the mathematical statistical reality of evolution, particularly as it pertains to the genetic progression through evolutionary space of the chemical compounds critical to our very existence. And he also attempts to modify Darwin's original hypotheses by proposing such concepts as the quasi-species, which replaces the emphasis on the wild-type (the most capable individual) with an emphasis on a large population of different but similar mutants who may average out to be equivalent to the wild-type but who define the competition for selection and occupation of the high peaks in the genetic landscape. And this is the focus of his book despite the title. He does endorse a chemical-biological beginning of life.

Manfred Eigen's view on the matter is somewhat cloudy. He concludes that exactly how it all happened is probably never to be determined, but he does make the point that, in his view, conditions on early earth plus the ease of composition of acids and proteins, as well as catalysts of various forms, made the transmission from the earthly inorganic realm to the organic possible. Eigen contends that it was very possible that various appropriate prebiotic products could come about in the early oceans, some of which would have catalytic properties. He cites several investigations that lead more or less to the conclusion that nature could have produced that which led to life (Stanley Miller, Sidney W. Fox, Leslie Orgel, Albert Eschenmoser).

In essence, the needed ingredients for life were more easily produced than expected and had the necessary chemical attributes that could lead to replicating systems. However, having suggested these tantalizing points,

Eigen retreats to his real interest: the evolution of that life that had already somehow or other come about.

There is one more recent scenario espoused by Nick Lane in his book *The Vital Question*. The answer is energy. Claiming that the primordial soup thesis and other scenarios do not account for the energy conditions needed to create life's organic structures, Lane identifies alkaline hydrothermal vents in the ocean's depths as the electrochemical flow reactors that do satisfy these conditions. These vents present a warm labyrinth of interconnected micropores that act as catalysts as well as membranes across which the acidic ocean fluids and the vents' alkaline fluids can allow an electrochemical flow. This in turn allows the synthesis of life forms. From the vents up to the ocean surface is a problem, but there appear to be ways to accomplish that feat. The process is complex, and a read of Nick Lane's book is both helpful and exciting.

For various reasons today's alkaline hydrothermal vents are not producing life-forms, but four billion years ago external conditions may have allowed such an outcome. A question. Did the vents themselves exist then? Nevertheless, Nick Lane's thesis stands out as very reasonable, even though I would still not dismiss the other scenarios. Yet.

Exactly how would the needed elements, acids, and proteins have combined to produce life? The jury is still out on the specific ways this was accomplished, but there seems to be a scientific consensus that the above-mentioned environmental scenarios as well as others provide plausible paths to follow. In addition, the basic forms of what we would call life have been replicated in the laboratory. The laboratory experiments to date may be simplistic and may show a lot to be desired, but they do show that natural causes can create some of the essential elements of life. The point is that there was no need of outside intervention to produce life. It could and did occur naturally.

What about the claim that life was brought to earth from some place out in space? It is hard to say this impossible. Earth has been and is currently showered with material from space every day. Organic substances could be among the arrivals. But this should mean that conditions somewhere out there were similar to conditions here on earth; otherwise, the imports would find it difficult to survive on arrival. For me, it seems logical that, if organic material from elsewhere could be created, then it could also be created here, assuming similar conditions there and here. I contend the outside help was not needed even if it might have occurred.

The theists, of course, deny that the just-related theses and experiments are valid. However, their denial is based on purely religious beliefs, not usually subject to any scientific critique. Some theists are scientists. That only proves they are human!

Probabilities and Proofs

Richard Dawkins again invokes the "anthropic principle" in the debate on the origin of life. And once again there are the statistics. He cites one billion to thirty billion planets in our galaxy and a hundred billion galaxies (I have read as high as one thousand billion galaxies and one hundred billion stars per galaxy, average). He writes in *The God Delusion*:

> If the odds of life originating spontaneously on a planet were a billion to one against, nevertheless that stupefyingly improbable event would still happen on a billion planets.

Dawkins's point is that with all the probabilities being what they are, there is always the chance that things came out as they did at least once. That we are here is nothing more than the establishment of that fact.

In *God, the Failed Hypothesis*, Victor Stenger devotes a chapter, "The Uncongenial Universe," to the debate on the beginnings of life. Let me repeat that Stenger's thesis is that there should be evidence of God's intervention where evidence would be expected. There should be a reasonable scientific explanation for cosmic and earthly events created or staged by God. Without such evidence of divine intervention, there is no reason to suggest either the need for or the existence of God's efforts.

I devote some space to Stenger's work because he does a good job of summarizing the pertinent scientific theories involved. Some of this review is a repeat from earlier chapters, but it is helpful.

Stenger begins the subject chapter refuting the arguments of Hugh Ross, Guillermo Gonzalez, Jay Richards, and others who contend that the cosmic and earthly physical probabilities are such that life has to be the result of design, read God. Stenger replies that the fact that earth presents the desired conditions for life as we know it is no indication that God did it. When it comes to probabilities, Stenger states that, given the numbers of galaxies, suns, and planets, the probabilities are good that life on earth came about as it did. No God needed and no evidence to the contrary.

In pursuance of the same old ID approach, there comes the argument that the universe and earthly conditions are "fine-tuned" to lead to life on earth and the human being. This refers to the thirty-three constants, mentioned by Hugh Ross and others, that must be exactly as they are for the universe and Earth to be as they are. Again, I cite Stenger's emphasis on the need for scientific evidence of divine intervention and his conclusion that there is no such fine-tuning. The reality of the universe as it exists borne out by the validity of the past centuries' scientific exploration proposes a universe exactly as one would expect, given the factors involved in Newtonian physics, the theory of relativity, quantum mechanics, and the resultant multitude of physics and chemical laws accepted by the scientific community. Stenger cites several examples of the lack of need for and evidence of fine-tuning. The simple explanation is that certain conditions occurred, and that life developed accordingly. Don't put the cart before the horse.

Stenger cites the work of physicist Anthony Aguire, physicist Craig Hogan, and theoretical physicists at Kyoto University, all of which would support the thesis that the universe could provide conditions that might lead to the creation of life. That means the universe as is could produce life without outside intervention. For example, carbon and oxygen, two elements essential to life as we know it, are among the easiest to produce through nuclear reactions on or near early Earth.

Stenger goes on to doubt any fine-tuning of the vacuum energy and other constants, while accepting that there are certain crucial conditions that must be met to allow the creation of life. But what's new? Everything that exists depends on certain conditions. The conditions determine what is going to exist.

Finally, Stenger engages in discussions of the immensity of the universe, the lack of order and structure, and the miniscule status of Earth in the universe. The universe is not congenial to the existence of humankind, and, in fact, God has wasted a vast amount of space and time if he was intent on creating humans. This is certainly not evidence of any intent to do so. Just the opposite, it shows no reason at all that would favor his supposed creation.

To sum up Stenger's contribution, there is no evidence, given the facts, that there is a divine being, nor is there a need for a god for us to arrive at the life we have today.

Scientists describe a series of constants, factors, and circumstances that are critical to our being what we are. When they cite something like thirty constants that are necessary for life-as-we-know-it to exist, there is the implicit assumption that life-as-we-know-it exists only because the factors remain exactly as they are. I have a problem with this view, and I have referred to it earlier in this book. I have not read or heard of any analysis that takes these numerous critical factors and juggles them so as to produce another combination amenable to the creation of life-as-we-know-it. Suppose factor A decreases, but factors B and C increase. There are innumerable different combinations and permutations that might arrive at the same result. If the constants were to change, would there not be a wide range of lifelike results somewhere in the universe? Why can't there be another solution? We need oxygen, but for billions of years organisms on Earth existed without oxygen in the atmosphere. Today we know of organisms that live in radically differing and extremely challenging environments.

Let me engage in what would be called far-out speculation. Investigations to date have basically concentrated on the miniscule particles that make up both inorganic and organic matter. Suppose we look at the other extreme. Suppose we assume an ancient oceanic "organism," a vast body of liquids, elements, and compounds. This "organism" on the size of the Pacific Ocean or more would over millions upon millions upon millions of years relentlessly produce compounds of innumerable sorts, all of which would decay according to environmental conditions and then be reconstructed according to these same environmental conditions, over and over and over again. Do we not see here a pattern that would eventually trip upon a variant that would assume by itself the repetition that the truly mindless monster "organism" had already repeated ad infinitum? Let there be an element of chemical organic beginnings or crystalline clay antecedents or a combination of these and other leads; it all tends to presuppose a transition to the life we now accept as reality. Or is this a different perspective on the primordial soup?

Summing Up

Summing up our discussion on the beginning of life, it seems there has been continuity between the raw elements of our Earth and the forms that we call "life." In effect, there was no beginning, per se. Investigations involving a number of pathways from the inorganic to the organic or prebiotic to biotic offer several plausible scenarios for developments leading to today's life-forms. There are significant objections to them, and more evidence is needed. None should as of this date be abandoned. At this stage there does not appear to be any need for God. There are too many other plausible possibilities.

CHAPTER 7

God Is a Human Creation

The Evidence in All Areas So Concludes

As we review the several disciplines that relate to the existence of God, it seems clear that God does not exist! God is a creation of the human mind, meant to alleviate the pains of life on earth and the inevitable death of the individual. Humans have created God in their own image!

Humankind's history from its earliest times over many thousands of years shows a human tendency to propose the existence of gods. Yet there is no evidence that the gods actually existed. Humankind's fundamental fears and desires bred a series of imagined supernatural beings that were supposed to ease human life on earth and in the hereafter. Much was and is based on faith, founded on the preaching of numerous dominating individuals and influential groups of sages. As the centuries passed, the myths and the histories were elaborated upon and tailored to the benefit of elite groups. Anything that relies on this historical record as proof of a supernatural reality must be held in extreme doubt.

Any number of religions propose a scenario in which a god or gods create the world around us and the animals that exist here. The idea that a deity or some supreme power created humans and the animals of the earth as opposed to the process of evolution is absurd. All are, frankly, fantasies. The scientific record is far too strong to dispute. Life existed billions of years ago and has taken an evolutionary path to where we are today. It's clear! It's not disputable!

Why do so many peoples of the earth believe in gods or a god? Beyond the physiological and psychological pressures to seek support in the supernatural, humans had to face the pressures of the civilizations they created. Society, culture, and power politics have forced people to believe. Any youth or in fact any individual who deviates from the god belief is ostracized in most of history's civilizations. I have been advised (I have no proof of the statement) that only 12 percent of today's progeny depart from their parents' religious beliefs.

Religions seem to place great emphasis on the beginnings of everything. The gods caused it all to come into existence. However, they are pursuing a dream. There are no beginnings! The universe as it exists is a derivative of a previous state, whether that be a collapsed universe, a resurgent black hole, an introduction from another cosmic plane, or any other of often suggested alternatives. God didn't create it. It has always been here in some form or other into infinity. Likewise, life on Earth as we know it was preordained by the nature of this universe. Life is a logical progression from inert matter to self-replicating systems that lead to the biological systems that we see today. No supernatural being was needed, nor was it involved.

Why?

We are all familiar with the *w* words associated with intellectual interrogation: *what, where, why, when, who,* and *whom.* We might add *which, whence,* and *whither,* and maybe more such as *how.* I propose that prehistoric humans and their cultures well into the relatively recent historic past concentrated on the interrogatives to the exception of *why.* Humans wanted and needed to know what the elements were and what they represented, and they needed to know what they should do to extract benefits or avoid punishment. They concerned themselves with who did what and the affected being. They did not question the reason for what was presented to them by their environment. Their task was to cope with it. Because humans could not find themselves in a position of command, their concerns led them inexorably to belief in the supernatural. Remember, however, that we are still dealing with the *what, where, when, who,* and *whom,* relative to the appeasement of the gods.

Somewhere in the historic past certain sages began to ask why things are the way they are and what that means. I have no evidence as to the timing, and the question *Why?* is a relatively modern philosophical inquiry.

In any case, the ancient propensity to create gods gained an impulse from the philosophers of the last roughly five thousand years who sought to justify their very existence on earth. Why do I exist? Why am I what I am? What is the reason for my being? Why do I have to die? What is the meaning of life? Question after question. Why? Recognizing their consciousness and their corporal vulnerability, humans decided to answer the *why* with the already established prehistoric foundation of god belief.

The answer to the questions above is painfully simple! There is no *why*. There is no meaning. Humanity is the result of a series of factors that led inexorably to where and what we are. A certain star happened to have a planet that allowed for the development of certain sorts of life-forms. Among the billions of possibilities in the universe, it just happened to occur here. Statistics being what they are, one could say either that it had to happen somewhere or that despite all the odds it did come about at least once. Evolution does all the rest! *Homo sapiens* developed through evolutionary processes into a thinking animal with an as yet incompletely explained consciousness. Meaning? Nothing at all! Why? No reason. It just came out this way. Quite frankly, the statement by so many that there has to be a reason behind our human existence exasperates me to no end. Now I will employ the *why?* Why must there be a reason behind your existence? Answer: there is no need for a reason other than that of your own ego and imagination. Is God involved here? No! Why should He be?

God's Work

Having classified God as nothing more than a creation of the human mind, let us conjure such a figure to address the unlikely conditions and situations his existence would have to entail.

God would have to be an infinitely old and enduring entity, which is surely in accord with theist thinking. As stated in the preceding text, I am convinced that there is no beginning for either time or space. Both are infinite.

I am also fully aware that in our universe the rules can be changed or bent, depending on the conditions, and that in other universes the rules may be very different. To be the figure the theists claim, God would rule over all of this for eternity. But for what reason? Does an over-watching

God make sense? Where is the utility? What has he done over the infinite past? Has he had an active hand in bringing about what exists today? Maybe, but how? What reason or need is there for God if the natural laws suffice? None! The theist says, of course, that there need be no reason for God. He is omnipotent, and our human judgments and reasoning have no meaning whatsoever on God's workings.

Whether there was nothing before the big bang or something there before the big bang, what was God supposed to be doing? Did God just exist there? Did God merely float in space- time? Was God space-time itself? Purportedly there was no time before the big bang. Nothing. So, no God. Would God's existence imply previous space-time or universes? What would make God trigger a big bang (or colliding branes or other dimensions)? Simply God's whims? Is there a reason hidden somewhere? The theist would say that we mortals cannot understand the mind of God. In any case, God had to exist before the big bang, otherwise there would be no claim to first cause.

All of this implies that God has always been here and always will be, as the space, time, energy, and matter that he oversees have been and always will be. It means that God reigns over a set of laws that govern these things, laws that may vary from cosmological place to place. Did he set them in play? Why, how, and when? Infinity being what it infers and is, God is more probably an observer. Is God playing with us like a cat with a mouse? Or is God an active loose cannon on an astronomical rolling deck? That is, God follows no human concept of logic and intelligence. He experiments. He incites conflict. He is malicious. He is kind and loving. He gambles. He is sure. He is a chameleon. Maybe. Or is he just there?

And earth and humankind? Why should God care? In his infinite space and time, he has potentially innumerable examples of earth-type developments and the evolution of the organisms thereon. He would let the rules determine where developments go. This may only be a distraction from the boring oversight of all of space and time. Does he know where humankind and all the other attempts for survival in this and other universes will end up? Maybe. But he will have seen earth's scenario many times over and can't be all that engaged. Things will work out as they will.

According to the theist view, God created humans in God's own image. What image? At what stage? The universe is fourteen billion years old. Did God decide that fourteen billion years later his image would be expressed on a tiny speck in the universe called Earth? Why the wait? Of course, time is meaningless for God, says the theist. But then what image did God anticipate? Blue-green algae? A dinosaur? A Neanderthal? Lucy? Martin Luther? To say that a supernatural entity created something in its image and that that image is a modern human being is ludicrous! It makes no sense at all.

What does God expect of us, and why would God expect anything at all? Is it faith? Why would an all-powerful supernatural entity demand and rely on faith from a tiny and obscure portion of its empire? Why would God care at all about your physical churches, temples, synagogues, mosques, and other sites of worship? Why would he endorse the enormous and elaborate bureaucratic organizations into which humans pour so much of their wealth? Would he truly care a whit about worship in any form? He would surely laugh at the uncounted numbers of prayers launched his way.

Would not a clear demonstration of God's existence be far more compelling than mere faith? Of course, theists point to Jesus, Mohammad, Gautama, and others as proof of God's intercession on Earth, but that is a very weak argument. Those claims are extremely suspect. Hiding behind the claim that the supernatural is not subject to reasonable, empirical, and obvious proof is also unacceptable.

In *The God Delusion*, Richard Dawkins denies that God could be responsible for the creation of life given the high improbability of his being able to adjust all the factors critical to that creation. I find that to be a dubious argument. It also inadvertently infers that physics couldn't do it either. If God does exist, probability considerations are immaterial. God would be able to "twiddle the knobs" as much as he likes to achieve whatever he likes. Better questions are those raised above. Why and for what reason is God necessary, and what evidence is there that points to his existence?

As one final note, I note that we humans have consistently referred to God as masculine. There are many feminine gods, but the guy on top is generally a male. It is clear to me that this is a reflection of most prehistoric and historic societies and evolutionary tendencies. Why have we not referred to the almighty as *it*? It is because we humans invented God in our image, and historically the male has been the dominant figure.

I have written this book in the first person, and in this light, I would like to end with a personal summation. After years of study of the history, bio, quantum, celestial disciplines I have become more and more convinced of my views regarding god belief. We observe the wonders of the universe with its hundreds of billions of galaxies and stars. We see a tiny speck at the edge of one of those galaxies called Earth, which displays its own wonders. We also note the trials and tribulations of living on that tiny speck. And because of these wonders and worries we entertain the vision of a supreme being responsible for it all.

This being in various forms is supposed to determine and judge all that happens throughout the universe to the extent that it even knows and judges our innermost thoughts and our futures in the here and hereafter. I find this to be incomprehensible. How could the egotistical selfish fantasies of an animal species on the smallest imaginable rock in an incomprehensibly vast universe decree the existence of a universal power apart from nature? Science has shown in ever more detail with every day that nature alone rules this universe. A supernatural supreme being is nothing more than a reflection of the fantasies of Earth's inhabitants. It is clear to me that the supernatural—God—is not only improbable but impossible.

Have I now denied humankind its righteous spiritual evolution, its right to question its very existence and its meaning? Does this mean that the spiritual is not needed? Not at all! It is our capability to fantasize and to dream that defines our mastery of the earth we inhabit. And seeking solace in the Almighty might fill a role in human consciousness. But none of this truly supports the actual existence of a greater force, an unembodied lord of all. It only supports, instead, the frailty of our human existence.

Despite all the arguments cited in this book, God, or gods or an all-embracing supernatural entity, do exist as virtual realities. Computers and cyberspace make the term understandable. Since at least 90 percent of humanity believes in God in some form or other, then we confront a virtual reality, and it is not going to go away.

But it is not true reality. Given all that we know, in contradiction to all that the theists have maintained for thousands of years, God was never present, and we were certainly not created in the image of God. All of the evidence points in the opposite direction; God was created in our image, and God is a human creation!

SELECTED SOURCES

Agusti, Jordi, and Maricio Anton. *Mammoths, Sabre Tooths, and Homonids.* New York: Columbia University Press, 2002.

Ali, Maulana Muhammad. *The Holy Qur'an.* Ahmadiyya Anjuman Isha'at Islam Lahore Inc., Ohio, USA, 2002.

Aquinas, Thomas. *The Summa Theologica.* Chicago: Encyclopaedia Britannica, William Benton, Publisher, 1955.

Ardrey, Robert. *African Genesis.* New York: Atheneum, 1961.

Armstrong, Karen. *The Lost Art of Scripture.* London, Penguin Random House, 2019.

Augustine. "Confessions," "The City of God," "On Christian Doctrine." Chicago: Encyclopaedia Britannica, William Benton, Publisher, 1955.

———. "On the Immortality of the Soul," "Man and Spirit," *The Speculative Philosophers.* New York: Random House, 1947.

Bageant, Joe. *Deer Hunting with Jesus.* New York: Three Rivers Press, 2007.

Behe, Michael J., *Darwin's Black Box.* New York: Free Press, 1996.

Bibby, Geoffrey. *Four Thousand Years Ago.* New York: Alfred A. Knopf, 1961.

Bock, Darrell L. *Breaking the Da Vinci Code.* Nashville, TN: Nelson Books, 2004.

Booker, Christopher. *The Seven Basic Plots: Why We Tell the Stories.* Continuum, 2005.

Bright, Bill. *A Man Without Equal.* Orlando: New Life Publications, 1995.

Brown, Dan. *The DaVinci Code.* New York: Doubleday, 2003.

Burdick, Alan. *Why Time Flies.* New York: Simon & Schuster, 2017.

Cairns-Smith, A.G. *Seven Clues to the Origin of Life.* Cambridge: Cambridge University Press, 1985.

Carroll, Sean. *The Big Picture.* New York: Dutton, 2016.

Cole, Juan. *MUHAMMAD Prophet of Peace Amid the Clash of Empires*. New York: Nation Books, 2018

Commins, Saxe and Robert N. Linscott. "Man and Spirit," *The World's Great Thinkers: The Speculative Philosophers*. New York: Random House, 1947.

Currie, Robin and Stephen G. Hyslop. *The Letter and the Scroll*. Washington, DC: National Geographic, 2009.

Darwin, Charles. *The Origin of Species by Means of Natural Selection*. Chicago: Encyclopaedia Britannica, William Benton, Publisher, 1955.

————. *The Descent of Man and Selection in Relation to Sex*. Chicago: Encyclopaedia Britannica, William Benton, Publisher, 1955.

Davies, A. Powell. *The Ten Commandments*. New York: New American Library, 1956.

————. *The Dead Sea Scrolls*. New York: Mentor Books, 1961.

Dawkins, Richard. *The God Delusion*. New York: Houghton Mifflin, 2006.

————. *The Greatest Show on Earth, the Evidence for Evolution*. New York: Simon and Schuster, 2009.

————. *The Selfish Gene*. New York: Oxford University Press, 2006.

————. *The Blind Watchmaker*. New York: W. W. Norton, 1996.

deGrasse Tyson, Neil. *Astrophysics for People in a Hurry*. New York: W.W. Norton, 2017.

Dembski, William A. *The Design Revolution*. InterVarsity Press, 2004.

————. *No Free Lunch*. Lanham, MD: Rowman & Littlefield, 2002.

Dennett, Daniel C. *Consciousness Explained*. New York: Little, Brown, 1991.

————. *Darwin's Dangerous Idea*. New York: Touchstone, Simon & Schuster, 1996.

————. *From Bacteria to Bach and Back*. New York: W. W. Norton, 2017.

Ehrman, Bart D. *God's Problem*. New York: Harper Collins, 2008.

————. *Misquoting Jesus*. San Francisco: Harper, 2007.

Eigen, Manfred. *Steps towards Life*, translated by Paul Woolley. New York: Oxford University Press, 1992.

Finegan, Jack. *Light from the Ancient Past: The Archeological Background of Judaism and Christianity*. Princeton: Princeton University Press, 1959.

Goodspeed, Edgar J. *The Apocrypha*. New York: Random House, 1959.

Gould, Stephen Jay. *Wonderful Life*. New York: W. W. Norton, 1989.

Greene, Brian. *The Elegant Universe*. New York: W.W. Norton, 2003.

———. *The Hidden Reality*. New York: Alfred A. Knopf, 2011.

———. *The Fabric of the Cosmos*. New York: Vintage Books, 2005.

Hamer, Dean. *The God Gene: How Faith Is Hard-wired into Our Genes*. New York: Doubleday, 2004.

Harbour, Daniel. *An Intelligent Person's Guide to Atheism*. London: Duckworth, 2001.

Harris, Sam. *Letter to a Christian Nation*. New York: Vintage Books, 2006.

———. *The End of Faith*. New York: W. W. Norton, 2005.

Hawking, Stephen. *A Brief History of Time*. New York: Bantam Books, 1988.

Hawking, Stephen, and Leonard Mlodinow. *The Grand Design*. New York: Bantam Books, 2010.

Hawking, Stephen. *The Universe in a Nutshell*. New York: Bantam Books, 2001.

Hawking, Stephen. *Brief Answers to the Big Questions*. New York: Bantam Books, 2018

Hesse, Herman. *Siddhartha*. New York: Barnes & Noble Books, 2007.

Hick, John H. *Philosophy of Religion*. Englewood Cliffs, NJ: Prentice-Hall, 1983.

Hitchens, Christpher. *god is not Great*. New York: Twelve, Hachette Book Group USA, 2007.

Holt, Jim. *When Einstein Walked with Godel*. New York: Farrar, Straus and Giroux, 2018.

Isbouts, Jean-Pierre. *The Biblical World: An Illustrated Atlas*. Washington, DC: National Geographic Society, 2007.

Johnson, Dominic. *God Is Watching You*. New York: Oxford University Press, 2016.

Keay, John. *India: A History*. New York: Grove Press, 2010.

Keller, Timothy. *The Reason for God*. New York: Riverside Books, 2008.

King James Version. *The Holy Bible*. New York: Thomas Nelson and Sons, 1950.

Krauss, Lawerence M. *A Universe from Nothing*. New York: Free Press, 2012.

Lane, Nick. *The Vital Question*. New York: W. W. Norton, 2015.

Larousse Encyclopedia of Mythology. New York: Prometheus Press, 1959.

Lessing, Erich. *Die Griechische Sagen*. Orbis Verlag, Munchen, 1977.

Lings, Martin. *Muhammad: Inner Traditions*, Rochester, VT, 2006.

Lopez, Donald S. Jr. *The Story of Buddhism*. San Francisco: Harper San Francisco, 2002.

Ly, Boreth. HAVC 124C: "Arts and Politics in Theravada Buddhist Traditions," Volumes 1 and 2. University of California Santa Cruz Copy Center Professor Publishing, Santa Cruz, 2014.

Margulis, Lynn. *Origin of Eukaryotic Cells*. New Haven/London: Yale University Press, 1950.

Martin, Paul S. and Richard G. Klein. *Quatenary Extinction*s. University of Arizona Press, 1984.

Maslow, A. H. *The Farther Reaches of Human Nature*. New York: Viking Press, 1973.

Miles, Jack. *Religion as We Know It*. New York: W.W. Norton, 2020.

----------. *GOD in the Qur'an*. New York: Vintage Books, 2019.

Muhammad Farooq-i-Azam Malik. *Al-qur'an*. Houston: Institute of Islamic Knowledge, 1997.

Narada. *The Buddha and His Teachings*. Taiwan: White Stone Publisher, 2016.

National Geographic. *Visual History of the World*, Peter Delius Verlag, Gmbh, KG, Berlin, 2005.

———. "Secrets of the Brain," National Geographic, February 2014.

———. "Seeing the Light," Washington, DC: National Geographic Partners, February 2016.

Newberg, Andrew. Eugene D'aguili, and Vince Rause. *Why God Won't Go Away*. New York: Ballantine Books, 2002.

Niebuhr, Reinhold. *Moral Man and Immoral Society*. Louisville, KY: Westminster John Knox Press, 2013.

Page, Jake. *In the Hands of the Great Spirit*. New York: Free Press/Simon and Schuster, 2004.

Pagels, Elaine. *The Gnostic Gospels*. New York: Vintage Books, 1989.

Pagels, Elaine, and Karen L. King. *Reading Judas*. New York: Viking Penguin, 2007.

Penrose, Roger. *Cycles of Time*. London: Vintage Books, 2011.

Persinger, Michael A. *Neuropsychological Bases of God Beliefs*. New York: Praeger, 1987.

Piccioni, Robert L. *Can Life Be Merely an Accident*. Westlake Village, CA: Real Science Publishing, 2010.

Pielou, E. C. *After the Ice Age*. Chicago: University of Chicago Press, 1991.

Piggott, Stuart. *Prehistoric India*. Baltimore: Penguin Books, 1961.

Quammen, David. *The Tangled Tree*. New York: Simon & Schuster Paperbacks, 2018.

Radhakrishnan, Sarvepalli, and Charles A. Moore. *A Source Book in Indian Philosophy*. Princeton: Princeton University Press, 1989.

Raffel, Burton. *Beowulf*. New York: New American Library, 1963.

Randall, Lisa. *Warped Passages Unraveling the Mysteries of the Universe's Hidden Dimensions*. New York: Harper Perennial, 2006

Reich, David. *Who We Are and How We Got Here*. New York: Pantheon Books, 2018.

Roberts, Neil. *The Holocene: An Environmental History*. Oxford, UK, Blackwell, 1998.

Rovelli, Carlo. *The Order of Time*. New York: Riverhead Books, 2018.

Rushdie, Salman. *The Satanic Verses*. New York: Henry Holt, 1988.

Rutherford, Adam. *Creation*. New York: Penguin Group, 2013.

Schopf, J. William. *Cradle of Life*. Princeton: Princeton University Press, 1999.

Shubin, Neil. *Your Inner Fish: A Journey into the 3.5 Billion Year History of the Human Body*. New York: Vintage Books, 2009.

Smith, Huston. *The World's Religions*. San Francisco: Harper San Francisco, 1961.

Smith, Huston, and Philip Novak. *Buddhism*. New York/San Francisco: Harper Collins, 2003.

Stannard, Russell. *The End of Discovery*. New York: Oxford University Press, 2010.

Stavrakopoulou, Francesca. *GOD An Anatomy*. New York: Alfred A. Knopf, 2021.

Stenger, Victor J. *God, the Failed Hypothesis*. Amherst, NY: Prometheus Books, 2008.

Swami Prabhavananda and Christopher Isherwood. *Bhagavad-Gita*. New York: New American Library, 1955.

Tabor, James D. *The Jesus Dynasty*. New York: Simon & Schuster, 2007.

The Economist. "A Survey of the Brain." London, 23 December, 2006.

Wade, Nicholas. *The Faith Instinct*. New York: Penguin Press, 2009.

Wilczek, Frank. *Fundamentals*. New York: Penguin Press, 2021.

Wing-Tsit Chan. *Chinese Philosophy*. Princeton: Princeton University Press, 1973.

ABOUT THE AUTHOR

W. R. Frederick is not the usual author on god belief with a professional stake in the debate. Born and raised on Long Island, New York, he is a graduate of the US Military Academy at West Point and possesses degrees in science (engineering), languages, business, and political-military strategy. He pursued a career in the US Army and a later career with Hughes Electronics. He has traveled widely. It is, however, a lifelong interest in ancient history, archaeology, and related religions that underlies this work, written in the first person to emphasize his own views. Mr. Frederick is also a professional oil painter. He resides in Los Angeles.

Printed in the United States
by Baker & Taylor Publisher Services